Living Through the Hoop

Reuben A. Buford May

Living Through the Hoop

High School Basketball, Race, and the
American Dream

New York University Press • *New York and London*

NEW YORK UNIVERSITY PRESS
New York and London
www.nyupress.org

Library of Congress Cataloging-in-Publication Data
May, Reuben A. Buford, 1965–
Living through the hoop : high school basketball, race, and the
American dream / Reuben A. Buford May.
p.   cm.
Includes bibliographical references and index.
ISBN-13: 978-0-8147-5729-1 (cloth : alk. paper)
ISBN-10: 0-8147-5729-4 (cloth : alk. paper)
1. Basketball—Moral and ethical aspects—United States.
2. Basketball—United States—Sociological aspects. 3. Basketball
players—Georgia.   I. Title.
GV885.7.M39 2007
796.323'62—dc22   2007023845

New York University Press books are printed on acid-free paper,
and their binding materials are chosen for strength and durability.

Manufactured in the United States of America
10 9 8 7 6 5 4 3 2 1

Dedicated to the young men and men who live their lives through the hoop and to the memories of Calvin Cody (1984–2006) and Frank Ellis May Jr. (1942–2006).

Contents

Acknowledgments

The preparation of this book has extended over many years, and many people have contributed to its contents. My own experiences as a player and the people with whom I have come into contact have greatly shaped the way I have thought about *Living Through the Hoop*. I would like to thank my mother for supporting my initial efforts to play basketball in the sixth grade. Her love and support have been an inspiration in many of my endeavors. I also owe my brother Tim thanks for his patience. Over the years he frequently stood victim to my burgeoning competitive spirit—a spirit so much alive that it merits its own "person" in the form of Reginald S. Stuckey. I thank my brother Khary, who chose to sing opera over playing basketball, for being a real-life demonstration of the range of possibilities for someone starting at a different position in the social structure.

Along the way I have had several coaches who were instrumental to both my appreciation for and understanding of basketball and its significance in my life and the life of so many others. My eighth-grade coach, Coach P., awarded me a Most Improved Player trophy. That trophy remains a reminder to me to always work hard at anything I undertake. Coach Lester Foster, under the strict orders from his wife, gave me the opportunity to play college basketball on the junior varsity team at Aurora University. Coach Don Holler, former head coach of men's basketball at Aurora University, taught me the X's and O's of the game. To both of them, I am grateful.

Beyond my coaches, the men with whom I came into contact around basketball at college had a profound impact on my life experiences. My "uncles," Sam Nicholson, David Bailey, Eric Liggons, and Revin Fellows, were all older, black, male college students at Aurora University who taught me how to be a man through basketball. My college roommates, who were also my teammates, showed me the fun side of living life and playing basketball. Victor "Slick Vic" White dropped me a dime, Ed "Monorail" Hill showed me the turnaround, and Maurice "Ice" Culpepper let me play with his deejay equipment. They each taught me how basketball helped to order their lives. I am grateful for those memories.

When I graduated college and began working, my dear friend Ken Watson challenged me to "conceptualize basketball" in writing. He forced me to "ponder" (I can hear his voice echoing this command in my head even today) basketball in the way that he had challenged me to do with so many other subjects. I continue to be reminded that the things he told me "back then" matter now. I am appreciative of his life-long support and tutelage. My advisers at the University of Chicago, William J. Wilson, Richard P. Taub, and Edgar Epps, helped me to develop personally and intellectually beyond the foundation that Ken Watson had provided. They were just a few of the many scholars at the university that made my experience there memorable. Many of my peers from my days at Chicago remain among my greatest critics and supporters. I am grateful to Alford Young Jr., Mary Pattillo, Mignon Moore, Jolyon Ticer-Wurr, Nick Young, Ray Reagans, Sandra Smith, Carla O'Connor, Peter Schneeberger, George Wimberly, Jeanine Hildreth, the late Eric Rhodes, and Fred Hutchinson for their support over the years.

I thank the many students—too numerous to list here—at the University of Georgia and Texas A&M University who were brave enough to let me know when they thought one of my ideas needed to be revised. Additionally, a special group of folks during my time in both Georgia and Texas proved to be indispensable to my overall quality of life. The Reginald Stuckey Crews at UGA and TAMU were vital support systems for the production of my scholarly work. It is only they who have the context for understanding Reginald in his fullness. I thank Kristin McKenna, Jessica Cheek, Jessica Martin, Kevin Samples, Terry Thompson, Dominique Holloman, Lindsey (Cadenhead) Kirk, Jerome Bramlett, Shanna Jackson, Trey and Pam Ezekiel, Karyn Lacy, Shannon England, and Eniola Alabi for having my back in Georgia, and I thank Christine (Timmins) Sheffield, Courtney Wolfe, Daniel Oelschlegel, Ricardo Vasquez, Lisa Ray, Brandy Bates, and Jennifer Whitely for their warm reception of Stuckey in Texas.

I owe thanks to Woody Beck, William Finlay, Leigh Willis, Scott Brooks, Karyn Lacy, Michael Messner, Norman Denzin, Elijah Anderson, Walter Allen, Jack Katz, Darnell Hunt, Gary Alan Fine, Mitch

Duneier, Mario Small, Simon Gottschalk, and Eduardo Bonilla-Silva for helping me think through a wide array of matters. At Texas A&M University my colleagues have provided a collegial environment. In particular, I am especially thankful to those colleagues who participate in the Race and Ethnicity Workshop. They compose an intellectual collective that has few parallels with respect to its diversity of people, methodological approaches, and intellectual perspectives in the study of race and ethnicity. Special thanks to Joe Feagin, Mark Fossett, Rogelio Saenz, Joseph Jewell, Sarah Gatson, Nadia Flores, Robert Mackin, Wendy Moore, Nancy Plankey Videla, Ed Murguia, and Zulema Valdez for creating that community. Portions of this book have benefited from the feedback and questions raised in talks at UCLA, Vanderbilt, UT-Austin, Northwestern, and UIC.

Heather Hodges, Dominique Holloman, Lyndsey Harrison, Ryan Jebens, Charity Clay, and Kenneth Sean Chaplin read earlier versions of the manuscript; their insights were useful for further developing my ideas. I am particularly indebted to Kenneth Sean Chaplin for his close reading of various versions of the manuscript. His questions and suggestions were the basis of considerable revision for the current text. I am grateful to the anonymous reviewers for helping me to tighten the focus of the manuscript. My editor at NYU Press, Ilene Kalish, proved to be indispensable. Her technical skills, knowledge of the subject matter, patience, and encouragement were invaluable to me as I attempted to capture the lives of young men. Additionally, Ilene's assistant, Salwa Jabado, provided superb administrative support. I also wish to thank Jim Alley for his help with the upkeep of my home and Betsy Jones for her assistance in getting the manuscript out the door.

It is difficult for me to imagine that I would have had any measure of success had I not had the support of my family. My stepdaughter, Tamarra, was an initial source of inspiration for coaching basketball. She and I grew closer around hoops. She showed me how important sport could be for bonding families together. My daughter, Regina, has been a wonderful distraction from the complexities of thinking about the world. My wife, Lyndel, has been the most important source of support for me as I have embarked on various scholarly projects. As an ethnographer, I have led an unusual life, spending countless hours among other people. Lyndel has so graciously shared her time. To her

I am grateful. I have been blessed to have a family that reminds me that I might be a sociologist "out there," but at home I am just Reuben, daddy, and husband. I thank them for their support.

Chapter 5 derives most of its subject matter from a revised and extended version of my article "The Sticky Situation of Sportsmanship: Contexts and Contradictions in Sportsmanship among High School Boys Basketball Players," *Journal of Sport and Social Issues* 25(4): 373–390. I would like to thank Sage Publications for permission to use this article.

Finally, *Living Through the Hoop* could not have been completed without the young and adult men whose lives were its subject. Although I cannot thank them individually for all they have done, I am grateful to them for sharing their time, love for the game of basketball, and intimate aspects of their lives. They have taught us much about sport, society, and self.

Preface

It was the fourth quarter and we were winning by twelve points with under one minute left in the game. The opposing team had just deflected the ball out of bounds near our basket. As the referee went to retrieve the ball, Coach P. shouted toward the end of our bench, "Reuben, go in the game for William."

I got to my feet but hesitated. Coach P., seeing that I was nervous, took my arm gently and ushered me toward the scorer's table. I stumbled along the sideline under the force of his pull. When we got to the scorer's table, the scorekeeper said to me, "Who are you going in for?"

"Uh, uh," I stuttered.

"He's going in for number 21," Coach P. said.

My stomach churned. When the referee signaled me, I ran excitedly onto the court to play in my first elementary school game. My teammates and the few spectators in the gym offered their supportive cheers.

Like all "scrubs" or "extended blowout players," I was the crowd favorite—the kid that got to play once both teams' starting players had established the game's outcome.

"Reuben," Coach P. shouted, "stand right by the free-throw line. Justin, you inbound the ball."

I followed Coach P.'s instructions as my hands began to sweat in anticipation of "live action." The referee handed the ball to Justin on the sideline. As I stood on the free-throw line I felt as though my every move was being watched and dissected by the coach, the other players, the referees, and the crowd. I was surprised a moment later when Justin threw the ball to me. I bobbled it but regained control, in the way only a clumsy twelve-year-old could.

I looked around for a teammate to pass to, seeming to hold the ball forever. As I tried to keep my balance, I could hear a low rumbling of voices in my head. I was confused. I didn't want to make a mistake and throw the ball to the wrong player. I was sure I wouldn't ever get a chance to make that kind of mistake again. The pressure was intense.

Slowly, the voices became clear, "Shoot it. Shoot it."

I turned toward the basket but was still afraid to shoot. My thoughts were racing. What if I miss the shot? My teammates would never let me live it down.

I had plenty of time to contemplate the outcome because the opposing team's scrubs weren't guarding me. They were following the universally understood but unwritten rule that scrubs did not play serious defense in the last minute of the game because scrubs were incapable of playing serious defense at all.

"Reuben, shoot!" Coach P. shouted, shaking me back into consciousness.

I grasped the ball firmly with both hands, squatted to the floor, jumped in the air like a frog, and pushed the ball up with a full body thrust. The ball left my hands and floated upward toward the gym lights in what appeared to be slow motion. Just as I became anxious that I might knock out a light, the ball began its descent. It was right on line for the basket.

Swish. The ball dropped straight through the net, and the crowd cheered before I realized I had made the shot. I could feel the sudden excitement of succeeding at something I had only dreamed about. As the crowd applauded I skipped back down the court to play scrub defense. I don't remember much else from that game, but I do remember that after that day my love for basketball began in earnest.

Although I lacked the skill of my other sixth-grade teammates, who had been playing organized basketball for many years, I was always enthusiastic about competing against them. Like many young black men growing up in the city of Chicago, it seemed as though basketball was the center of our being. However, after I graduated from middle school, I was discouraged from trying out for the high school basketball team. There was such a saturated pool of athletic talent at the local high school that I could only watch as all my former school teammates were cut one by one from the team. Despite this, my desire for hoops never died, and I continued to play informal basketball games at the local outdoor court, sometimes weathering extreme midday sun and humidity for hours only to come home and pass out from the enervating heat.

When I reached college at Aurora University in 1983 I again

thought about playing organized basketball. There were only a few black men at this small liberal arts college, and most of them were basketball players. My initial bonding with them was based on our mutual love for the sport. Through their encouragement I went out for the team my sophomore year and made it. I spent the next three years playing college basketball, and when I graduated I felt that I might never enjoy bonding with other men within the context of organized basketball like I had in college. Fortunately, many years later I met the young men and coaches of the Northeast Knights, who shared my love of basketball. Only then, with this enduring love for the game in mind, did I begin to seriously ponder the powerful affects of basketball. Why did I love the sport so much? Why did so many other young black men as well?

When I moved to Georgia in 1996, I joined the Northeast Knights girls' basketball program because my stepdaughter was playing and the school was looking for volunteer coaches. I was a sociology professor at a local university, and my research was focused on the ways in which African Americans construct notions of race through their interactions with one another. In particular, I was writing about the ways in which African American men understand the meaning of race within the context of a neighborhood tavern in Chicago. This research became the basis for my first book, *Talking at Trena's: Everyday Conversations at an African American Tavern.*[1] I spent my days teaching and writing and then my afternoons running drills with my stepdaughter's team. Coaching was both fun and inspiring. Best of all, I was around basketball all the time.

In 1998, after my stepdaughter graduated, the head coach of the boys' basketball program at Northeast High School invited me to be an assistant coach on his staff. I readily accepted. As I worked with the boys' team, I became struck by the powerful hold that basketball seemed to have on so many of the players. At the same time, I became increasingly aware that many of the male college students whom I taught and played informal pickup basketball with at the university had continuing aspirations to be walk-on basketball players for the university basketball team. It was intriguing that some college students believed that they were just as capable of playing big-time college basketball as those scholarship players already on the team. In most cases these players had been accomplished high school athletes and could have been excellent practice players for the university team.

Few, however, had the necessary physical stature and basketball skills to be true contributors on a major university basketball team. Yet they still believed. I wondered what it was about basketball that had such a strong pull on so many young men. After my second year of coaching, I decided to formally study the young men who played for the Northeast Knights.

By the time I began my study I had already established rapport and credibility with the players and coaches through my previous years of service to the girls' and boys' basketball programs. I spent a great deal of time with the young men and coaches. From mid-October to early March of each year I met with the boys for practices and games for approximately twenty-five hours a week. Immediately following practice and games I recorded fieldnotes. Some nights we returned home so late that I waited until morning to reconstruct my observations from scant notes I had written on the usually dim and often loud bus ride home. I also recorded observations when we were not in basketball season. The summer months of June and July were crucial periods of development for the young men, and I coached them during that time.[2] I also conducted eighteen exit interviews with young men who had completed their final year of varsity basketball at Northeast High School.

I draw on these fieldnotes and interviews to explore the nuanced ways that these young men live everyday life through basketball.[3] I examine how the young men meet the challenges of safeguarding their lives in dangerous neighborhoods, come to develop a masculine identity, and understand the complexities of race. I argue that while their focus on basketball is profoundly beneficial in helping them to move through high school, their devotion to it consumes their identities in such a way that many of them aspire to a post-high-school career instead of focusing on more viable or realistic goals. In order to understand their motivation I consider the role of mass media, their community, and the coaches in influencing some of the young men to focus on basketball as a means of climbing the social ladder. In concluding my study I discovered that inasmuch as this is a story about young men and basketball, it is also a story about the ways that inequality and race help systematically structure the kinds of choices young black men make.

Beyond my continued love for the game, I also am an ethnographer. "Ethnography" is a method by which sociologists explore the

social world around us. This affinity for ethnography, which often involves logging hours of observational fieldwork and laborious note-
taking, is grounded in my many years of journal writing. I have maintained a personal journal since the age of eleven and have honed the
skill of capturing personal experience. Ethnography is much like journal writing, although it is a more systematic form of observation and
data collection and necessitates that one also be reflexive about docu-
menting one's experience. As an ethnographer, I immerse myself in
the lives of those whom I study and document these experiences. Essentially, this means I take an active role in what is happening around
me. As such, my own "perspectives, experiences, and emotions become equally important to the accounts gathered from others."[4] Thus,
it is critical that I investigate, in my writings about others, who I am as
I help to produce the narratives that I presume to collect.[5] My experience, then, is not only important to me but at the same time central to
understanding how any given research project unfolds,[6] perhaps in
this case all the more so since I have much in common with the players of the Knights.

One final note is in order. Since so many of the young men have
shared intimate details with me about their lives, I have used pseudo-
nyms for people and places throughout the text.[7] Although some
young men asked me to identify them by name, I chose not to because
by identifying them I would also identify young men who wished to
remain anonymous. In the end, it matters not who is specifically identified because this story could be about any young black man trying to
make sense of his life by living through the hoop.

Introduction

It was early January 1998, and Tamarra, my stepdaughter, and I had just finished practice with the Northeast High School girls' basketball team. Before leaving the school we decided to hang around to watch the middle school boys' team play. The game was being played in the gymnasium at Northeast High School. It had been arranged by administrators at the high school and middle school to accommodate the large crowd.

As we made our way to our seats Calvin Cody, a thirteen-year-old Northeast Middle School player, caught my eye. He had just dribbled the ball down the court in a flash, put it behind his back, and then through his legs. After eluding two defenders, he stopped on the left of the free-throw line, elevated high above another defender, and shot a jump shot that went through the hoop touching nothing but net. "Damn," I said in a whisper to myself. Before I could digest what he had done, his teammate Arturo stole the ball from the opposing team and laid it in for two more points.

"Who are those guards playing for the middle school?" I asked Tamarra.

"Oh, that's Calvin Cody and Arturo Mills," she said. "They can ball."

"I see they can play," I said, as I leaned back against the bleachers.

"Calvin is Coach Benson's little nephew," Tamarra added. "He and D. Benson are cousins, and Calvin plays just like D. Benson."[1]

"Calvin is a little too flashy for me, but he can play," I said.

"There's really nobody that can hang with him at any of the middle schools," Tamarra added, "and little Turo is really good too."

As I watched Calvin and Turo score basket after basket I was impressed with their basketball skills. Although they were both under six feet, they seemed to hold unlimited promise. What I did not know at the time was that Calvin, Turo, and many other young men at

Northeast High School would teach me more about basketball and life than I could have imagined.

They would be among the first group of young men that I would coach at Northeast High School in the fall of 1998. In a sense, we would all begin our basketball careers together. They would show me the everyday challenges that many of them faced with drugs, alcohol, and violence in their neighborhoods. I would instruct them in the finer points of executing a team offense to defeat their opponent. They would teach me about what it meant to become a man when you live in places that define manhood by how tough you can be, how many women you can have, and how much money you can hustle. I would demonstrate to them the importance of teamwork on the court. They would reveal to me both the simple and profound ways that race and inequality influence how they lived and how they played. I would show them the importance of playing tough defense. And through it all they would make clear to me that basketball was one of the few things on which they could pin their hopes for a better life.

Indeed, basketball was a beneficial influence for many of the young men in very tangible ways. They could enjoy enhanced social status with the girls because they were high school athletes. They could "say no to drugs" and be respected by their peers simply because they were members of the Northeast Knights. They could avoid street life by occupying their time in the gym "shootin' rock" instead of standing on the corner "slingin' rock." They could be in the presence of black men who were accountable to their families, held regular jobs, and tried to live a "respectable" life.[2]

And yet, although I discovered how basketball was beneficial to the young men in many respects, I also learned about the downside of their intense involvement in the sport. Many of the Knight players counted on basketball to transform their lives well beyond high school.

Athletic scholarships and even professional careers in the NBA were deeply sought-after goals. Despite the grim reality, these beliefs are supported by the very coaches (myself included), school supporters, parents, and community members who push the young men to work harder on the court. We often espouse the belief that individuals, irrespective of their initial starting point, have an equal opportunity for social mobility in most American institutions, and, thus, an individual's ability to move up the ladder is simply a matter of whether he or she has worked hard enough. I would argue that in order for our sociocultural institutions to be maintained and perpetuated such deceptions occur systematically.

This point is supported by sociologist Harry Edwards's observation that sport, as an institution, "has primary functions in disseminating and reinforcing the values regulating behavior and goal attainment" in the United States.[3] Such is the case with basketball, wherein ideas about the American dream, equal opportunity, and social mobility through hard work are reiterated constantly. Sociologist Howard Nixon suggests that Americans in general believe that there are opportunities for mobility through sport, but even more so among black males. He states, "The spectacular financial success and fame of athletes from modest social origins would seem to give substance to these images and reinforce the ideology that explains them. Indeed, professional sports careers and athletic scholarships to attend college have been counted among the most important tickets to success for black American males."[4] The commonplace acceptance of such values is so engrained in our understanding of social life in the United States that some individuals—for instance, the young men of the Northeast Knights—may clearly recognize the limits of how far they can rise within this society and yet continue to pursue hoop dreams irrespective of those limits.

The young men believe and make choices about their lives based on the view that *sports enhances mobility* rather than from the perspective that *sports impedes mobility*.[5] That is, they believe that sports are an effective avenue through which to attain higher social status, rather than a waste of time and energy that detracts from efforts they could put forth in alternative pursuits to mobility. These young men attempt to live the American dream of a "good life" through basketball.

Such hoop dreams have consumed the lives of many young men, including basketball prodigies like William Gates and Arthur Agee, whose lives and careers were the subject of the highly acclaimed 1994 documentary *Hoop Dreams*. Unlike *Hoop Dreams*'s story of two elite players, *Living Through the Hoop* focuses on how average players like the Northeast Knights' Calvin Cody and Arturo Mills swallow the intoxicating euphoria of athletic success, only to choke on the reality that there is an enormous pool of athletic talent with whom they must compete beyond the realm of Northeast. Most of the Knights have little chance of continued athletic competition beyond high school, but they share similar aspirations as those held by their more athletically gifted counterparts who are being recruited by top colleges and universities to play for thousands of scholarship dollars and the chance to play on national television. In contrast to the elite high school basketball players who are the center of media attention, the subjects of this study possess few exceptional characteristics. Yet their lives, because they are suggestive of the majority of young black men who play high school basketball, are perhaps even more important to our understanding of the relationship between sport and society than the lives of those few who have succeeded at the higher levels.

At its core, this book is concerned with how players live their lives through basketball. However, my goal is not to take the reader on a chronological journey through individual players' basketball careers. Rather, I seek to penetrate the world of high school basketball—a world that consistently yields players for the hoop gristmill—as it continues to remake itself and shape the lives of successive cohorts of young men. I approach this task by presenting aspects of the young men's lives as they navigate their communities, contemplate the meaning of race, develop notions of masculinity, reconcile sportsmanship with the need to win, and experience the effects of the "dirty trick."

In chapter 1, "A Look Through the Hoop," I describe the social world of the Northeast Knights, painting a picture of a basketball team with players who are considered average within the broader context of high school basketball. I provide an overview of the kinds of players that play for the Knights, the community and school contexts in which the young men play and live, and the relationships among coaches, players, and parents. The descriptions in this chapter provide details for understanding the young men's lives.

Although the Northeast Knights might be composed of players like those that compete at many high schools throughout the country, the Knights program is unusual in at least one key respect: team selection. In chapter 2, "For the Good of All," I examine the Knights' no-cut policy. A departure from most teams, this unconventional approach to competitive sports is embraced by most of the players and coaches. I argue that the resultant team dynamic might well guarantee the team's failure annually if it were not for the cohesive group culture of the Knights that stems from Coach William Benson's benevolence. Understanding the no-cut policy is crucial to understanding the success of the Northeast Knights, both competitively and as an institution that offers unconditional support and stability in the lives of these young men.

Although adolescents are generally confronted with the temptation to consume alcohol, use drugs, or engage in criminally deviant behavior, some communities offer these temptations more readily. In chapter 3, "The Three D's: Drinking, Drugs, and Deviance," I examine the players' behavior within the context of the desolate and dangerous neighborhood conditions in which many of the young men have spent their childhoods. On the positive side, I look at the community status bestowed on the young men because they are members of the venerated Northeast Knights basketball team. I also examine the players' brushes with the law, their loss of loved ones through violence, the prominent lure of alcohol and drugs, and those former Knights lost to one of the "three D's." Ultimately, I reveal the ways in which the players' personal motivations, the opportunities created by the Knights program, and the community's overall respect for the players help most of the young men steer clear of the streets' temptations.

In chapter 4, "Race and Hoops Everyday," I investigate how the players make sense of the popular notion that blacks have superior athletic ability. In this chapter popular texts on race and sport, like John Hoberman's *Darwin's Athletes* and Jon Entine's *Taboo*, receive explicit consideration.[6] I explore the young men's interpretive capacity to square conventional notions of race and athletic ability with their experiences. I demonstrate the young men's belief that race, in and of itself, is not a proxy for athletic ability. Furthermore, I argue that the players' conceptions of athletic ability are grounded in a belief that everyone has an opportunity to be successful, irrespective of race. This taken-for-granted notion of fairness echoes the young men's on-the-court behavior. More important, this same notion of fairness supports their aspirations for the hoop dream.

I also explore the players' and coaches' experiences confronting racism within their athletic participation. I reveal how the coaches' deep-rooted experiences with racial hostilities within the context of sports shapes their thinking and thereby shapes the directives that they give the young men who compete in often racially hostile environments.

In the time the young men spend with the coaches, they garner and emulate the behavior patterns expected of men. Furthermore, the athletes' interactions with one another help to reaffirm these expectations. In chapter 5, "Knight-Style Masculinity," I explore the nuanced ways in which the young men and coaches construct masculine identities through gendered behaviors, expressions of sexuality, and balancing tense relationships with girls and women. I also consider the young men's perceptions of "hypersexualized" black males and their social relationships with young white women, which are frequently perceived as deviant. All these factors structure the young men's understanding of themselves as young black males.

In chapter 6, "Sportsmanship and the Need to Win," I consider the ways that the players evaluate their on-the-court behavior with regard to fair play and sportsmanship. I reveal the players' understanding of context—for example, team goals, coaches' expectations, and community influence—for determining what is and is not sportsmanlike behavior. Despite the normative examples of sportsmanship, players and coaches continue to define their behavior not only by team standards and their immediate group context but also by their own experiences. These shifting interpretations demonstrate the complex ways in which sportsmanship becomes purely a question of context. I suggest that the young men's use of context to define sportsmanship is similar to their use of context to understand their life chances and opportunities for social mobility.

In chapter 7, "The Dirty Trick," I tie the book's implicit and explicit themes together to reveal the complicity that coaches, parents, schools, and mass media share in driving the young men into the saturated arena of athletics. I then expose the central byproduct that the Knights experience from their participation in boys' high school basketball. Finally, I expand the scope of the book to encompass institutionalized deceptions as they play out in other social contexts. In the end, institutionalized deceptions help perpetuate the fallacy of a pure meritocracy. This is key for maintaining the stability of our social structure. The "dirty trick" of basketball is exposed to the extent that it relates to similar "dirty tricks" throughout society.

While in the field, an ethnographer touches many lives and is touched by many lives in return. For me, the emotional ties to Calvin Cody, a young man whose exploits figure prominently throughout the book, remind me of the significance of sociology for the people we study. In the epilogue, "The Death of Calvin Cody," my reflections on his life explore the moral and ethical complexities of the "dirty trick" as they were lived by him.

I have also included a methodological appendix in which I discuss the ethnographic approach, qualitative interviews, and the sample group used for this study. I also explore the complex roles a researcher must negotiate while in the field. Finally, I discuss my motivation for representing the world of the Northeast Knights in the way I have chosen.

There are rare times in researchers' lives that they can invest the same kind of time and energy in projects of interest as they might in the things they really love. Although researchers may have a passionate interest in their projects, most of that interest tends to be tempered by some scholarly distance. This is not the case for me. The activities of research and personal satisfaction are very much interconnected. Ultimately, however, my aim as a researcher is to present a sociological understanding of the social worlds that I have experienced intimately. It is with this aim in mind that I proceed to explore the almost spiritual bond between the men and young men of Northeast and the sociocultural significance of basketball—and athletics more generally —to those who live, play, and watch hoop.

I

A Look Through the Hoop

Mama, just go back up in the stands. This is between me and my coach!

I was anxious as we passed through the metal detector and entered the gymnasium. Not only was it my first game as an assistant varsity coach of boys' high school basketball, but it was also my first game on the road—and in Forest County of all places. The folks at Forest County were well known for packing out their gymnasium to cheer on their Raiders. They were hostile too.

What made matters worse was that, at just thirty minutes up the road from Northeast, some of our players had kinfolk that went to school at Forest County. This game would be for bragging rights. It would also be one of the few places where the opposing team's players and fans would be black like us.

On a few occasions in the past, the competitive energy had spilled from the court and ended up in the parking lot, with fistfights among spectators from both schools. What stuck out to me most about our loss the previous year was the fiercely competitive and physical nature of the game.

As the players got dressed in the locker room I walked around as tense as I had been the first time I had ever played. A few minutes later Coach Benson entered the locker room to give his last set of instructions to the team before we went out to warm up.

"Now, gentlemen," Benson said, "let me tell you something. You represent Northeast. Take pride in that. Don't be out here embarrassing your family letting guys outplay you. You know, from the time we came through the door all I heard everybody talkin' about was a party. They're supposed to be having this dance after they beat us. Well, gentlemen, let's cancel that fuckin' dance. Remember, don't let that backside man push you out of the way to get the rebound. If the ball's on the floor, you need to be on the floor."

The players nodded in silence, and Benson waited to let his words sink in. "Now let's get the prayer," Benson commanded.

We circled around and held our hands up in the center of the circle. As we began to recite the Lord's Prayer, I became keenly aware of the deep echo of our combined twenty-five voices, "Amen!"

"Knights on three," Lance, a junior captain, said, "1-2-3."

"Knights," we all responded.

Our players, twenty-one in all, lined up according to height and ran through the locker-room door. As they took to the floor clad in their red uniforms with black trim, the Forest County crowd booed. Instantly, those boos became cheers as the Raiders entered the gym from the opposite locker room. They were wearing their signature white uniforms with green trim. Their twelve players moved easily through warmup drills as their fans danced to hip-hop music in the stands and sustained a high-pitched chatter.

The horn sounded, and it was time to introduce the players. The public-address announcer introduced our team first. As he announced our last starter, "Number 4, Clifton Bolton," his assistant shut off the lights in the gym.

When the lights went out, the Raiders' fans cheered, and then the up-tempo music began.

"And now, your Forest County Raiders!" the public-address announcer shouted.

The fans stood and screamed as the announcer called the Raiders' starting lineup. Under a bright spotlight, each Forest County player ran to center court.

After the Raiders were introduced, we all stood around a few minutes waiting for the gymnasium lights to illuminate. I was already exhausted from the pregame hype.

The two teams met at center court for the jump ball. For the first time I noticed that Forest County had the clear height advantage over our team. All their players stood at about 6'5" or taller. They were lean and athletic. Our tallest starting player, Lance, stood at 6'2". But what we lacked in size we made up for in tenacity. That was Coach Benson's gift. He was a motivator.

When the referees tossed the ball up, Forest County's lean, athletic center easily outjumped Lance for the ball. The Raiders scored first, but we scored several baskets consecutively from steals we made from our full-court-press defense.

During the first quarter I was surprised by how much Benson relied on the other coaches for feedback and assistance during the game. I debriefed the players about their performance as Coach Taylor substituted them in and out of the game and Coach Bowden provided Benson with critical statistical information. We finished the first quarter with a six-point lead.

At the start of the second quarter we began intensifying our press defense by aggressively pursuing every pass the Forest County players made. Those Raiders couldn't handle our persistent pursuit of the ball. We inched the lead up to ten points. Our leading scorer, Clifton Bolton, scored eight of those points on a variety of shots. He was not very big at 6'1", 180 pounds, or very quick, but he had a precise jump-shot, an arsenal of creative moves to the basket, and an "I can score on anyone" attitude.

At halftime we left the floor with a ten-point lead. Benson came into the locker room and gave what I would later learn was his typical halftime speech.

"Listen," Benson said, "you know they are going to come at you with that half-court trap. Don't forget what you're supposed to do. And I told you we still not blocking out to get the rebound. We gotta have rebounds on the backside." Benson paused then said, "Coaches, what you got?"

"We gotta rebound," Coach Taylor said.

"We gotta keep pressure on the ball," I added.

"We gotta take the open shot," Coach Bowden said.

After we fired off this relay of suggestions to the players, Benson said, "Does anyone have anything else for the good of the organization?"

The players were silent.

"Shit, gentlemen," Benson said, "let's get the hell outta the locker room. We can't win the damn game in the locker room. And don't walk out there."

The players collectively sprung from the locker-room bench, jogged through the gym door, ran back onto the court, and began shooting warmup shots.

As the players shot around, I thought, "That's it? That's all we need to talk about?" In the past, I had always noted with curiosity the brief time that Benson and the Knights were in the locker room. He took about three minutes out of each halftime, whereas most coaches typically kept their players in the locker room nine minutes of the ten-minute halftime. I thought, "I hope we've given them enough information."

We began the second half with the ball. We scored several lay-ups in a short span and pushed the lead up to eighteen points. Our defense remained consistent, and we were making our open shots. As the third quarter came to an end, I felt I was well on my way to my first victory as an assistant coach of boys' basketball.

In the fourth quarter, however, the momentum shifted. The Raiders were playing harder and with more confidence and aggression. They changed from a zone defense to their patented 1-3-1 half-court trap, sending two players to double-team the ball each time we passed it to the corner. Benson had warned our players about this half-court trap in the locker room, but once the Raiders started their pursuit on defense we were rattled. We began to turn the ball over and gave Forest County several uncontested lay-ups.

As the clock ran down to under thirty seconds left in the game, the Raiders had cut our eighteen-point lead down to a mere two-point lead. We had the ball, and our plan was to hold it until we were fouled or the final buzzer sounded, but Clifton got trapped in the corner and couldn't provoke the foul, and he instead attempted to throw a cross-court pass to Larique. At 5'9", 154 pounds, Larique was quick, but he couldn't get to Clifton's pass fast enough. One of the rangy Raiders stepped in and stole the ball. He passed it to his teammate, who had already begun streaking down the floor. Just like that, the Raiders tied a game that we had led for thirty-one of thirty-two minutes. The Forest County faithful erupted. I could hardly hear anything.

Coach Benson called a timeout. As the players walked over looking dejected, Benson started fussing at Clifton for dribbling into the trap with the ball: "Haven't I told you to stay your ass out the damn corner?"

Clifton just nodded.

"Larique," Benson said, "you gotta get your ass over there to get the damn ball. You know they going to double-team him. Get your ass over there!"

Larique nodded.

I clapped my hands and offered encouragement, "We okay."

The horn sounded for us to come out of the huddle.

"Run your damn press breaker and protect the ball," Benson commanded. "When we get down on our end we going to hold the ball and run spread. We'll get the ball to Clifton for the last shot."

The boys nodded silently and then returned to the court.

Clifton stepped out of bounds and threw the ball in to Larique. Larique waited for the defense to clear, and then he began dribbling the ball up the court. *10-9-8-7 seconds.*

Right on cue, Larique eyed Clifton breaking across the middle of the lane. *6-5 seconds.*

The Raider guarding Larique knocked the ball loose. *4-3 seconds.*

As Larique tried to secure the ball, he unintentionally kicked it, and it rolled out of bounds at half court.

"Raiders ball," said the public-address announcer.

There were 2.8 seconds left on the clock when the Raiders' coach called a timeout.

"Dammit!" coach Benson shouted as he threw to the ground the white towel he'd been using to wipe his hands.

The Knights hesitantly walked back to our bench. All the players on the floor had played for Benson at least one year, so they knew what was coming.

"Shit," Benson yelled as the players got closer. "Y'all trying to give the fuckin' game away. Fuck it. If y'all ain't gonna play any better than this, we don't even have to get off the bus next time. We just won't play no more games this season."

Benson looked around as if he were contemplating a way to take back all the mistakes we had made that night. *Buzz.* The horn sounded.

"Set up your half-court press," Benson said. "Whatever you do don't let them get the ball inbounds close to the basket. We can still win this game. We got this. Knights on three, 1-2-3."

"Knights!" we shouted.

The team exited the huddle with renewed confidence and took their positions on the defensive end of the court. When Forest County came out of the huddle, they set up with a player at half court and the other three players close to the basket. Our defenders covered the players close to the basket to prevent the easy pass inside.

All the players for both teams were in position. My stomach began to churn as the referee handed the ball to the Raider standing out of bounds.

As the Forest County player began to wind up and throw what he thought was an uncontested pass to half court, Clifton, who had been inching forward in anticipation of the pass, ran two steps to half court and intercepted the ball.

2.7 seconds. Clifton took one dribble.

2.2 seconds. Clifton dribbled once more.

1.8 seconds. All the coaches started shouting, "Shoot it! Shoot it!" We feared that he would run out of time. Clifton ignored our commands.

1.3 seconds. Clifton took one hard dribble and exploded up toward the basket.

0.3 seconds. Clifton extended his arm and released the ball over the front of the goal.

0.0 buzz. Time expired as Clifton began to descend from his leap, and the referee signaled *basket good.*

Clifton hit the court then sprang up in the opposite direction and ran directly to the visitor's locker room with his teammates chasing behind him. The Raiders' faithful were stunned.

In the locker room the players piled on top of Clifton. He had thirty-three points that night, but none more important than the last two.

As the coaches entered the locker room, Benson said, "Shit. Everybody up."

The Knights gave Clifton some room and gathered around Benson.

"Listen," Benson said, "I told y'all we had the game."

The players nodded with approval and gave out high-fives to one another.

"Clifton," Benson continued, "that's the way to make it hurt. It's those close games that really hurt. Shit, I guess we canceled that party."

We laughed.

"Now get your shit on," Benson said with a little laugh, "and let's get the fuck outta this small town."

We huddled up, raised our hands in the middle, and Lance shouted, "Knights on three. 1-2-3."

"Knights!"

The Northeast Community

Northeast is like many small- to medium-size metropolitan areas. The population is approximately 105,000. Sixty-four percent of the population is white, 27 percent is black, and 6 percent is Latino. Twenty-eight percent of the population of Northeast lives below the poverty level.[1] This racial composition, coupled with poverty rates that disproportionately affect blacks, helps to explain its reputation as an undesirable environment. The majority of the players who play for Northeast hail either from Flat Shoals, Hillside, or Eastridge housing developments. An example of the general distribution of the team over communities is the 1999–2000 team. Of the twenty-eight players from this team, sixteen were from these neighboring housing developments, nine were from nearby working-class communities, and three were from affluent neighborhoods. With the exception of one player, all the players were black.

Flat Shoals, Hillside, and Eastridge were built in the early 1940s as affordable housing developments for low- and moderate-income families. Today, these housing developments continue to be homes for low-income families, primarily blacks in Northeast, but because of concentrated poverty and other structural factors, there has been an increase since the 1970s in crime, drug use, and social disorganization in these residential areas.[2] The social conditions of these housing developments offer a formidable barrier to enjoying the innocence of youth.

Many of the players live near drug houses—neighborhood homes in which the sale of crack cocaine is the primary function—or on blocks where gunplay and violence occur often. In fact, during the 1990s, four of the Knights' former players from these neighborhoods were murdered after they were no longer playing basketball for the team. Two were shot, and two were stabbed to death. One player, Thomas Thurmon, was murdered while he was an active member of the team. During the 1997 basketball season, Thurmon, at that time a junior, was shot to death while riding in a friend's car. A day later the shooter, twenty-two-year-old Phillip Winston, turned himself in to the police and admitted killing Thurmon supposedly in self-defense. Winston, however, in his statement to the police admitted that in actuality Thurmon resembled someone who had threatened to kill him. Thurmon's murder had been a case of mistaken identity.

Although the entire school mourned Thurmon's death, many of the players recognized his death as just another reminder that they lived in a high-risk environment. In their community, survival was based on one's ability to compete against the constant allure of fast money obtained through drugs and crime and to be confident, aggressive, and, above all else, willing to fight in any way necessary. Many of the former players, who have internalized this outlook and confidence, projected an attitude of aggression and have also successfully channeled these feelings into mainstream activities. Some of the Knights attended college and started successful careers. These former players remained a source of encouragement to the players and to Benson, who believed in trying to help these young men face the difficult odds of the circumstances and environment into which they were born.

Northeast High School

Over sixteen hundred students attend Northeast High School, which is located in the metropolitan area of Northeast, Georgia. Approximately 55 percent of the students are black, 35 percent are white, 7 percent are Hispanic, 2 percent are Asian, and 1 percent are multiracial. Two-thirds of the students hail from working-class to upper-middle-class black and white communities in Northeast.[3] One-third of the students are from families that live below the poverty level.[4] Most of these impoverished students are black and live in one of three low-income housing projects located in a three- to five-block radius of Northeast High School.

About 51 percent of the students entering as freshmen receive their high school diploma within four years. This completion rate for high school is dismal, yet it is on par with Georgia's statewide average of 55 percent.[5] Northeast High School had gotten its graduation rate up to 53.4 percent in 2003 but dropped slightly to 51.4 percent in 2004. Sixty percent of Northeast High School graduates go on to four-year colleges and universities (approximately 1 percent attend very selective schools), and approximately 5 percent attend two-year community colleges. A small percentage of those students who drop out go on to obtain their GED (general equivalency diploma). Most go on to work in places like fast-food restaurants around metropolitan Northeast.

During my time there, the school went through three principals. The third, Dr. Elizabeth Morris, began in 1999. Dr. Morris had over thirty years experience in education and had done a more effective job in maintaining discipline in the high school than did her male predecessors. The school had two full-time armed police officers and several surveillance cameras that were installed throughout the halls in the late 1980s. Still, there were disciplinary problems. These problems mainly involved truancy, prank bomb threats, school fights, and a gradually increasing gang problem in the area.[6]

Until recently the tension among students at school was related to loose neighborhood affiliations throughout Northeast. These affiliations were simply identified as a North versus South conflict. However, during the influx of Latinos to Northeast in early 2000, there was a rise in gang affiliation among both black and Latino populations.[7] Individuals, especially Latinos, were claiming allegiance to organizations in Northeast that were offshoots of renowned gangs like the Crips and Bloods of Los Angeles, California. These affiliations were highlighted in a special report on gangs in metro-Northeast conducted by the Northeast newspaper in December 2003. Until that report, the Northeast police chief refused to acknowledge what he termed "groups" as gangs. After that report, the Northeast Police Department created a gang task force and attempted special intervention in Latino neighborhoods like Steep Cliff and black neighborhoods like Flat Shoals, Hillside, and Eastridge. The threat of these street gangs brought an additional concern for parents who were trying to rear their children in these neighborhoods.

Despite the tension created by deviance at the high school, many students participated in, or were supportive of, the school's extracurricular academic and sports programs. These programs were well established and provided a source of pride for the Northeast community.

The notoriety of the school for its athletic success is in no small part due to the accomplishments of the boys' basketball program. Under Coach Benson, who began coaching at Northeast in 1987, the team averaged twenty wins per season in the 1990s and was regularly in the top ten of the Georgia Coaches' Poll. Additionally, the Northeast Knights won several state region championships, played in postseason tournaments, and twice went to the state tournament's Elite Eight.

The Young Men Who Play

Harry desperately wanted to be a Knight. But he lived in Rockgate and went to William Ford Middle School, one of two feeder schools for Northeast High School. William Ford Middle was about twenty minutes from the high school, and the other feeder school, Northeast Middle, was just five blocks away. Consequently, William Ford Middle was not as socially or athletically connected to the high school as Northeast Middle.

Harry was concerned that his middle school team would not give him enough of a chance to play for the Knights. But the Knights' coaches did get to see Harry play, and they recognized his talent despite his 5'11" height. As he did for all the young men graduating from Northeast Middle and William Ford Middle, Coach Benson made certain that Harry knew about summer basketball workouts at the high school. Like Calvin and Arturo, Harry gladly joined the Knights program the summer before his first year of high school. He, like so many others before him, played four years for Coach Benson and helped continue the winning basketball tradition at Northeast High School.

Typically, only the more dedicated basketball players worked out with the Knights during summer workouts. Most of the other players became a part of the team during preseason conditioning in the fall semester. Still others only came out once they had heard that we "brought the balls out."[8] These players were committed to football workouts, summer camps, vacations, summer school, or work and were unable to, or chose not to, participate. Those players who worked out during the summer were at an advantage when the school year began. They had become familiar with our practice drills as well as our offensive and defensive strategies over the summer.

By the time basketball season rolled around, Coach Benson's no-cut policy meant that the team composition consisted of players from a variety of neighborhoods, social backgrounds, and skill levels. We had players who had been playing basketball since elementary school and those who had only decided to join the team in their senior year of high school. For instance, one year the team included players whose parents worked as a dentist, lawyer, service-sector employee, civil servant, schoolteacher, and janitor, among other occupations.

Despite the social diversity of the players' families, the most consistent participants on the team were from the low-income families of Northeast. Their parents were typically working poor or received some form of federal assistance. Some players, like Calvin Cody, lived with a single grandparent or another extended family member.

Conspicuously missing from the Northeast Knights program was the white athlete. On average, there was only one white male athlete who chose to come out for the Knights varsity basketball team each year. This was especially noteworthy given that the high school's student body was approximately 35 percent white and Northeast Middle School's basketball team was composed of almost 50 percent white players each year. Furthermore, there were white players who participated on the ninth- and tenth-grade teams but ultimately chose not to return to the team for subsequent years. They typically cited a desire to devote all their time to another sport like baseball, soccer, or football.

Although in the past there had been tall players, few Knights during my time were tall. The average player was about 6'2". We had a few players that were as tall as 6'5", but they tended to be our weaker players. Our most skilled athletes played the guard position and over the years ranged in height from about 5'5" to 6'2". They were the focus of our offensive output and defensive pressure. They also were usually two-sport athletes, playing the "speed" positions in football or running the sprint events in track. Given the average height of the Knights, there were rarely games in which our players were taller than the opponents.

Since Coach Benson had been around Northeast for most of his life, he had often coached the younger brothers and sons of his former players. For instance, Arturo's older brother Bill Fields played for one of the earlier teams. Unfortunately Bill did not finish his career with the Northeast Knights because he began using and selling drugs and, ultimately, went to jail. Still, Coach Benson often talked to Arturo and his teammates about the positive contributions that Bill Fields made to the Knights program.

Perhaps one of the most interesting characteristics of some players was their direct family ties to Coach Benson. Benson coached four of his own nephews. These nephews were sons of one of Benson's five brothers and two sisters.[9] I watched all four of Benson's nephews come through the program over the time that I was involved at Northeast. These players felt some pressure from their familial relationship with Coach Benson. For instance, after his senior season at Northeast, Calvin Cody, who was the last nephew to play under Benson, made these observations about being a Northeast Knight under the direction of his uncle:

> For me it's like putting more pressure on me to play under him because I know he just ain't going to put me in just because I'm his nephew. So I gotta work harder than what everybody else is doing.

During Calvin's career his teammates understood that he was given the team leadership role because he was the best player and not because he was Coach Benson's nephew.

In addition to the family relationships between Coach Benson and his nephews, some of the players had direct family ties with one another. There were two sets of brothers, Ishmael and Aaron, and Terry and David, who played two years apart. Another player, Raphael, had a younger brother, Sadeek, who participated on the ninth- and tenth-grade teams. Although Raphael and Sadeek had the same mother, they had different fathers.[10] Beyond the players who were brothers, the most typical familial connections between players were that of distant cousins. However, these familial relationships had little impact on the kind of relationships that the cousins developed with one another as players. In many instances, it was only after becoming involved in the basketball program that the two young men learned that they were related. Ultimately, familial relationships such as these were de-emphasized, and teammate relationships were stressed.

Despite the emphasis on team and teammates, it is interesting that few of the players actually considered themselves to be friends with other players. Only a small cluster of players exchanged phone numbers or attended weekend activities together. When asked about whether basketball helped them to develop friends, most of the players believed that their good friends were not involved in basketball. Indeed, most of the young men had established their identities outside basketball. Benson was well aware of this. He even complained to the players, "Shit we got thirty damn players, but only about seven of y'all will stick up for each other. Y'all would let somebody outside fuck with your teammate. You supposed to look out for your teammate." Thus, while the players tolerated one another, few developed close ties with their teammates.

In sum, the typical player for Northeast High School was from one of the low-income areas surrounding the school, had played basketball at the middle school level, was involved in more than one sport, and may have had distant familial ties to other players. These players worked together because of the appreciation they had for the rich history of success at Northeast High School and their admiration for Coach Benson as a "player's coach."

The King of the Knights

When I first watched the boys' basketball team play, their unorthodox substitution patterns and the large number of players intrigued me. During games, Benson, a thin, brown-skinned man standing at 6'8", would bark instructions with the intensity of a crazed man. One need not be right behind the bench to hear the obscenities flow from his mouth. In a voice slightly higher than alto he would scream phrases laced with expletives like, "You do what the fuck I say you do!" "Throw the Goddamn ball!" "Well, get your ass over there!" His style of talk and intimidation was a familiar sound that I recalled hearing and imitating as a young man at outdoor courts around Chicago. Still, if you observed closely, you could see that Coach Benson, at age fifty, was about much more than the prolific profanity that flowed from his mouth.

After joining the team I learned that Benson's style was rooted in his own experiences as a native of Northeast, an athlete, and a black man. Benson grew up near the Eastridge housing project two blocks from the high school and played basketball at Northeast under the guidance of legendary coach Paul Carson—a very successful coach and the first black man to coach at the school. The desegregation of the school, like that occurring at many public schools in the United States during the 1970s, meant that coaches and players now had to consider race more prominently in their everyday lives. Although Northeast High School was racially mixed, the basketball team was predominantly black. Northeast players continued to confront racial hostility when they played against high schools with all-white teams. Such racial hostility, especially in the Southern states, profoundly shaped the lives of people like Coach Benson. As a black male, he was confronted with the daily realities of inequality based on race. Like other blacks, he had learned to "live with it" and to "keep striving," yet these experiences undoubtedly became a fundamental part of his life philosophy.

As a Knight, the young Benson was little more than a role player —a substitute for more skilled players. Benson once remarked about his playing days at Northeast, "I always felt that I didn't always get the opportunity to show what I could do." After graduating from Northeast High School, Benson played college basketball at a historically black college, Taylor-Smith College, where he started as a freshman. Benson had a successful college career—his college team competed for conference championships, and he received Most Valuable Player honors. After graduation Benson attended Capel State University, another historically black college, where he earned a master's degree. Two years later he landed back at Taylor-Smith as an assistant coach of the women's basketball team. He later took over the men's program at Taylor-Smith and led the team to a conference championship.

After his successes in collegiate coaching, he returned to Northeast High School to be closer to his family and to take over the program and teach physical education after Coach Paul Carson's retirement. Having the opportunity to play at Taylor-Smith helped Benson develop his coaching philosophy. "At Taylor-Smith I got a chance to grow as a player. I learned that players need an opportunity to grow. That's one of the reasons I don't cut players. Instead I try to put players in a position to be successful."

Despite his unorthodox approach to team selection and his prolific use of profanity to communicate with players, Benson was well liked by most of his current and former players. One former player, a college graduate, even commented, "Coach Benson might not have been the best with X's and O's, but I wouldn't have wanted to play for any other coach." Benson exhibits a burning desire to win, and his players appreciate that competitive fire. Such characteristics first drew many of the young men to play for the Northeast Knights.

The Other Men Leading the Knights

In the spring of 1998, two years after I had begun working with the girls' basketball team at Northeast, Coach Carla Pickens, head coach of the girls' basketball team, called a meeting with her assistant coaches to inform us that she was resigning. After our meeting with Coach Pickens, I saw Benson in the lobby of the gym, and he said, "So they bringing in a new coach?"

"Yeah," I said.

"Are you going to still be working with them?" Coach Benson asked.

"I don't know. I have to meet with Coach Stones first," I said.

"Well shit, if it don't work out you should come over here with us. I got a spot on the ninth-grade team. You can coach that if you want to."

Although Coach Benson had provided encouragement and support to me while I coached with the girls' team, we had never really had extensive conversations. Thus, I thought it was unusual that he would approach me to make such an offer. I suppose that he could tell that I felt disappointed about having to deal with the coaching change in the girls' program. I had been Coach Pickens's assistant coach for two years and had established a significant role in team practice and game strategy.

I contemplated Coach Benson's offer. The next day I met with Coach Stones, the new coach of the girls' team, and we both determined it would be best for the team if I left the girls' program. After that meeting I found Coach Benson and told him that I wanted to join his staff.

Just like that I was now a member of the coaching staff for the boys' basketball team at Northeast High School.[11] I joined a staff that had been with Benson for many years. I was brought in as an assistant coach on the varsity team and head coach of the ninth-grade team. I replaced Coach Carlos Armstrong, who left Northeast high school to become a principal of one of the elementary schools in the area. I joined Coach Rick Bowden, who had been Coach Benson's top assistant coach on the varsity team for twelve years, and Coach Cornell Taylor, who had coached the junior varsity team for nine years. Over the years, Bowden and Taylor transitioned out and were replaced by younger coaches. I soon became Coach Benson's top assistant coach. Coach Odell Henry, a clean-cut, dark-skinned man who had a youthful flare, joined us. He was in his midtwenties and often dressed in the latest hip-hop fashion. He was good friends with another young coach, Milton Frye, who was a former player for Benson and had played on one of the Knights' most successful teams. Also joining the staff was the only white coach, David Shore.

In addition to the coaching staff, we had Sammy Hunt as our scorekeeper and statistician. Hunt had served in this capacity for almost fifteen years. He was a tall, slender, white male about 6'6". He often wore a baseball cap to cover his receding hairline. Hunt had a bright smile that he flashed when a young man or coach shared a humorous quip. His overall joyous and positive attitude was grounded in the happiness that he got from working closely with the young men of Northeast. For a long time I had observed Hunt, and, to me, he seemed out of place with the Northeast Knights. It was not just because he was the only white male that I observed working with the program until Coach Shore arrived. Rather, it seemed Hunt had a genuine appreciation for the difficult social conditions that some of the young men faced. His understanding of these social conditions and his willingness to help these young men were not characteristic of what one might expect of an upper-middle-class white male.

Indeed, Hunt's initial involvement with the program was grounded in his experience with a young black male, Steve Tills, whom he had "adopted." Before Hunt became a paraprofessional at Northeast Middle School in 1988, he worked at the local Young Men's Christian Association (YMCA). He was in charge of organizing games, taking care of equipment, and keeping the score for a recreational league. It was during this time that he met Steve, who was involved in the recreation program at the YMCA. Steve had a difficult home life, and he was just one of several young men whom Hunt adopted at the YMCA. Hunt's efforts gave many of the young men, especially those who lived in the rough Eastridge neighborhood, a fighting chance of surviving difficult home and neighborhood social conditions. He took on the role of a surrogate parent for those players whose parents were otherwise occupied.

The Parents of the Knights

Few parents of the young men were visible participants in the activities of the boys' basketball team. The lack of participation by the boys' parents had always been a point of contention for many of the girls' parents when I was a coach of the girls' basketball team. Since both

boys' and girls' parents formed the basketball booster club, the complaint from the girls' parents was that the boys' families were not
actively involved in fundraising, concession-stand work, or other
booster club activities. There was much legitimacy to their argument,
especially given the number of players that participated on the boys'
team. The no-cut policy meant that the boys' varsity team was composed of twenty players on average, yet only three or four parents a
year consistently supported the activities of the team.

It is worth noting that, unlike the boys' team, the girls' team consisted of both more white players and players who were primarily
from two-parent, middle-class families. For instance, in the 1998–1999
season six girls were white, and two of their families were well known
for their participation in political and financial activities in the city of
Northeast. In short, the girls' parents had both the work-schedule flex-
ibility and financial resources to participate in booster club activities
and to travel and support the team at home and away games.

The difference in race and class makeup of the girls' and boys'
teams is interesting. I speculate that the interrelationship between race
and class at Northeast High School might provide one explanation for
the disproportionate representation of white middle-class females on
the girls' team compared to the disproportionate number of black
lower-class males on the boys' team.

The proportion of blacks that were in poverty at Northeast High
School was considerably larger than the proportion of whites in poverty. If one were to sample the black and white populations ran-
domly, it is likely that a white student selected would be middle class,
whereas the black student would not. These class differences might
play out in sports participation in the following way: since girls' basketball was a game that relied on skill more so than boys' basketball,
where the stereotypical dominance of the black male athlete had been
well established, it was more likely that the white female athletes
might feel confident enough to try out for the girls' team, unlike white
males for the boys' team.

The white female athletes' confidence might stem from the fact
that as middle-class athletes, these girls' families were capable of pay-
ing for training and the use of facilities where the athletes could develop their basketball skills and thus their confidence. Their black
female counterparts, on the other hand, who were more likely from
one of the low-income communities, were not in a position to pay for

training. Additionally, if these young black female athletes wanted to practice, they would have to compete with young black males for use of the public courts. Thus, it would be less likely that black female aspiring athletes would have the opportunity to refine the skills necessary for competitive varsity basketball.

I speculate that as the Women's National Basketball Association continues to develop, young, low-income, black females' perceptions will be altered such that they too will desire to have lifestyles in the limelight like their black male counterparts. Furthermore, as the prominence of the women's game increases, poor parents may be willing to expend finances to help move their daughters through the necessary training for a successful career in basketball. Although the women's game is not nearly as prominent or as financially viable for its participants as the men's professional game, it still provides a measure of success beyond that achieved by many individuals from lower-income neighborhoods.

The reasons for the lack of family support varied for the young men on the Knights. Some of the young men lived with elderly grandparents who had limited resources and often battled health ailments and thus gave limited visible support to the team. These grandparents had assumed responsibility for the young men, through diverse means, often at great personal expense.

Other players lived in single-parent households, where the sole wage earners were unable to attend games because they were working. Typically, these parents worked more than one job or were scheduled to work during evening hours. Such situations prevented the parents from attending games and supporting their sons. The young men who grew up in such households had become accustomed to their parents' work responsibilities. It was a great sacrifice for these parents to attend games—a fact revealed to me early on in my time coaching at Northeast.

When I first started with the ninth-grade team there was a parent who worked during her son's games. For our first home game Ms. Blake had taken off work early that day to come watch her son Trent play. Trent was a starter for me, but he was not playing well. He seemed to have a difficult time following my directions. I pulled Trent from the game at the start of the second quarter and did not let him play any more in the first half. After halftime I inserted another player in the game to start the second half. We were playing well and slowly inching the lead up. At some point during the fourth quarter Trent's mother came down to the bench, leaned over my left shoulder, and shouted at me, "When is Trent going get back in the game? I took off work early to see him play. When is he going to get back in the game?" Before I turned and said something rude to Ms. Blake, Trent said, "Mama, just go back up in the stands. This is between me and my coach!" I was relieved that the young man took responsibility for making certain that his mother's parental authority and my coaching authority remained separated. At the same time, I learned the kind of sacrifice that single working parents would have to make in order for them to see their sons play.

Although most of the parents did not support the team by participating in booster club activities or attending games, there were a few active parents, mostly a core group of three or four each year. They typically worked in middle-class occupations that provide both financial resources and flexible schedules that allowed for participation. These parents were unique in their support because they were typically willing to provide for the entire team, giving unselfishly from their own pockets. They provided pregame meals for the team, gave players rides home, and attended home and away games. Largely through their support for their sons, all the players benefited.

Because these parents were so few, and the basketball program budget was so small, Coach Benson had to constantly approach individual members within the community for their support of the team. In seeing the difficulty that Benson faced in one instance, my wife and I volunteered to feed the players and coaches for one pregame meal. We purchased a relatively inexpensive meal and spent approximately $200. Since the Knights play about thirty games annually it was easy to see how difficult it becomes for a core group of parents to maintain their financial support over the season. Thus, Coach Benson turned to church leaders, friends, and others to meet the team's needs.

The booster club members often questioned the need to feed twenty players a pregame meal (these objectors were usually parents of girls who had their own money to purchase meals). As coaches of the young men, we were aware that in some instances the pregame meals might be the best meal that a player received during the week. This was the rationale for our constantly seeking out sponsors for meals.

Over the years, there were parents whose support was more disingenuous—that is, it was contingent on the prominence of the role their son played on the team. These parents were involved with the program because they wanted to help their son gain in some personal way—for example, playing time or an athletic scholarship to college. These were also the parents who were prepared to express their unhappiness to coaches about their son's playing time. As Coach Benson's first assistant, I was given primary responsibility for deciding when and which players were substituted into the game. This meant I sometimes received pressure from parents about the decisions I made —despite the fact that the decisions were based on the conversations that Coach Benson and I had over time to determine which players might work best in which situations.

On one occasion, the father of one young man who was a substitute player on our team came to practice to meet with me regarding his son's scholarship chances and playing time. Our discussion ended when the father physically threatened me and challenged me to "step outside." When I refused to continue the encounter the father angrily left the gym. We had no further contact. The father had been involved with the basketball program but was primarily concerned about how the program would help his son get a scholarship. Oftentimes this happens because parents have an unrealistic understanding of what college coaches are looking for in players and what their sons are capable of doing themselves. This disjuncture between the players' ability and the parents' expectations helps the players to create unrealistic expectations about their athletic future.

Beyond the parents who seek personal gain for their sons and those who fail to support the young men during basketball activities, there was one unique parent. Mr. Thompson, the father of Ricky and Sylvester Thompson, became seriously involved with the team. Thompson is a 6'1", 225-pound, black male. He had been a kickboxing instructor and had competed in tournaments for several years. In addition to his full-time job as a building subcontractor, he owned a gym for training fighters. For two years during my time as assistant coach, Thompson volunteered as a conditioning coach for the Northeast Knights. He brought the exercises and discipline from his own athletic training to the Knights program. He joined us in the summer of Ricky's senior year and Sylvester's junior year. For two days a week

Thompson would teach the young men martial arts conditioning and techniques. They worked on agility, speed, and footwork. After his first summer, Thompson continued to travel with us to every game and was an unofficial coach on our bench. His support contributed to the team's success.

The Playing Field of Wilmington County

Against the backdrop of the "rough areas" in which the Northeast Knights players grow up were the suburban schools where the team had to go to compete. Since Northeast High School was one of only two large high schools in the Northeast community, the Knights had to travel to Wilmington County to compete with other schools of its size. These schools were newly built—less than fifteen years old—and located in mostly white middle- to upper-middle-class communities in Wilmington County. For instance, Western High, a Wilmington County school, is located across the street from family dwellings valued at $325,000. For the most part, all twelve schools that competed in Northeast's basketball region shared these socioeconomic characteristics. Not only were the players from the Wilmington County schools of a higher socioeconomic class than most of the Northeast players, but also most were white. In fact, only one of the twelve schools in Wilmington County had more than four black players on their boys' varsity basketball team during the time I coached.

Such socioeconomic and racial differences enhanced the already competitive spirit of the contests among schools. When I first joined the team and attended several practices, I kept hearing Coach Benson admonish his players for not practicing hard, despite the already overwhelming physical nature of the practice drills. I failed to understand why Benson would badger his players to be so aggressive in practice. There was excessive physical contact—like elbows to the face and hard slaps on the wrist. Most referees in games would rarely tolerate such behavior. Benson would sum up his admonishments by saying, "You and I know that you are not going to get any calls when you go to Wilmington County. You better be ready to take a beating and keep on playing." Older players, having played in Wilmington County previously, also acknowledged what they perceived to be unfair play and officiating when they played there. One player told me, "It's rough in Wilmington County. They really give you cheap shots. You gotta get a big lead because the referees will try to give the game to the home team. Nothing but a lot of home cookin'.'"

I perceived much of what Benson and the players were saying about Wilmington County as overblown statements about an opponent that the players and coaches despised. But on my first trip there, I immediately got a sense of the biased officiating and the unregulated rough play about which the players and Benson had complained. Even after that first game, I tried to maintain an objective position regarding officiating, but it seemed that every time we played in Wilmington County there was systematically unfair treatment.

In addition to the referees' and opposing players' behavior, the fans at these schools were hostile. Several times during the season the fans shouted obscenities at our players. Some fans, as we entered the gymnasium, made racist comments like, "Look at the little black monkeys" or "Here comes that gang of niggers." These fans were rarely reprimanded since Benson spent little energy during game time trying to identify the offenders to school officials who, in Coach Benson's eyes, probably shared the fans' sentiments. In some cases, however, the offending fans were identified by school security and removed from the gymnasium. It was in watching the players play within Wilmington County that I better understood the complex meanings that basketball had for the young men. Playing in Wilmington County was one of the few ways the young men could be treated with respect by defeating "them white boys." Even if the Wilmington County fans and players didn't respect the accomplishments of the Northeast Knights, the Knights were always proud of winning.

Basketball expresses the beauty and pain that the young men from Northeast High School meet with as they negotiate their everyday existence. It is as if dribbling, passing, and shooting a basketball can wipe away, in one stroke, the complex problems that they face. Through playing basketball the young men learn to hope for something more out of life than their communities can offer. In the short term this hopefulness is positive, as it keeps the young men off the streets. But, ultimately, these hopes are seldom realized, as there is no real future for them in basketball. Yet this hoop dream keeps the young men focused on making it in spite of difficult circumstances.

2

For the Good of All

I told myself, "I know I'm going to have my chance one day."

Smitty J tugged on his shorts as he bent over to breathe. He had just finished running sprints with half of the forty-two young men who wanted to play for the Northeast Knights. He was a scrawny freshman at six feet and about 160 pounds. He hadn't shown any particular basketball skills on previous practice days, and I didn't think today would be any different.

Since it was only our third day of full fall practice, the coaches had not yet met to divide the players into teams by grade or skill. I was biding my time and being patient with most of the young men. Clearly though, some of the boys just didn't belong. I was set on pointing out each one of these boys to Benson; I thought Smitty J was one of them.

"Next group," I barked. "Ready, go!" The second group of boys took off sprinting to the far end of the gym. Smitty J was still bent over trying to catch his breath and clutching his stomach. I looked at him and thought, *Look at him, he's weak. He doesn't have any basketball skills. He needs to go ahead and quit.*

"What's your name?" I asked.

"Smitty J," he replied between breaths.

"I'm Coach May," I said. "You alright?"

"Yeah."

"Then you better get ready to run; your group is next," I said. I turned to look at the next lineup of young men, most already leaning forward in anticipation of the next sprint. "Next group. Ready, go!"

Smitty J took off and stumbled just behind the group. He was dragging one foot and holding his side.

"Run, Smitty J!" I shouted.

Smitty J frowned at me. His response had been the same over the two previous days. He consistently made disapproving gestures to coaches when they commanded him to perform a certain drill. His looks seemed to be a direct challenge to our authority to run the team.

Although it was only my second year of coaching at Northeast, I knew that no matter how much I wanted to boot a player from the team, it was Coach Benson's policy not to cut players. I must admit to feeling frustrated as I watched guys who couldn't play get in the way of those guys who could.

After practice the coaches met to have our first discussion about the new and returning players. When we got to our discussion of the first-year students I said, "Well, of the freshmen, I think Smitty J is the weakest. I wish we could go ahead and let him and some of those others go too."

"Well, Coach May," Benson said, "I really like that kid Smitty J."

"Why? He can't shoot and he's uncoordinated," I replied. "He would be the first player I cut."

"Coach, he's just young," Benson, admonished me. "You gotta develop players. All they need is a chance."

I listened to Benson, but I didn't really accept what he had to say. I knew there were some young men who wouldn't ever be able to play no matter how much of a chance you gave them. They just weren't athletic enough to compensate for their lack of skill.

"Well, he wouldn't be the first player I would work with," I replied.

"Don't worry. He'll be alright," Benson replied.

Of course Benson had no intention of cutting any player from the team, so our discussion was moot.

At the time we discussed the future of this group I did not know that by his senior year at Northeast, Smitty J would be one of our starting forwards and a reliable rebounder standing at only 6'2". More important, I did not know that Smitty J would be the tough gritty kid that we could count on time and again to play against stronger, taller players, an often demanding physical challenge that few players could reliably handle. Smitty J wasn't afraid of any opponent.

Although I had no sense of his future basketball accomplishments, I did have an idea that he might be the kind of quick-tempered player, prone to physical altercations, that Coach Benson would assign one of the assistant coaches to watch during games. For this reason alone I would have cut Smitty J from the team. But Benson could see Smitty J's tenacity, and he knew that a kid like him would belong to the streets if he didn't have something else to focus on. Fortunately for Smitty J, Coach Benson wouldn't let him feel the humiliation of being cut from the Northeast Knights.

To Cut or Not to Cut

Perhaps one of the greatest sports tales in recent years is that of former National Basketball Association (NBA) All-Star Michael Jordan. Many have considered Jordan, who led the Chicago Bulls to six NBA championships in the 1990s, as the all-time greatest professional basketball player. Yet, ironically enough, Michael Jordan was cut from his high school basketball team during his sophomore year. As the story goes, after he was cut Jordan dedicated himself to improving his game that summer. He was determined to prove those coaches wrong. Each morning he arose from bed at 6:00 a.m. and worked on basketball drills and lifted weights with the assistance of his dedicated junior varsity basketball coach. By the time Jordan had finished that summer's intense workouts he had become stronger, faster, and more skilled.

That fall Jordan returned to the varsity team at his high school for his junior season. As we know, Jordan became an outstanding player for his high school team, excelled in college, and became a premier professional player. Still, Jordan had experienced the initial humiliation of being rejected by his high school team. This feeling is common for many young athletes who try out for high school teams. When they are cut from the team, few are able to return and enjoy success like Jordan's.

The masses of young men who believe they are the next great professional basketball player, combined with the intense pressure that administrators and community members place on high school coaches to win, means that most coaches must select some players and reject others. High school basketball coaches nationwide routinely cut thousands of prospective high school players during fall tryouts. These cuts may have a profound impact on both the psyche and development of the young men being rejected. In some instances, rejection fuels motivation for improvement, such as with Michael Jordan. In others, these cuts can fuel feelings of failure. Despite the range of possible responses that individual players might have to being cut, the reality is that this "survival of the fittest" policy is consistent with most American institutions as well.

Players who have survived team cuts may easily rationalize that they can be successful in basketball because a process that is widely recognized to select the best players has affirmed them. Furthermore, by having made the team, these young men buy into a system in which their coaches will push them even further, both physically and mentally, to work harder and commit themselves to the team's success —ultimately with the belief that they are capable of continued athletic success beyond high school. This is a key motivational tool for coaches who have constant pressure to produce winning teams. Within this context the notion that "you are only as good as your weakest player" becomes a real consideration. If coaches expect to win, they must select quality players—even those substitute players who will only play a few minutes in the game—so that the team is internally competitive. Once the players are selected, coaches use various means of motivation to build players' confidence in their own skills. Without this confidence, players would fall victim to the pressures of competition and lose games. This process, however, has the consequence of encouraging players who have little athletic talent to acquiesce to the notion that they too can compete in basketball at the next level.

Although teams that use tryouts and cuts frequently have nonstar players who aspire to compete in basketball beyond high school, this problem becomes far more pervasive on those teams, like the Northeast Knights, who use a no-cut policy.

In high school basketball, a coach who uses a no-cut policy at a school with a sizable student population is unusual. On the one hand, with a large pool of talent, such a coach could expect to have his pick of the litter, and yet on the other hand, with so many possible players the team could easily become overwhelmed. Given the possible impracticalities of such a no-cut policy, I read Coach Benson's longstanding choice to field his team in this fashion as an altruistic one. The players have far more to gain than the coaches or even the team as a whole. One of the main drawbacks of the no-cut policy is that in allowing a large number of players to participate on the team, the building of team cohesion that occurs within small-group interaction can be jeopardized. In the sport of basketball, such cohesion is a necessity for winning.[1] Despite this threat to his team's success, Benson allows all who come out for the team to remain.

This is not to suggest that Benson's motivation for helping these young men is selfless. Indeed, it's reasonable to wonder whether humans can act without self-interest. Some have even suggested that acting selflessly is an act of selfishness in and of itself, given the gratification that one might receive from an unselfish act.[2] That said, I can't help but admire Benson for his choice because in my opinion the policy had a tremendously positive impact on the team.

What Constitutes the No-Cut Policy?

Coach Benson's no-cut policy is grounded in his belief that young men should be given an opportunity to be successful. He explained to me that the policy is rooted in his own experience as a black male, native of Northeast, and a one-time resident of the Eastridge housing project located just two blocks from the high school. Given the difficulties that these young men face because of enduring racism and their limited economic opportunities, Benson sees the team as a "safe space"—a place where the boys will always be given a chance and a place where they will not be rejected.

Each fall approximately fifty players for the varsity team alone come out to compete for an opportunity to play for Coach Benson and the Knights. Instead of being subjected to the rigorous physical tests and intense competition that most coaches use to help them select the right players, Benson puts the young men through fundamental skill training and physical conditioning. Traditionally, high school coaches make their team selection after a few days of workouts and evaluations, usually reducing their team roster to twelve to fifteen players. In most instances, the names of the players that "made it" are displayed prominently on a list attached to the coach's door. This public display intensifies both the glory of making the team and the humiliation of being rejected since all those who participated, and anyone else who happens upon the public list, are made aware of who did and did not make the team. Benson's approach avoids the sting of rejection. Some players may receive more of an opportunity to perform in drills, but all players are allowed to participate and are allowed to continue attending practice. If and when players do decide to leave the team, their departure lacks the stigma of rejection.

Although Benson's no-cut policy is well received by most players, who enjoy the opportunity to spend time with a large group of teammates, many parents consider the policy a hindrance to having a successful basketball program because the policy limits playing time. This is especially true for players looking to demonstrate their abilities to college recruiters. Yet, given the longstanding success of the Northeast Knights, these detractors have little opportunity to build enough momentum to force a change in policy or get a new coach. The players are aware of the added tension that exists between parents and Benson.

Initially, I agreed with the parents. I assumed that so many additional players would bring unnecessary problems, especially the limits to playing time. From my past experience, I knew that even teams that carried just twelve players usually had at least two or three players that thought they should be playing more. When these players complained, they negatively affected team chemistry and cohesion, which ultimately affected team success. Thus, I believed that having twenty to twenty-five players on the team would mean we would have even more dissatisfied players on our hands.

This was definitely the case one year when we had twenty-eight players on the roster but could only dress twenty-three players because we didn't have enough uniforms. We tried to compensate by having the last five players on the roster rotate with the two lowest-skilled players who were dressing. This resulted in having some of the younger players who were better skilled in uniform as opposed to older players who were not as skilled. Other factors that determined whether a player dressed were dependent on Coach Benson's evaluation of a player's individual situation, including whether a player faced disciplinary action for some disapproved behavior, whether a player had a personal crisis that affected his weekly practice performance, or how long a player had "paid his dues" in the program. Benson typically made his dressing roster about an hour before each game. Since I was responsible for handing out the team uniforms, I was the coach that had to inform the players that they would not be dressing. This was probably one of the more painful responsibilities for me. It was gut-wrenching to pass out uniforms to all those dressing and have remaining players look at me with frustration as they discovered that they would not dress. Typically, Coach Benson did not give an explanation to the player.

Since a large number of players participating in a traditionally noninclusive varsity sport would create more distractions, it would seem that Benson's goal of positively influencing many young men contradicted his competitive desire. Yet Benson's stated goal of winning was always evident in his talk to the players: "I don't care if it's five people out there on the floor in wheelchairs, you play to win. If it's old folks from the nursing home and they step between these lines, then they're going to get their ass beat." By giving each player enough attention, criticism, and encouragement to keep him involved, Benson was able to reconcile his winning philosophy with his desire to help as many young men as he could. As Benson pointed out to me, since most of the kids hail either from Flat Shoals, Hillside, or Eastridge housing developments, they would have greater opportunity to get into trouble if they were not with us.

Community Context and Collective Support

It almost goes without saying that the players on the Northeast Knights basketball team enjoy playing basketball.[3] But beyond their enjoyment of basketball, the players are aware of conditions outside basketball that compel them to be a part of the Knights when they would otherwise have quit or been cut. Although these conditions are not uniform for each player, the majority of players face similar struggles, so much so that I would say that the players share an "idioculture" that supports the team's no-cut policy.[4] An idioculture "consists of a system of knowledge, beliefs, behaviors, and customs shared by members of an interacting group to which members can refer and that serve as the basis of further interaction."[5] For something to become part of a group's idioculture, it must be known by the members of the group, have a usable social meaning, be functional to address a group's problems, be appropriate within the group's hierarchy status, and usually be triggered by some experienced event.[6] The Northeast Knights' no-cut policy meets these criteria. Coach Benson's desire to be inclusive forms the basis on which the young men and coaches form an idioculture that provides beliefs and behaviors that help them manage the no-cut policy.

As mentioned, underlying the no-cut policy is Benson's recognition of the difficulties that many of the Northeast youth face within the broader community. Since most of the players hail from low-income housing developments and attend schools that provide few resources, their opportunities are limited. They can't afford special athletic camps to help them with their skills, nor can they afford lessons or expensive equipment. The players recognize these limitations and are, for the most part, supportive of the no-cut policy. For instance, Byron, a starter, suggests that he is comfortable with the no-cut policy because he recognizes that everyone should be given an opportunity to succeed or develop.

> *May*: Well, what do you think about the no-cut policy? Is that a good
>   thing or a bad thing?
> *Byron*: It's a good thing. Everybody should have a chance.
> *May*: So it's a good thing, even if people like Yurell and Nathan . . .
> *Byron*: They can say they had a chance to play.
> *May*: Yeah. Alright. You ever feel like they were—people like that
>   were a distraction at all?
> *Byron*: Oh, naw. They just played hard. They came at you.

Byron suggests not only that the players are given a chance to play but that the team can benefit from the marginal players' competitiveness. Yurell and Nathan, the two marginal players mentioned, had limited basketball skills and physical ability and had demonstrated a limited mental capacity for understanding the nuances of the game. Although Yurell and Nathan were not documented as mentally disabled, Benson had coached several players who were learning disabled or who had Attention-Deficit/Hyperactivity Disorder (ADHD).[7] Occasionally, Benson would joke with the other coaches, "I should be getting paid extra money for all of the kids they send me that they don't want to deal with." In addition to working with any young man who wanted to come out for basketball, Benson would often have "problem" youth, who were "given permission" by their teacher to come to the gym during Benson's physical-education class period. Many of the teachers viewed Benson as a stabilizing force for these "problem" youths at Northeast High School. These "problem" youths not only were disciplinary problems but also included students with special needs. For instance, William was a deaf member of the team. Given his limited skill and his physical stature (5′3″, 180 pounds), it's likely that had Benson held tryouts at the beginning of the season, William would have been cut.

Byron's comment about Yurell and Nathan, "they can say they had a chance to play," suggests that these players can take pride in the fact that they were members of the Northeast Knights basketball team. This is a significant point, given that for many of the youths there are few things about their lives and surroundings of which they might feel proud.

The fact that Coach Benson has an overall concern for the youths in Northeast is not lost on his players. Turo also recognized that Benson was concerned with the feelings of those individuals that would most likely be marginalized by being cut.

> He doesn't cut anyone 'cause he feels for them. He don't wanna cut nobody. 'Cause, like, they might feel, like, hurt and disappointed. So he keeps people on the team or whatever, and they roll and have fun with us.

Turo suggests that the no-cut policy is grounded in a desire to protect the youths and their feelings. Indeed, it is easy to understand this approach when one considers the tough circumstances in which many of the Knights grow up. There are constant reminders of those who have fallen victim to the deleterious conditions within their neighborhoods. In fact, Benson was himself a resident of the Eastridge neighborhood and has lost family and friends to violence and drugs. The most recent event occurred in May 2004, when Benson's twenty-four-year-old nephew was shot in the back and killed after an altercation with another male in the Cookman Square Homes—a housing development five minutes from Northeast High School.

Another player, Ricky, also recognized the utility of the no-cut policy:

> *Ricky*: Yeah, [the no-cut policy was good] because it didn't, as far as, it didn't break any kid's heart as far as coming out and stuff.
> *May*: Yeah. Do you think it had any negative impact on the team at all?
> *Ricky*: Naw, not really . . . 'cause, like, even if some of them that didn't get cut or whatever, and they still on the team, they still

may have supported the team, like during the games and stuff. I've seen them down there [at the end of the bench] clapping the team up.

In each case Byron, Turo, and Ricky—all starters—indicate that the no-cut policy had positive outcomes for both their teammates and the team. For some players these outcomes may have been nothing more than having the opportunity to choose whether they would continue to play basketball. For instance, Jaris, an infrequently used substitute player, recognizes the degree to which the no-cut policy gave him the freedom to choose what he would do rather than being forced to leave the team:

> Actually, I kinda liked the way y'all did that [the no-cut policy] because if you are a player and you see that you're not—if they're [the coaches] not, like, using you or whatever, you could leave—unless you just wanted to stay there [on the team] and learn and try to get better for next year or something. It's kinda straight to me 'cause most people, like, if you didn't make the team, it's like heartbreaking or whatever. But if you just wanted to stay around and just, like, help the team or whatever—like fix water and tote bags—I guess that was cool.

Jaris's comments suggest how the beliefs, attitudes, and behaviors related to the Knights' idioculture reflect the players' understanding of the community circumstances that make the no-cut policy functional for the young men. As sociologist Gary Fine suggests in his discussion of idioculture, "For an item of culture to be overtly functional to a group, the group must define itself, either implicitly or explicitly, as having a problem, and then the cultural item may be proposed as a solution to the problem."[8] The problem, identified by Benson and later affirmed by the players, is one in which there is a constant threat to the lives and the well-being of young black males within Northeast. Since there are few positive alternatives in Northeast for expressions of masculinity and manhood beyond sports, the players at Northeast High School identify with being a part of the team.[9]

Irrespective of their individual ability, the players are capable of recognizing the benefits that accrue to them, because they choose to continue as Northeast Knights. For instance, Meshaq, a marginal player who would have surely been cut if Benson held tryouts, reflects on the ways he benefited from the no-cut policy:

> *Meshaq*: I liked it because it gave me a chance to really try to show you what I could have did and what I can do. You know . . . it really helped out players like Nathan and me. We were like the bottom of the food chain really. . . . So it really gave us both a chance to try and do something. Even though he was kinda crazier than me. But, you know, we had fun, you know, playing the sport that we like to play.
>
> *May*: Did you get frustrated by having to sit on the bench a lot?
>
> *Meshaq*: Not really, because sometimes I'm like, "I'm glad he [Benson] didn't put me in that spot." 'Cause I don't know what I might have did.
>
> *May*: Okay. But other times you felt, you know . . .
>
> *Meshaq*: Sometimes I wanted to get in there [the game] and just make somebody move out the way. Make a little statement right quick. [I laugh.] You know, go to the hole hard and lay it up. . . . Just make a statement, then he [Benson] can take me out.
>
> *May*: Do you think by having that many people—more people than we had uniforms for—was that a bad thing?
>
> *Meshaq*: Not really, because everybody was able to come to practice, you know. And really, during practice, you should be able to work even harder to try to move up. So that would have gave them more chance right there. I remember last year I didn't even get a jersey, but, you know, I still kept working.
>
> *May*: During games or during practice?
>
> *Meshaq*: No games. I didn't get no jersey, but, you know, I was still cool with it though.
>
> *May*: Did you feel like—were you disappointed that you had to get water or carry bags or anything?
>
> *Meshaq*: Naw, 'cause I told myself like, "I know I'm going to have my chance one day."

Meshaq was a player with an aggressive disposition. In fact, he had a reputation among his teammates and the people around his Eastridge neighborhood as a "fighter" who would not hesitate to engage in physical confrontations. His participation on the basketball team was a special point of pride for him. He recognized how playing ball gave him an opportunity to "stay out of trouble." He would only need to turn to his younger brother, Oshay, for a prime example of the dangers of street life. Oshay, at sixteen, had been to the Youth Detention Center several times for burglary and theft. Meshaq once told me, "I tried to tell him to get involved with sports or something, but he won't." If Meshaq himself had been cut from the Knights team, he too could have easily been "out in the streets."

Meshaq's teammate Pooty Cat, another player who grew up near Northeast, agreed that he too had been saved by his participation with the Knights. For him, the greatest advantage was having something to do after school:

> Say, like, you know, you'll have something to do after school. You ain't gotta go home, you know what I'm saying. You be outside and no telling what you might get into.

Ultimately, it is this kind of feeling of belonging that Coach Benson tried to build among his players. Benson structured the team selection process on the basis of the context of individual and community influences. These elements are best understood as helping to create an atmosphere that facilitates the team's success despite its unusual organizational structure.

Practical Problems and Players' Perceptions

I sometimes think of the basketball team much like a business organization that operates within a competitive market.[10] The basketball team seeks to effectively compete with other teams in much the same way as businesses seek to outperform their competition. Like a business whose structure affects its productivity, a team's structure can affect its chances of consistently winning. In the case of the Northeast Knights, the team has consistently had success despite having a team structure based on a no-cut policy that encourages players with limited skills to become a part of the team.

The Northeast Knights competed in a region with twelve teams from Wilmington County—a predominantly white, suburban, middle- to upper-middle-class community.[11] Most teams in this region had rosters with no more than twelve to fifteen players per team. The

Northeast Knights' team structure was an anomaly noticeable to referees, opposing fans, and players alike.

When we visited high schools within the region to compete, referees and opposing fans were quick to note our team's structural difference. For example, the referees—who were responsible for making certain that the number of players dressed in uniform matched the number of players in the score book—could be seen counting our players over and over again as the players moved through pregame warmups. Typically, it only took a few moments for the referees to display a look of frustration from having to re-count the players several times. At one game, a referee, amazed by the twenty-two Knights in warmup, asked his partner, "Does the Georgia High School Association even allow this many players on a varsity roster?"

Nowhere in the rule book was there a statement regarding the number of players to be fielded by a varsity basketball team. The only point at which the number of players on the team becomes relevant, insofar as the rules are concerned, is during the state tournament playoffs. The rule mandated that only twenty people, including players, coaches, and staff, be permitted free admission into the playoff facility. We circumvented this requirement by arranging for players to gain entrance on official coaching passes that permitted a coach to bring an additional person to the game. Thus, all the players on our roster were able to dress and compete during our trips to the state tournament.

In addition to the referees' perceptions, fans of the opposing team frequently noted our numbers in their pregame commentary with shouts of "Man, look at that army. There are a lot of them." Some of the Knights found this structure problematic from a practical standpoint. For instance, Turo, a three-year starter for Northeast, in the following exchange describes his perception of the no-cut policy and its impact on the team. His perception of the Knights' organizational structure is particularly interesting, given that his playing time—a concern for most players—was little affected by the fact that there were many players.

> *May*: Do you think having twenty players on the team was a good thing?
> *Turo*: No. [He laughs, then I laugh.]
> *May*: No?
> *Turo*: No.

May: Why not?

Turo: I say you should have at least twelve to fifteen players.

May: Twelve to fifteen players? Why do you think having twenty is not a good thing?

Turo: I don't know. I just think that's too many people. All of them ain't going to be able to play, because you ain't going to be able to blow a team out every game. . . . I know I wouldn't like to be sitting on no bench the whole game.

Turo recognizes the practical implication of having so many players with so little time available to compete. When the Knights team was successfully defeating its opponent by a "blowout" then all the Knights were guaranteed the opportunity to play. Yet, as Turo points out, "you ain't going to be able to blow a team out every game." Thus, the question becomes, What are some of the internal tensions that result by having a team structure that is all-inclusive?

May: You think Coach Benson knows that having a lot of people on the team is not a good thing? 'Cause, you know, you said you didn't think it was a good thing.

Turo: I don't think he knows it because—I don't think he . . . He couldn't cut nobody really.

May: But, I mean, like you said, it wasn't a good thing, and you figured as a team, since everybody couldn't play, if you had fewer people on the team, it'd probably be a better team. You think?

Turo: Yeah. You know how you have people on the bench and they never get in? Then they start talking about the team and stuff. That put the team down, and then somebody get to arguing.

One of the problems, according to Turo, is that some players become disgruntled if they do not have an opportunity to play. Although Turo suggests this as a problem that the Knights face, this is also a point of contention for teams that have only twelve to fifteen players. This problem exists even at the professional level, where some professional players have demanded to be traded to another team so that they might achieve greater playing time and an opportunity to be recognized as a star performer.

I would argue that if the Northeast Knights did not have an idioculture that helped them bond together, then when the number of players on the Knights' roster grew beyond the traditional twelve to fifteen players, the conflict around playing would intensify and negate the team's cohesiveness and thus effectiveness. Jaris, an infrequently used substitute player, recognized this difficulty when I asked him whether there were too many people on the team:

> Not really. Well, somewhat, because they always used to whine about the bench—like it was crowded on the bench or whatever. But like if you wasn't—I guess everybody wanted to play. If we having a good game, everybody wants to get in and play.

Jaris was ambivalent about the degree to which he felt comfortable with the team's no-cut policy. For him, the no-cut policy offered an opportunity to be a part of something. Yet it was also a hindrance to the overall team experience.

As simple as it might be, the team's tension around sitting on the bench brings to light the Knights' divergence from traditional team structure. Most facilities are not set up to accommodate a team of twenty or more players and four to five coaches. The mismatch between team size and accommodations means that players have to devise innovative ways to sit together. For instance, players pushed individual seats together so that two players could share a chair, or players sit in the bleachers directly behind the bench. Despite these innovations, as Jaris suggests, players continue to "whine about the bench." This "whining" is consistent with the kinds of responses that many professional basketball players demonstrate when they have displeasure about a playing circumstance. Such responses from professional players are well known to the Northeast Knight players, who are frequent consumers of televised sporting events and of the sports media's coverage of the players' (seemingly) every move.

Team Productivity, Coaches' Strategies, and Players' Responses

Most coaches will tell you, "You play the way you practice." The idea behind this phrase is that the more consistently players work at developing a skill in practice, the greater chance that they will be able to perform that skill at the required time in the game. Indeed, this is the reason why so many coaches spend time drilling shooting skills. Players who can effectively shoot and score improve the possibility that a team can win. In this regard a no-cut policy for team selection can have an impact on team performance outcomes by simple mathematics. For instance, if twenty to twenty-five players are allowed to join in practice drills in a two-hour practice period, then each player will take fewer repetitions than if there were only twelve players. In short, this means that the better players will have reduced time to further develop their skills. Those Northeast Knights who are marginally skilled are therefore consuming practice repetitions that are typically available on other teams for more accomplished players.

Despite the limitation presented by an excessive number of players practicing, one could argue that the no-cut policy is a competitive advantage because it provides a steady pool of athletes who compete for the Knights should one become injured, quit, or become academically ineligible. However, the disparity between the skills of those proficient players and their substitutes is so great that the loss of a significant player has a real effect. There is little competitive advantage to having only a "warm body" to replace a player who previously contributed a great deal to the team's success.

Given the possibility that nonessential players might consume essential players' repetitions, Northeast coaches developed practice strategies that improved the opportunity for better players to participate in practice more than their marginal counterparts. Simple steps were taken to limit marginal players from multiple repetitions. Although these marginal players were given the opportunity to participate in drills, they were not given repeated opportunities. In some respects, then, the marginal players were treated with a degree of second-class status. If the marginal players were not prepared to sacrifice their own workout time but demonstrated dissatisfaction with their role, then their subsequent behavior could alter the cultural climate of team practice—usually for the worse.

Because of the no-cut policy at Northeast, the team is certain to have players that will not help them to win games.[12] Just by their mere presence, these players alter the team's goal of winning in favor of their own desire to play, both in practice and in games. If they do not get playing time, these players can become disgruntled, and their dissatisfaction can be contagious. Thus, coaches walk a fine line between the individual player's satisfaction and the team's success and cohesion.

The no-cut policy is perhaps the greatest coaching challenge at Northeast because each player needs to feel that he can positively contribute to the basketball program. Coach Benson must emphasize to each player that he is contributing and that he will have the opportunity to contribute more in the future. To this end, Benson encouraged individual players, whether starter, role player, or marginally used substitutes, to work hard in practice. Still, players like Yancey, a rarely used substitute, perceived Benson's encouragements to be disingenuous. These feelings drove Yancey to question the utility of the no-cut policy altogether:

> *Yancey*: I thought maybe he [Benson] was just stringing some guys along, 'cause usually in the locker room, maybe if we lost a game, he's going to say to this player right here like, "Get ready." Then the next time you come to practice he doesn't even use that player. I wouldn't say he was stringing them along but just getting their hopes up that maybe sooner or later they would play.
>
> *May*: Is that a good thing or a bad thing?
>
> *Yancey*: It could be good and negative in a way on that player. 'Cause that player is saying to himself, "Okay, now I know I gotta work harder because he may put me in that situation." But if that player keeps working harder and he knows he's not playing, then that's just going to bring his self-esteem back down, and he's not going to work that hard like he used to.
>
> *May*: Would it be worse to get cut or to be strung along?
>
> *Yancey*: I'd rather get cut. Just let me know if I didn't make the team. 'Cause that would make me wanna work harder that next year to make the team, to show him that I can play.

Yancey suggests that Coach Benson's encouragement to work harder fell on deaf ears. Indeed, Benson consistently selected the higher-skilled players to play, and only on occasion would lesser-skilled players be given an opportunity to play. Ultimately, players like Yancey became disgruntled. In this way, the no-cut policy had a negative effect on some players. For Yancey, a marginal player, perhaps being cut would have forced him to face the reality that he had to work harder to get better. Yancey's preference for a "survival of the fittest" selection process is consistent with the ways competition and selection work in free-market capitalism.

Other players central to the team would have also welcomed the challenge of being cut. They too seek the clarity of a system that eliminates those who are not good enough. For instance, Turo, a three-year starter and team leader, suggests that being cut, if he were not capable of making the team, would have provided him with important motivation for improvement:

> *May*: You think it would have hurt you if Coach Benson had cut you?
> *Turo*: Not really. I would have came back the next year and worked harder. I would have worked harder.
> *May*: Yeah, but even if you had worked harder and Benson had cut you, would it have hurt you?
> *Turo*: Yeah. I would want to transfer and come back and play y'all and beat y'all.

Turo's recognition that he would have been hurt by being cut is important. He, like so many of the other players, is aware of the kinds of struggles that result from an inclusive team-selection policy. Turo and Yancey are examples of young men who would have taken their rejection from the team and used it as a means of motivation. Their attitudes are consistent with an overall ethos that supports competition. And yet they both accepted the no-cut policy as an important positive attribute of being a Northeast Knight.

Imitation as Flattery

The Knights' unusual selection process also had an effect on the teams in the region, especially since the Knights were consistently successful.[13] Other teams in the region attempted to change and modify their own team structures as a result of viewing the Knights program as successful and therefore worthy of imitation.[14] However, as far as I could tell, these teams' attempts to replicate the Knights' success using the Knights' team model without the cultural infrastructure to support it ultimately proved unsuccessful.

For example, one year Missionary High School dressed nineteen players. During their two games against Northeast High School their strategy was to match their platoon of players with the Knights' platoon of players. Each time the Knights substituted five players off the floor, Missionary did the same. In both games in which the Knights played Missionary, the Knights won.

The following year, the head coach of Missionary reverted back to the traditional twelve- to fifteen-player team composition. Although I was unable to question the Missionary coach about his decision to revert to the team's structure, I speculate that the coach found managing additional players to be problematic. I do not mean, however, to suggest that there are no alternative explanations for Missionary's return to a traditional team structure. In fact, it is reasonable to suspect that the pool of talent from which Missionary's coach could have selected his team might have declined measurably after the year he attempted to fill a roster of twenty players. But at no other time over the seven years I coached at Northeast High School did Missionary attempt to dress and play more than fifteen players. Similarly, Ford Heights, another school that attempted this approach, also discontinued its use after one year. Thus, I surmise that both coaches were merely experimenting with a team structure that they viewed as successful.

When Benson saw Missionary and Ford Heights' replication of the Knights' team structure he simply restated the well-known phrase, "They say imitation is the highest form of flattery."

The Power of Not Cutting

Benson's leadership and the players' acute awareness of the challenges of their neighborhood environments fostered the collective attitude necessary for assuaging the tensions that arose from carrying additional players on the team. Within the context of team formation, the young men learned how to assume nonconfrontational roles that did not detract from the overall competitive orientation of the team. As a condition of being part of the team, some players accepted the possibility that they would have to share a uniform with another player on the team. But, as Meshaq pointed out, as long as he was a part of the Knights in any capacity, he had an opportunity to demonstrate what he could do. The no-cut policy gave him the opportunity.

As the players begin participating in team practice, they come to understand that they are competing for a place within the structural hierarchy of the team. Just as workers in an organization understand that they are competing with others for additional resources (for example, increased salary), so too do the players understand that they are competing with one another for more playing time and the opportunity to perform. Thus, the no-cut policy circumvents the harsh and instantaneous exclusion that comes from tryouts and cuts, ultimately encouraging the players to believe that they continually have the opportunity to successfully demonstrate their abilities in much the same way that others are convinced that they have the opportunity to freely pursue the American Dream. These themes of equality and meritocracy echo throughout the young men's experiences as Northeast Knights. They provide the basis on which the players hold out hope for future basketball success despite long odds.

Many of the Knights believe that as long as they are close to the game they have a chance to demonstrate what they can do. The no-cut policy encourages the players to keep playing the game instead of risking being swallowed up by the streets. Admittedly, this approach to team selection perpetuates a belief on the part of average players that they have the capabilities to play at the next level. In this regard, the seed for mobility through athletic participation is planted. But I am sure that Smitty J, that scrawny, quick-tempered freshman, was better off as a Knight, rather than a victim, first of my intention to cut him and second to the lure of drugs and violence in his rough Cookman Square neighborhood.

3

The Three D's

Drugs, Drinking, and Delinquency

Oh, man. They smoke, drugs, they do everything like that. You can't put it past them.

If we lost another game our season would be over. We had finished the regular season sixteen and six, winning the last ten out of eleven games for an impressive run to the state playoffs. We were slated to play the Trojans of Tresom High School from Atlanta in the first round of the state playoffs. Earlier in the season at a Christmas tournament they had defeated us by ten points. Although they were bigger than we were, we had rebounded well but lost the game because of our inability to protect the ball in the last two minutes of the fourth quarter.

For this game we would have to travel to Tresom since they had a higher seed in the state tournament. After a two-hour bus ride, our players seemed eager to play. As the boys got dressed, the other coaches left the locker room to watch the end of the first playoff game; I stayed behind issuing out uniforms. The players waited for Benson to come and give his pregame talk after they got dressed. Some of the boys pounded basketballs hard against the floor and locker-room walls. Others paired together and stretched. Most of them were listening to CD players and bobbing their heads to the music and lyrics of rappers like Master P, Three Six Mafia, Juvenile, Ruff Ryders, and Hot Boys. I could easily distinguish the lyrics blaring from the boys' headphones:

I need a hot girl . . . I need a hot and spicy ho I can shop with.
Give my ho 10 g's, tell her to spend the shit . . .[1]

Benson came down to the locker room for his talk. He pulled a chair up and sat down and said, "Everybody up." The boys pulled off their CD players, grabbed the balls, and sat on the bench in front of Benson.

"Gentlemen," Benson began, "tonight is a chance for you to make a statement about what this team is all about. What you have done to this point doesn't matter. The only thing that matters is what you do from here on out. This is an opportunity to show people who you are and what you're about. Now, to do this, you gonna have to get after it like there is no tomorrow, 'cause if you don't, there won't be a to-morrow."

The players sat focused on Benson and listened as he spoke plainly, "You know, they say it's not the size of the dog that matters but the fight in the dog. Have you ever seen some of them little dogs? Some of your most vicious dogs are them little biddy dogs about like this." Benson held his hand out about a foot from the floor.

"Ha, ha," the players laughed.

"You'll see those big dogs barking, and the little dog is just stand-ing there quiet. See 'cause he sizing the big dog up. He's just waiting for the right time to get his ass. So when the big dog gets too close, that little dog jumps all on his ass. He locks his jaws on the ass of the big dog and won't let go."

The players continued to laugh.

"I ain't kidding. What's the name of those dogs? You know the lit-tle ones? They be all on that big dog's ass. That big dog is running around in circles, and that little dog is locked on to his ass until the big dog just gets tired and stops running. The big dog is like, 'Damn, would you get off my ass.'"

"Ha, ha," the players laughed.

"Gentlemen, I wanna see y'all get on Tresom's ass like that little dog. They might be bigger than us, but you know how to get after it. Just jump they ass and lock on just like that little dog. This is your chance to do something that you won't have a chance to do again. You won't ever come this way again."

As the laughter subsided Benson surveyed the room. When he was satisfied that the players had gotten the message he said, "Let's go get after it. Now let's get the prayer." The coaches and players started rising up from the benches and circled together.

As we circled Benson said, "Gentlemen, don't panic if we get into trouble early. This is the state playoffs. Teams are going to throw everything they have at you. We can handle anything that anybody can throw at us. This is your chance. Your time is now."

From the moment the referee tossed the ball up for the jump, this game was different from the last time we had played Tresom, and everyone on our team knew it. Perhaps it was Benson's speech, perhaps it was the adrenaline of the state playoffs, or perhaps we were missing Curtis Duster.

Curtis was only 6'4" and 185 pounds, but his arms were extremely long and he was an excellent leaper. He scored well around the goal, and we could count on him to get at least eight rebounds a game against taller and stronger players. But his biggest attribute was his defensive presence. He jumped so high that he was able to block jumpshots from inside the paint without being called for goaltending. But, Curtis wasn't there.

After the first quarter Tresom High School led the game by ten points. Our players looked more discouraged than I had seen all season. Tresom was scoring on almost every possession because we had no one to match against their big players in the paint. I couldn't help but think how many shots Curtis would have blocked if he had not been arrested a few days earlier.

At the end of the first half Tresom was ahead by twenty points. Benson entered the locker room at halftime and said, "Some of y'all need to get off y'all ass and play. We can't wait around. We don't have some players with us tonight, but does that mean we are just going to lie down? Shit, if y'all don't get off your ass, I'ma put some of these JV players in. They can't do no worse than what y'all doing. Now let's go. We can't win the game from in the locker room."

The Knights seemed renewed for the second half, but just like the first half, Tresom couldn't be stopped on the inside. *We miss Curtis*, I thought.

Curtis had been arrested a few days before the state tournament when the police conducted a drug raid on his aunt's home. Apparently, his aunt had been running a drug house, and Curtis happened to be in the house when the police raided it. "He was just in the wrong place at the wrong time," Benson had said.

By the beginning of the third quarter there was no amount of motivation that the coach could provide because we all realized that our players were no match for Tresom on this night. It seemed as if all of us wanted the game over. We had missed the state playoffs the previous year, and this year we were getting outplayed. By the time the final horn sounded Tresom High School had thumped us by fifty-two points. We were all embarrassed.

On the bus ride back to Northeast, Benson sat in his usual seat at the front of the bus. He leaned over to me across the aisle and said, "May, we missed Curtis tonight."

"Yeah we did," I said, "but I'm not sure Curtis could have made up the difference of fifty-two points."

"You're probably right," Benson replied, "but Curtis wouldn't have been scared."

"That's for sure," I said.

We both sat back in our seats for the long bus ride back home. *These rides are always longer when you lose,* I thought.

As Benson sat back in his seat I heard him mumble, "Drugs."

Temptations

Like many other adolescent boys, the Northeast Knights are confronted with temptations about drugs, alcohol, and other delinquent behavior.[2] Given that many of the Northeast Knights hail from low-income areas where drug use and distribution is performed openly, these boys seem all the more vulnerable. Although these young men live in a small metropolitan area, parts of Northeast resemble the urban ghetto that sociologist Elijah Anderson describes in his study of inner-city North Philadelphia, *Code of the Street*:

> In the impoverished inner-city neighborhood, the drug trade is everywhere, and it becomes ever more difficult to separate the drug culture from the experience of poverty. The neighborhood is sprinkled with crack dens located in abandoned buildings or in someone's home. On corner after corner, young men peddle drugs the way a newsboy peddles papers.[3]

Like the young men of North Philadelphia, many of the Knights face constant pressure within their neighborhoods to be involved in drugs —if only through witnessing constant drug use or seeing the material benefits of drug sales. During my seven-year tenure I witnessed at least three Northeast Knights quit the team and turn to habitual drug use or to selling narcotics. Coach Benson mentioned that during his time at Northeast he knew of several more players addicted to drugs or arrested for drug-related crimes, some even dying as a result of criminal violence.[4] One of Coach Benson's latent goals for the Northeast Knights basketball program is to quell such activities by immersing the young men in basketball as a way of life. During the school year we had the young men practice seven days a week and do school work during afterschool study hall four times a week, and we generally consumed the young men's "free time." As Meshaq, a player from Eastridge, suggested, "To be honest, we see y'all more than we see our mothers."

In 2003 a school policy was rewritten to explicitly prohibit a seven-day-a-week practice schedule. Coach Benson was disappointed with this policy because he felt the school administration had failed to appreciate both the athletic and social significance of keeping the boys active with basketball. Although I grew fatigued during the season from such intense workouts day in and day out, over time I began to appreciate the rationale for Benson's holding practice seven days a week, even on Christmas and Thanksgiving holidays. These young men were in constant danger of engaging in delinquent behavior, and having practice offered them a "safe haven" and a largely positive activity on which to focus their energies.

In this chapter I show how the community contexts in which the young men grow up help them to view basketball as a prime means of not only survival but also mobility. Within their low-income communities the young men are provided with seemingly clear choices to either participate in delinquent behavior or to seek status in some form of athletic participation. These choices are predicated on taken-for-granted stereotypes of black males that flow from media portrayals of the "aflete" or "hustla." For instance, the young men see players like Shaquille O'Neal, star center for the NBA's Miami Heat, on television programs like *MTV Cribs* driving his car with custom "extras" through the 'hood, or they watch black actors like Terrence Howard, in movies like *Hustle & Flow*, "come up"—gain status—by pimping and rapping in the 'hood.[5] Within their own neighborhoods the support that the players receive reinforces the notion that they are capable athletes who may one day move beyond their neighborhoods. Interestingly, even the drug dealers, gang leaders, and other disreputable characters within the young men's communities become supporters of the young men's athletic aspirations.

Calvin and the Crackheads

The crackheads were standing along the side of Calvin's house as I stopped my car. They were milling around and waiting impatiently for something. Calvin opened my car door and said, "I'll be right back, May." He got out of the car, walked across the street, and went into his grandmother's single-story, wood-frame house. The four-room house was located on the southwest corner of Wilson and Pike streets near the Eastridge housing development. There was an empty lot directly behind the house. From the street I could see that a few more "hypes" were standing by the back porch waiting. I sat watching the crackheads and taking in the enormity of Calvin's situation. Thirty seconds later Calvin emerged from the house with his gym shoes in hand. As he walked to the car, I contemplated the daily challenges that he must face just getting to and from school. Calvin's house was only four blocks from the school, yet I had never seen this area up close until I had to run him home to get his shoes. I had heard about his living situation from Mr. Hunt and others, but seeing this area made it real to me. It reminded me so much of the many densely populated drug areas I had seen growing up in Chicago. The dangers of living in such a place were well known to me.

It was common knowledge around Eastridge that the corner where Calvin lived was the gathering place for drug-addicted "junkies" and "hypes" that wanted to purchase a variety of drugs. In fact, some players and community members speculated that Calvin's twenty-three-year-old half-brother, Terrence, who also lived in the house on Wilson and Pike, was the "best thing in Eastridge"—that is, the largest distributor of illicit drugs in the area. While Terrence maintained steady employment at a manufacturing plant, he also ran a drug business right behind Calvin's grandmother's house. This meant that Calvin was frequently exposed not only to the constant temptation of drugs and money but also to the possible violent byproducts of the illegal drug business.

Like many of the young people who live in Eastridge, drugs had touched Calvin's life in many ways. He and L.C., Calvin's twenty-year-old half-brother, left their mother's home and moved in with their maternal grandmother when Calvin was fifteen years old. His mother, Lucille, who also lived in the Eastridge area, had started using drugs. Shortly after Calvin moved in to help take care of his grandmother, Lucille died of complications related to pneumonia. Her frequent drug use made her body unable to fend off the illness. Calvin took her death hard. He was close to his mother, perhaps even more so because he had not known the identity of his real father for very long.

Calvin's relationship with his father was similar to that of others whose fathers conceive them but do not parent them. Calvin first learned of his father's identity at the age of thirteen. He had believed that L.C.'s father was also his father until one day his aunt introduced him to his biological father, Nathan, a neighborhood drug addict. Nathan was Coach Benson's younger brother. I once met Nathan in front of the coach's home and wondered if he had really been the great athlete that the coach had bragged him to be. Nathan had consumed so many drugs that his skinny body now appeared as only a shadow of its former athletic self. Although Nathan continued to struggle with drugs, Calvin pointed out during his interview that Nathan was seriously "trying to get his life together." Fortunately for Nathan, his mother lived in the Eastridge area and was willing to help him try to get back on his feet.

If Calvin's brother, mother, and father are examples of all those who have succumbed to the pressure of drugs while living in Eastridge, then his aunt, uncle, and maternal and paternal grandmothers are examples of people who continue to successfully navigate the rough Eastridge area. All of Calvin's relatives in Eastridge lived within a two-block radius of one another. Given his living environment, I wondered how Calvin dealt with the pressure to be involved with drugs. His response revealed how the pressure was alleviated through a number of factors, including the status of his family members within the neighborhood. I asked, "So how is it that you live around all those drugs?"

> Calvin: Shoot, I'm used to it. It's just I done seen it all of my life, and I
>   see that they ain't getting nothing out of that.
> May: One of your teammates suggested that your oldest brother,
>   Terrence [a purported drug dealer], got you respect. Do you

> think people respect you, like over in Eastridge, because of your
> brother, or how do you think?
>
> *Calvin*: Really, I think 'cause of my grandmother. She's been over
> there, like, in the house she staying in now, I think she stayed in
> there for, like, sixteen years.

Calvin suggested that he had less pressure on him to engage in drug
use or sales because of the respect that people in the community gave
his family, especially his grandmother. His family's status within the
community was not only related to his grandmother's community status or his brother's purported drug-dealing status but also to the fact
that several members of Calvin's family were part of a long list of
Eastridge athletes that played basketball for the Northeast Knights.
This list included his uncle Coach Benson, his father, and three
cousins. As Benson observed, it is because of this respect that other
people in the neighborhood looked out for Calvin:

> Basically, a lot of the people around there, a lot of guys, you know,
> they kinda respect him and stuff and they say, "Hey, naw man, you
> go over there [away from the drug dealing] man." And then they will
> kinda—you know, if somebody is trying to do something to him,
> they going to take up for him.

Calvin's ties to both drug dealers and upstanding citizens came to
bear on his everyday existence. Those individuals involved in drugs
discouraged him from getting involved because they perceived him to
have the athletic talent to move beyond the rough life in Eastridge. Although Calvin recognized the positive aspects of being respected by
drug dealers in his neighborhood, he believed that his involvement in
the Northeast Knights basketball program more significantly curtailed
his probable delinquent behavior. As he noted, "Basketball helped me
out a lot." The protective function of the Northeast Knights was not
lost on Calvin's teammates, who recognized him to be in a difficult situation. Several players named Calvin as an example of an individual
that "was helped out by playing basketball."

Calvin's survival was also significantly influenced by Benson's
presence, whose own personal experience in the Eastridge area made
him well aware of the struggles that players like Calvin confront as
they grow up. I always felt that my participation with the team could

have a broader positive impact on young men like Calvin. Benson often boasted to the players, "How many high school teams have a Ph.D. on their staff?" As an African American man, my participation offered the players a proximate example of the alternative life possibilities available to them. Some players who had the opportunity to talk to me about my profession would ask me general questions about college life. I did not realize how important these brief interactions might be until my last year of coaching, when one young man presented me with a plaque that read, "Coach May, thank you for teaching me how to be a man." Still, like Coach Benson, I recognized that these players were products of their environment and still engaged in drug use. As Benson pointed out to me after I asked him whether his players used drugs, "Oh, man. They smoke, drugs, they do everything like that. You can't put it past them."

Although Benson may have helped prevent players like Calvin from engaging in drugs, drinking, or delinquency during their time in the Northeast Knights program, there was little any of us could do once the players moved beyond the reach of Northeast. For instance, there were special athletes who passed through the Northeast sports programs who were tabbed for athletic success at the college level. David Colt was one such athlete. He played football and basketball at Northeast and went on to Big South University on a football scholarship. However, his fast track for athletic excellence was derailed by "a puff of smoke."

David and a Puff of Smoke

In the spring of 2003 I sat in my office reading the Northeast newspaper. I scanned the headlines until I came across a story about six Big South University athletes who had been arrested for possession of marijuana. As a fan of college sports in general, I was not surprised that athletes had been arrested for drug possession. After all, 2003 had been a year of scandals for many college athletic programs. In the article it was reported that BSU police received an anonymous call from a student who complained that the athletes were smoking marijuana in a player's dorm room. I began to read the list of players involved in the scandal. When I got to the third name, my eyes widened and remained fixed on the name DAVID COLT. "What?" I said aloud. "I don't believe that. I know he wasn't smoking." David Colt of all people. The fun-loving, amicable, big guy who had played football and basketball for the Northeast Knights was now listed among a group of weed-possessing, deviant, college athletes. I sat back in my chair and contemplated the probability that there had been a mistake. Surely there was an explanation.

I had known David well. In the previous two years I had spent twenty-five hours a week with him in three months of basketball. In that time, he never seemed like the kind of young man who would be involved in a drug scandal. He did not travel with that kind of crowd. From all indications, he and his older brother Tommy—who also played football and basketball for Northeast—were two of our "good kids." Despite his 6'2", 300 pounds size, David was more of a jolly comedian than an aggressive brute. He rarely used the profanity that was commonly used by other players when joking and teasing with the other boys. His demeanor seemed to fit his family's conservative middle-class background. They attended church regularly and proclaimed Christian beliefs as a foundation for their family. David's parents, both educational administrators in the Northeast community, supported his participation in athletics but expected high academic performance. David had done well athletically and academically in high school.[6] Instead of choosing to attend school out of state, he decided to stay near Northeast and attend Big South University on an athletic scholarship.

When David completed his senior basketball season at Northeast High School, I had the opportunity to interview him for my study. I asked him specifically about drug and alcohol use. He denied using either. This denial resonated with me when I read the news account of his arrest.

David's story became an important reference point for the discussion of drugs in the interviews that I conducted that spring, allowing me to personalize questions about whether the players used drugs and alcohol. During the time that I worked with David, I was under the impression that he did not use drugs. My assessment was based on his daily behavior, his friendships, and his statements during the interview. Still, it was possible that David's behavior and his account to me were acts of deception. If this was the case, David had done an outstanding job of deceiving not only me but his teammates as well. Most of them agreed that they did not think David had used drugs.

The inconsistency between the media report and David's statements to me raised questions about the credibility of respondents' self-reports of deviant behavior. Although I could not empirically verify David's statements denying drug or alcohol use, I attempted to cross-check all the players' responses by asking them to tell me about other players who they thought used drugs or alcohol. This proved to be an effective means of identifying those players who used drugs or alcohol. The names that were given to me were consistent through most of the interviews. Additionally, most of the players who were named as drug or alcohol users had admitted to me during their interview that they had in fact indulged in drug or alcohol use. Since David had not been identified as a user by other players, I surmised that his statements denying drug and alcohol use during the interview were truthful. Thus, I assume that his college environment ultimately influenced David to experiment in a variety of behaviors that were inconsistent with how others had viewed him during high school. David's change in behavior had a profound effect on his athletic opportunity. In the end, the marijuana-possession incident became the basis on which David and the coach at Big South University mutually agreed that it was in David's best interest to transfer. He transferred to a smaller college and sought to get his athletic career back on track.

Although David's incident with drugs occurred during college, it is clear from the reports of the Northeast Knights that drugs and alcohol are also a part of the adolescent experience in high school. Thus, drug and alcohol use was a matter that the young men frequently confronted. It can have a profoundly alluring affect. I have watched its power in the lives of three young men with whom I came into contact through the Northeast Knights basketball program.

Drugs: The Body Snatchers

Tyson Baylor

I walked Tyson to his mother's car and said, "Ms. Baylor, let me just tell you. Tyson has been telling you that he has been practicing with us, but he refuses to come to practice and he just hangs out here. I know he told you we get done with practice at eight, but he is only a freshman and we finish practice at six. I don't want you to think he is with us when he is just hanging out."

"Okay, thank you," she said to me. She then turned to Tyson and said, "Why are you doing that?"

Tyson just turned his head as if he were frustrated by the situation. "Get in the car," his mother commanded. Tyson opened the car door and got inside. That day when Ms. Baylor drove Tyson away was one of the last times that I would see him around Northeast High School.

When Tyson was a freshman he had come out for the freshman team. As the head coach of the freshman team that year, I was excited by the prospect of having Tyson play for me. He was 6'6" with a wiry build. He was not a very skilled player, but his athletic ability was profound. The main problem with Tyson, however, was that by the time he had reached high school, he had been exposed to too much street life with too little guidance. From the first day of conditioning exercises it was evident that he was a smoker. I stayed on him to make him run and get into shape, but he hardly improved. I told him, "Tyson, you need to stay away from smoking if you want to get better." But he refused. Like one of his teammates said, "Tyson loves that weed."

Tyson had worked out with the team for about six weeks. He played his first freshman team game and was an instant success. Still, he was hard to motivate. Most players, when they have success, want to build on it, but each day Tyson seemed further distracted by what was "out there." One day, Harrick, one of Tyson's teammates, complained to me that his gold nugget watch had been stolen from his locker in the team locker room. Harrick suspected Tyson because another player had seen Tyson put the watch in his pocket and leave the gym. When I asked Tyson about the watch he denied having anything to do with it. For several weeks I spent time trying to recover the watch from Tyson, and to recover Tyson from the streets. When I realized that Tyson was consistently missing practice, yet hanging around after school, I confronted him. I could not get him back to the gym for practice, so I let his mother know. It was then that she took him home.

For the next two years I occasionally saw Tyson hanging out at school. His eyes were always red, and he smelled of marijuana smoke. By the end of his sophomore year he had become one of the 49 percent of the freshmen who enter Northeast High School but fail to graduate. After dropping out, Tyson spent his days just hanging around in the Rockgate neighborhood where he had grown up. Although Rockgate is working class—generally populated by factory workers and service-sector employees—and several miles away from central Northeast and places like Eastridge, there were elements of the drug culture that thrived in that area. Tyson was swept up by that culture and began selling drugs. The last time I heard anything about Tyson was a few years later. There was a brief statement in the Northeast newspaper that described his arrest and conviction on possession of crack cocaine with the intent to distribute. I couldn't help but think, "All that promise, all gone."

Cameron Faulk

Like Tyson, Cameron Faulk lived in the Rockgate area. He was a vibrant young man who had just graduated from middle school when I first met him. His mother had brought him to the basketball program as soon as we started our summer workouts. It was a great opportunity for us to get to know him and for him to get to know us before he actually began school at Northeast. Although he was only 5'8", he was skilled, athletic, aggressive, and quick. He had all the talents needed to be another quality guard for the Northeast Knights. Cameron also had a quick temper and an attraction to street life. Both of these characteristics made him vulnerable to the pressures of the streets. We worked hard to keep him with us, but Cameron did not even finish summer workouts.

When Cameron entered school his freshman year he did not go out for the basketball team. He left school after his sophomore year and took over the "family business" when his uncle was arrested for selling drugs. A few years later, at the age of seventeen, Cameron followed his uncle to the penitentiary for possession of crack cocaine with the intent to distribute—another young life lost to the streets.[7]

Curtis Duster

Perhaps the most unsettling case during my time at Northeast was that of Curtis Duster. He was another young man with raw athletic ability but few basketball skills. He was also a silly and playful kid. He stood at 6'4" and walked with a monster's lurch. The other players would often affectionately call him "Goofy Curtis." Curtis had the proclivity for trouble in the classroom because of his silly antics. Not only was he silly, but he was also resistant to authority. He would attend class and distract other students, and he would goof off even more when he was verbally reprimanded. He had been taking Ritalin since middle school to help make him focus in the classroom and be less disruptive. Curtis was well aware of the drug's function but became less willing to take it once he got to high school. He had discovered that he hated the side effects. The drug made him sluggish, and he often seemed distant during practice. It was shortly after he began manipulating his own Ritalin dosage (he would feign taking the drug in front of his teachers) that he also began showing up to basketball practice reeking of marijuana.

I remember one day pointing out to Coach Benson that Curtis had been smoking. Benson called Curtis over and said, "Listen, that smoking ain't going do nothing but get you in trouble. You gotta leave it alone. You doing well in basketball, and we need to count on you." Although it was rumored that Curtis had failed to give up smoking and hanging out, the Northeast coaches rarely had any trouble with him. It was as if we were the only ones who could keep him focused and in control. Although we were able to get Curtis to work harder and do better in school, he still had his bad days, even at home. Curtis's mother complained that he was getting out of control at home. Each time Benson spoke to Curtis he showed improvement for a few weeks. Finally, Curtis's mother felt like she could not keep him in line and decided to "put him out." She sent Curtis to live with his aunt. This was perhaps the worst place Curtis could have been sent to live because his aunt lived in an area full of drugs.

When Curtis moved in with his aunt he began missing team practice. On the days when he did make it to practice, he looked like he had been smoking marijuana. However, this situation quickly came to an end because the police conducted a drug raid on his aunt's house. When drugs were discovered in the house Curtis was arrested for possession. He never finished high school, but once he got his legal troubles straightened out he began working as a day laborer. Although Curtis's story indicates a measure of success, his case is more troubling to me than Tyson's or Cameron's because Benson and the other coaches had spent two and a half years trying to keep Curtis on track and despite those efforts, we were unable to keep him safe from drugs. Yet, for all the Tyson Baylors, Cameron Faulks, and Curtis

Dusters who have failed to fight the temptation of drug use and sales, there are many Northeast Knights that survive such temptation.

Dodging Drugs and Alcohol

Like other high schools in the United States, Northeast High School is a place where young people begin to use drugs and alcohol on a regular basis. The players on the Knights team recognize that drugs and alcohol are a part of the youth culture at their school. Although many of the players were presented with the opportunity to engage in drug or alcohol use, most were able to resist using. The young men offered a variety of reasons for declining to use drugs or alcohol, most often because of their negative effects.

I related to many of the young men's experiences with drugs and alcohol. I had grown up in a single-parent family and in the early 1980s attended an urban public high school where drugs were readily available. There was even a strip outside the front of the school, known as "reefer row," where students smoked marijuana in plain view of all who passed, including teachers and school security. As for the players, the availability of drugs and alcohol and the consequences of their use were apparent to me during my adolescent years. The Knights' experiences differed from my own in that they were high school athletes who had high status throughout the school and were often invited by classmates to participate in social events. At these events some of the young men encountered drugs and alcohol. Most often, the strategies that the players employed to avoid drug use were grounded in their pride as members of the Northeast Knights. Furthermore, most of their peers did not pressure them to engage in consuming drugs or alcohol because they respected them as athletes. For instance, I asked Harry, a high-status player, how he had been able to avoid using drugs or alcohol at social gatherings, despite frequenting places where drugs were abundant and alcohol was flowing. Harry responded, "I be around people that smoke weed all the time. They know I don't do it, and they won't even let me do it." According to Harry, his peers respected the fact that he was an athlete who did not "use," and therefore they did not pressure him. Harry's comment about respect is comparable to Calvin's comments regarding his ability to avoid drugs and alcohol even while living in a virtual drug house.

Despite the risks of being associated with individuals who used drugs and alcohol, Harry continued to hang out at parties where drugs and alcohol were present. This fact was especially interesting given that Harry's own father, Big Harry, had admonished him not to hang in the wrong place—a suggestion that was emphasized when Harry was a young boy and saw his father arrested. I asked Harry about his father's arrest because I had heard about Big Harry's incarceration:

> *May*: Has your father ever been in trouble before?
> *Harry*: Uh huh.
> *May*: Drugs or locked up or anything?
> *Harry*: Yeah, being in the wrong spot at the wrong time. That's what he gets on me about. I was with him. But I was young though. 'Cause it was something of mine that I had to give to this little boy 'cause I needed to take it to him. And the boy daddy was a dope fiend. And I was in the car 'cause they used to stay right there on Essex. [Essex is not far from Harry's house in Rockgate.] I remember because I was looking around the car, and I remember I just seen a whole bunch of police cars just came. They jumped up and busted the door in and everything. Everybody inside got in trouble. But my dad didn't get in trouble that bad because the police came to the school and asked me questions, and I told them what happened and he told them the same thing. So he didn't get in a whole lot of trouble.

Harry was aware of the consequences of being caught in the wrong place at the wrong time because of his father's experience, yet he was still drawn to social gatherings where people might be using drugs or alcohol. His attraction to such social gatherings was not unique to him. Even players who were less popular, and more conservative about sex, drugs, and alcohol, were attracted to the parties where young men and women might engage in drug or alcohol use. This is because, despite being a relatively large community, Northeast is densely populated with crosscutting networks among blacks of various lifestyles. Players often have friendship and family ties to people all over the city. Thus, it was no surprise that a player like Ricky Thompson, who was considered pretty reserved by his teammates, could be found at the same parties as Harry.

Respect

One recurring theme throughout all the players' commentary about avoiding drug and alcohol use is the notion of respect. The players spoke frequently about the respect they were able to garner from those within their communities. Being an athlete seemed to create such a high level of status that players only needed to reject drugs and alcohol on one occasion before those around them understood that the athlete did not intend to engage in drug or alcohol use. The extent of respect accorded to high school athletes seems to resemble that which is accorded professional athletes, but on a smaller scale, in that they are treated with almost celebrity-like status. In some ways, then, high school basketball represents a microcosm of the broader professional sports world in which athletes are accorded respect by adoring fans who think of them as having superhero-like abilities and virtues. This type of respect also helps to make those on the Northeast Knights feel that they are likely to have a future as a professional athlete.

Beyond the young men's recognition that others have respect for them, the players are also aware that the easiest way to avoid drugs and alcohol is to remove themselves from circumstances that create greater opportunity to use. More important, they realize that they should avoid circumstances in which their presence might be misconstrued. As Byron, a player who was disappointed after learning of David Colt's arrest for possession of marijuana stated, "You just don't be in the room with somebody smoking marijuana. That's stupid." Jaris mentions specific strategies to avoid circumstances in which they could be guilty of drug or alcohol use by association:

> I got friends that drink, but I try not to stay where they are. Like, if they drink that's on them. But I'll, like, I'll hang with them or whatever, but if they get, like, in a car or whatever, I don't too much try to get in the car 'cause they can get caught or something and I'll be in trouble too. My mother tells me, "If you get in trouble," like, say for instance, if I was to get locked up or something, she's like, "You going stay in there 'cause I ain't even coming to get you. You mess up one time, you going stay in there for a minute. I'll come get you out later, but that just lets you know what it feels like, and that you shouldn't be doing what you did wrong."

Jaris used his mother's admonitions regarding the consequences of any kind of delinquent behavior as one reason for avoiding the more risky behaviors associated with adolescent peer culture. Jaris's mother was a single parent who diligently watched over her three sons. She spent a lot of time with the basketball team because both Jaris and his younger brother were players. Her support of their participation in basketball seemed to create a level of loyalty in Jaris, who demonstrated a willingness to follow her directives. Jaris's mother clearly laid out the threat of having to deal with incarceration. Yet the idea that she would permit him to languish there as a consequence of his lapse in judgment seemed to have a greater effect on Jaris's behavior than the threat of being arrested. Ultimately, I believe that his mother's support for institutional discipline was essential to keeping Jaris from engaging in drugs or drinking.

Jaris was not the only player who viewed the prospects of going to jail as a risk not worth taking. Pooty Cat, whose friends sold drugs in the neighborhood, was also afraid of being arrested, yet his fear did not prevent him from hanging with his delinquent friends. He reasoned that his friends respected him enough to discourage him from using or selling drugs. Still, Pooty Cat's friends envisioned him ultimately joining them on the corner once he completed his high school basketball career. Their reasoning was based on the desolate conditions of their impoverished neighborhood. They had witnessed other young black men who had failed to make it in mainstream society because of the inadequate cultural and social resources provided in their neighborhood. Indeed, their understanding of their own social limitations was part of their motivation for "getting in the drug game." Pooty Cat, on the other hand, feared incarceration enough to keep him focused on basketball throughout high school:

> I got some friends that sell drugs. . . . My mother gets concerned. Like, during the day she'll let me hang out with them, but when it gets kinda nighttime police stuff, she be telling me, "Get out from up there off the corner with them" and stuff. 'Cause you know, like, being an only child, sometimes you get bored being in the house, so you gotta go outside and do something. You know what I'm saying? You just be kicking it with them even though you know they sell drugs and stuff. None of them ain't never told me to sell it for them,

but they like, "When you finish school you going be out there with us," and stuff like that. But I ain't goin' be out there 'cause I don't wanna go to jail. I'm too small to be going to jail. Them boys try to handle me in jail [physically pin him down]. So I ain't going that way. That's why I don't do it.

Although Pooty Cat did not engage in the sale of drugs, his concern for being arrested was a legitimate one given that young black males are consistently the victims of racial profiling by law enforcement officers. Consequently, Pooty Cat need not be engaged in criminal activity to be confronted with situations in which law enforcement officers would infer his criminal culpability based on his race.[8] The use of racial profiling by law enforcement is especially problematic for blacks from low-income neighborhoods because these residents, unlike middle-class blacks, lack the resources necessary to combat such police harassment.[9] Thus, young black males like Pooty Cat need the support and guidance of significant others in order to offset the negative influences of living in low-income black neighborhoods.

Pooty Cat's mother, like Jaris's, played a key role in his decision-making. As an only child, he was permitted to interact with the young men in his neighborhood, but his mother laid down strict rules about whom he could associate with and when.

Interestingly, Pooty Cat shared his feelings of vulnerability regarding incarceration. In his joking comment about being "handled" in jail, Pooty Cat lacked the overinflated self-worth that some athletes possess. Such self-inflated perceptions can be the source of athletes' desire to act above the law. Yet I felt that, in general, the athletes within the Northeast Knights basketball program were humbled by Benson's consistently high expectations. Benson admonished his players in spite of their on-the-court success. He was quick to point out to the players, after a win, "I'll tell you the fuckin' problem. You done got damn satisfied. You won't work. But let me explain something to you. You won't get anything if you don't work." With admonitions like these, Benson was able to keep, to some degree, his athletes' egos in check on and off the court. Although many of the young men were able to avoid drugs or alcohol, some players still experimented. Just as participation in sport is a valued activity in their communities, so too are drugs.

"Dibbling and Dabbling" in Drugs and Alcohol

I was a junior in college the first time I sampled alcohol with my peers. Up until that time my mother had been successful at limiting the exposure that my brother and I had to alcohol and drugs. My mother had managed to climb up the ladder of social mobility, moving us out of various low-income communities where open-air drug markets and corner stoops for drinking were the norm. I suspect that our limited exposure to these places, my mother's own limited use of alcohol and drugs, and her watchful eye inhibited both our interest in, and desire for, experimenting with drugs and alcohol. Like Jaris and Pooty Cat, whose mothers also played a key role in their avoidance of alcohol and drug use, my brothers and I were able to avoid these substances until much later in life.

Many of the Northeast Knights suggested that they had avoided drugs and alcohol, but several had sampled both. Many of the players had actually experimented with these substances before they even got to high school. James talks about his experimentation during his middle school experience:

> Well, I done tasted alcohol. But as far as, like, getting drunk, no, I've never been drunk. I tried a cigarette when I was younger. I tried a Black and Mild [cigar]. I only tried them both once, and that's it. . . . I was like, okay. The cigarette, I was probably, like, just going into middle school. But the Black and Milds, probably in eighth grade at a party.

When I asked James why he did not smoke or drink after experimenting in middle school his response was typical of the other Northeast Knights:

> I done been around reefer, and I done had people ask me about it, but they know I don't smoke, and they respect that. . . . Like now most of the people know I don't smoke, so they don't even ask me. They might smoke it around me, but they know I don't smoke.

James's statements were consistent with the other players who did not feel pressured to use more drugs or alcohol. However, athletes like

Tyson, Curtis, and Cameron, all of whom were unable to establish an identity as occasional or nonusers of drugs or alcohol, were the players who ultimately left the Northeast Knights program because the appeal of drugs and alcohol became so great that each was willing to trade his athletic participation for substance use. Thus, those young men who remained members of the Northeast Knights were more likely to be occasional substance users if at all.

Given the influence that parents have over their children's overall development, I became curious about the extent to which parents' use of drugs or alcohol had influenced players like Pooty Cat to drink. Since limited parental consumption of drugs and alcohol has been suggested as a mitigating factor against the influence of peer substance abuse for some populations of adolescents,[10] I questioned Pooty about his mother's consumption habits:

> *May*: What about drinking?
>
> *Pooty*: I done drunk some liquor a couple of times. Like some Paul [Masson wine]. It's some red liquor. I don't too much. I don't do it like all the time.
>
> *May*: Does your mom keep liquor in the house?
>
> *Pooty*: Naw. She don't drink.
>
> *May*: At all?
>
> *Pooty*: Naw.
>
> *May*: She smoke?
>
> *Pooty*: She used to. She just told me when she smoked it made her eat a lot and stuff, you know what I'm saying. . . . She gained weight. And it was hurting me, killing me, all that smoke in my face.

For many of the players, their experimentation with drugs or alcohol may have had more to do with their level of exposure to drugs and alcohol by parents rather than by peers. In Pooty Cat's case, his mother did not use alcohol; therefore he was less likely to engage in regular alcohol use.[11] Furthermore, although Pooty Cat was permitted to spend time with his peers "up on the corner," his mother closely monitored his behavior, which mitigated the influence of his peers.

Like Pooty Cat, Shamar also experimented. His experiences with drugs were grounded in a core group of friends from his old neighborhood. Shamar had tried marijuana in the seventh grade and alcohol in high school. His peer group had been instrumental in both events. He smoked marijuana for the first time with two friends his age and a few older guys. He used marijuana infrequently after his mother had observed him high on his first instance of smoking. He said, "My mother was like, 'Shamar, you been smoking? I'm going to kill you.' After that I didn't hardly smoke." By the time Shamar reached Northeast High School he had experimented with drugs and alcohol enough to know his tolerance. He had "throwed up real bad" after drinking with his friends and decided that an occasional drink was enough.

All the players who drank or smoked described their activities as part of a group process. They experimented with their peers. Generally, in such situations, having the courage to sample the substance was far more important than whether one could ingest large quantities. As Joco said, "We might go to 'The Place' and drink on occasion. Not like heavily. We'd go to a party and drink a little bit. It was cool if you just drank a little bit." For the Northeast Knights, peer interaction seemed to have an influence on drinking and smoking, but parents' limited use of substances seemed to lessen the likelihood that the young men would become regular users of drugs and alcohol.

Perhaps the most interesting theme that recurred in the young men's recollections of avoiding extended drug and alcohol use was the level of respect that their peers seemed to have accorded them. The players suggested that there was something inherent in their status as a Northeast Knight that absolved them from engaging in drug and alcohol use. Three possible explanations for this reported respect come to mind within the context of Northeast. First, it appears that the alcohol- or drug-using friends of those athletes who rarely use substances have a vested interest in helping the athlete maintain his status as a member of the Knights. The status of the athletes helps bolster the status of the nonathletes who use drugs or alcohol. As long as their friends are members of the Northeast Knights, associates who hang around athletes can claim part of the athlete's status by asserting, "my boy is a Northeast Knight." These claims mirror those that members of a professional athlete's entourage might make to invoke the privilege or status accorded the professional athlete. If the athlete were to lose status, so too would the hangers-on.

Second, the respect accorded to the athlete is based on a community expectation that high school athletic programs be successful. This expectation influences the overall attitude of nonathletes toward athletes who use drugs. Since winning is key, nonathletes view nurturing and protecting skilled athletes from the deterioration that results from frequent drug and alcohol use as part of their community responsibility. If these athletes perform well, they bring esteem to the communities from which they hail. Although this might seem a simplistic view, one only need consider the nature of intense rivalries with nearby high schools to get a sense of how the success of these high school athletes is tied to the overall disposition of a community.

A third explanation for the respect is that other members from the Northeast community view athletes and their potential as important to the overall community. The athlete with promise might well reach the upper echelon of his sport and thereby be a source of pride for the people from that community. In many respects, this athlete has the potential to put his community on the map. The community members pin their hopes on the success of this high school athlete. The athlete is a symbol of hope for the people, many of whom he is not even aware of, who can little hope for their own successful escape from within a desolate neighborhood. Irrespective of the basis of their respect for athletes, it is clear that others in the Northeast community help the athletes hold the line on drug and alcohol use. In short, because members in the community believe these young men have promise, they hold the young men to a higher standard than they hold average citizens.

One final note on the use of drugs: As stated previously, winning is important to players, coaches, and community members. Given the importance of winning, it would seem that athletes might do all that they can to enhance their athletic performance. This includes the use of performance-enhancing drugs. Yet none of the players interviewed acknowledged that they or anyone they knew had used performance-enhancing drugs like steroids. Only one player, Capleton, discussed having used creatine (a weight-gain agent) to bulk up for competition.[12] This over-the-counter supplement can be purchased at most nutrition stores. Capleton quickly discontinued the use of creatine because he complained that the weight gain inhibited his speed. Coach Benson and the other coaches never, to my knowledge, endorsed the use of performance-enhancing substances. Indeed, such an endorsement would run counter to their objective of liberating the young men from circumstances that hinder their opportunities.

Although most of the Northeast Knights avoid drug and alcohol use, and those that do use do so in moderation, the young men are still confronted with opportunities to engage in other delinquent behavior.

Delinquency: Getting into Trouble

For many of the players, the biggest attraction to delinquent behavior is associated with the sale of drugs. Within their communities, the selling of drugs in open-air markets is a regular occurrence. As in the case of Calvin, these young men are exposed daily to the viability of selling illicit drugs. They see boys their own age exchange cash money for product. This simple exchange does not require the young men to conceptually understand the theories of a market economy that associate capital and earnings with some abstract notions. In the drug exchange, all is laid bare. The more products sold, the more cash received. The simplicity of such exchanges within a largely complex capital system makes the selling of drugs appealing to many of the young men growing up in low-income areas. Elijah Anderson, in *The Code of the Street*, captures the complex social and economic issues that young black men consider in determining the viability of selling drugs:

> For many impoverished young black men of the inner city, the opportunity for dealing drugs is literally just outside the door. By selling drugs, they have a chance to put more money into their pockets than they could get by legal means, and they can present themselves to peers as hip, in sharp contrast to the square image of those who work in places like McDonald's and wear silly uniforms.[13]

Since participation in the drug culture would lead to a greater likelihood of violent behavior, most of the boys choose not to sell drugs. Shamar, for example, refused to sell drugs because, by participating in basketball, he came to think, "Man, you know, I just think about it, and I'll be like, 'Hey I got everything going for me, so it ain't worth getting locked up for.'" Shamar's sentiment is consistent with the young men who remained members of the Northeast Knights throughout their high school careers. They had clearly made choices to avoid some of the pitfalls that their adolescent peers had confronted.

Although none of the Northeast Knights who remained part of the team throughout their high school careers chose to participate in the drug culture, some of them did get into "trouble." The young men's "trouble" was most often along the lines of behavior considered innocuous or "boys will be boys" behavior.[14] "Boys will be boys" behavior is delinquent, but from a social standpoint it is considered more or less acceptable. For instance, egging, shooting slingshots, joyriding, or firing BB guns are often thought of as harmless adolescent activities. Although many people see these behaviors as part of the acceptable process of coming of age, such risky and confrontational actions also are thought to be the basis for male domination. Irrespective of the ideological interpretation given this common delinquent behavior, it is clear that members of the Knights have experienced it. For instance, Shamar describes coming in contact with the police after driving his oldest brother's car without permission:

> I had my brother's blue Explorer, and he didn't know—me and my homeboys Leo and them. My mother and father were gone, and my homeboys set me up, telling me, "Come on, man, let's ride out, man. Ride for a minute. We just goin' to go through the Southside." . . . We had the music up in there. We were riding all good, then the police— all of a sudden—the police pulled up beside me and he looked. He said, "Hey, stop the jeep, stop the jeep right now," My boys said to pull out [run]. I said, "I know this man right here. He ain't going do nothing. Man, I know him." [The officer knew Shamar's grandmother from the community.] He [the officer] pulled over. Man he was mad. He was like, "I should put you on my knee and spank you." He took me out of the car and was like, "What the hell are you doing?" and all that. Then like, "You let your friends stick you up a tree," and all that. I got in trouble with my mom, and me and my brother almost got to fighting when they found out.

Delinquent behavior such as that described by Shamar typically occurs in groups. Shamar's recollection of his own behavior stands as a testament to the influence of a player's "homeboys." Shamar's involvement with these friends caused his grandmother great stress. One day, after he got in trouble in his first year of high school at Ford Heights, his grandmother sat him down for a long talk. At that time his cousin Larique was also visiting their grandmother's house. Larique listened as their grandmother told Shamar, "You gotta straighten out. You gotta quit being friends with those boys." Larique, who played for the Knights, interjected to Shamar, "Man, you need to come over to Northeast, man, and get away from Ford Heights. Their basketball at Northeast is better anyway." Shamar asked Larique to talk to Coach Benson. At the same time, Shamar told his grandmother that he wanted to go to Northeast. She responded, "You don't know nobody over there." Shamar was insistent and said, "It's gonna keep me out of trouble." Ultimately, Shamar's family let him transfer from Ford Heights to Northeast, where he got involved with basketball.[15] Shamar acknowledged during the interview that Benson helped shape him up, otherwise "I'd probably be selling drugs in the hood somewhere."

Some of the delinquent incidents in which the players were involved stemmed from an ongoing Northside-Southside conflict. Calvin experienced such an incident during his junior year. He had purchased an early 1970s Chevy Nova and added some window tint and stylish tire rims to his car, giving it a distinctive look. Since he owned a car, he could move about Northeast more freely. A few days after Calvin had purchased his car, I arrived at practice to discover that Calvin was not present. When I asked Coach Benson where Calvin was, he informed me that Calvin had been arrested. I stood in disbelief. According to Benson's account, Calvin and his friend Larry had gone to a party on the Southside, and some guys tried to jump on Calvin outside the party. These young men from the Southside had a grudge against Calvin that dated back to Calvin's time at Northeast Middle School.

The Southside boys' grudge had been brewing since Calvin's seventh-grade year, when his Northeast Middle School Eagles team defeated all the middle school basketball teams in the city to win the city championship. Students from one school, Sexton Middle, had developed an intense rivalry with the Northeast Middle School Eagles. In fact, several threats had been made to the Northeast Middle School Eagles a week before the Sexton-Northeast Middle School game at Sexton in Calvin's seventh-grade year. To allay fears and possible tension, the principal of the Northeast Middle School had the Eagles escorted to and from Sexton by the Northeast police. As Coach Benson indicated, the recent conflict between Calvin and the boys from the Southside was rooted in "jealousy over Calvin in middle school."

On the night the incident occurred, Calvin and Larry discovered that the boys from the Southside were waiting for Calvin outside. He and Larry returned to the party to avoid the boys, who were intent on attacking Calvin. After the party the boys were still outside waiting. Larry, concerned about his and Calvin's safety, pulled a gun from his waistband and started firing shots as he and Calvin exited the party. Calvin and Larry made it to Calvin's car and started home. A by-stander identified Calvin's car as he drove away from the party. It took the police little time to pull Calvin and Larry over. The police searched the car and found the gun that had been fired. Calvin and Larry were taken into custody; however, Calvin was able to avoid serious charges, since the firearm did not belong to him and he had no prior criminal record. Coach Benson, some of Calvin's teachers, and other community members testified in court as to Calvin's character. Calvin's brush with the law got him probation. He served his probation diligently while staying clear of further problems.

Although players like Calvin found a source of support from their coaches and teammates, there was occasional tension between players that could lead to conflict. This conflict could stem from the rough play and competitive nature of basketball at Northeast, or in school, such as over a girl. Rarely, however, did this conflict result in physical altercations between teammates. In the seven years I coached at Northeast only one conflict resulted in a fight between players.

Smitty J, a player with a quick temper and aggressive disposition to go with it, jumped on Turo in the locker room because Turo had joked about Smitty J's mother. The other players intervened and pulled Smitty J and Turo apart. Coach Benson, who believes in swift but variable discipline, talked to both players and reiterated to each of them that they were teammates and should not fight. I was disappointed with Benson's discipline, since I thought such behavior merited more severe punishment. Yet I understood Benson's decision not to bench either player, because the fight occurred on the eve of our first-round playoff game. When we lost the game the next evening, both players and coaches viewed the fight as a distraction from our goals.

Smitty J was easily one of the most aggressive and volatile players that I had seen at Northeast. In games, he was the player coaches had to watch out for because he frequently lost control and flailed around in a demonstrative manner. His anger was usually provoked by players from opposing teams. These players had somehow crossed an imaginary boundary of physical contact that Smitty J found unacceptable. For instance, during one game Smitty J had been going for a rebound when he and a player from the opposing team collided. The Knights came up with the ball as Smitty J fell to the floor. While he was down and the rest of the team was running to score a basket, the player from the opposing team intentionally kicked Smitty J as he ran back to play defense. The referee blew the whistle to stop play because there was a foul on our offensive end. Smitty J, who had just picked himself up from the floor, ignored the whistle and ran full speed from the far end of the court. He ran directly to the player that had kicked him, but just as Smitty J was about to swing, Benson grabbed him by the jersey and pulled him back. Once Benson was between Smitty J and the opposing player Benson shouted, "You don't do anything. You let the referee handle it." Benson turned and pointed at the referee and said to Smitty J again, "You let him handle it."

Smitty J's behavior on the court would make one think that he would have larger discipline problems at school. Yet few players, including Smitty J, were "problems." Indeed, there were occasions when some players had been suspended for fighting; however, based on both the school administration's report and the students' versions of the fights, the players were typically fighting in self-defense. Coach Benson frequently talked to the boys about avoiding conflicts in school because it mattered little whether the players fought in self-defense or were aggressors; they still had to serve a suspension that included being unable to compete in athletic activities. Especially during playoff season, Coach Benson emphasized that players should be most wary of those individuals that want to "start something just 'cause they are jealous."

Conclusion

Open-air drug markets, single-parent families, poverty, and criminal violence are realities for the players. Thus, these young men grow up in environments that are rarely conducive to visualizing broader opportunities for success beyond the typical icons of "'hood rich" drug dealers and criminals who loom "large" in poor, urban areas. Tyson, Cameron, and Curtis easily demonstrate the power of the environmental pull that seeks to draw the boys away from visions of what their lives could be like, to realities of what many peoples' lives are like around them. Each day, the young men witness friends and family members who succumb to the withering pressure and temptation of drugs and violence. Indeed, this is a story often told, both within the deleterious communities themselves and to the public at large.

Yet within the same communities from which Tyson, Cameron, and Curtis hail are young men who believe they have opportunities to live better lives. They avoid the call of the streets because, as Calvin points out, "I see that they ain't getting nothing out of that." Instead of being consumed by the troubles of their communities, these young men turn to basketball as a saving grace. From an early age, they see basketball with hope, as a seed of opportunity and mobility that can germinate and grow. As the young men spend more time competing and practicing, they become more invested in the belief that basketball will save them. The players' coaches further support this belief. The coaches' affirmations continuously build the players' confidence that hard work in basketball will help them escape their neighborhoods.

4

Race and Hoops Everyday

Y'all scared of playing them white boys.

Over the three years that I played basketball for Aurora University, we never had more than four white players on our team; but those players were key to our team's success. When they failed to perform in pivotal games, often against opponents whose players were predominantly black, then my black teammates and I sought explanations rooted in stereotypes. A black teammate of mine once said, "The white boys get scared every time we play a black team." I agreed, although I had little grounds on which to evaluate his judgments of our "scared" white teammates. Maybe it was just a "feeling" we had. No doubt, this "feeling" was rooted in our belief that blacks were natural athletes and whites were not.[1] We thought of our white teammates as crafty, intelligent, and skilled shooters, whereas we thought of ourselves as quicker, stronger, and more aggressive than they were. How could we think otherwise? Everything we had been exposed to, including media representations of black athletes, told us we were better built for the game of basketball.[2]

Sometimes these explanations of black athletic superiority were laced with creative arguments about physiological makeup. Whether blacks were indeed superior athletes or not, both we and our white teammates believed it to be true.[3] Race did matter to us. Thus, it was easy for us to surmise that our white teammates became intimidated when faced with the prospect of competing against black players, whom we all thought were superior athletes. We had learned that "white men can't jump" and that "blacks were bred to be physically superior."

For the young men involved with the Northeast Knights, issues of race are very real. Racial issues run subtly through the core of the boys' and men's lives on a day-to-day basis. Occasionally, however, the men and boys talk explicitly about the ways in which race affects their lives. What follows is a sampling of the players' and coaches' discussions when race was made explicit. First, I examine the players' views of athletic ability at the nexus of race and social environment and how these views generally challenge conventional wisdom about race and athletic ability. Second, I explore the coaches' experiences with race and racism to understand how historical experiences influence the way they come to view issues of race and how these issues play out in the young men's lives.

I argue that race is the theme that underlies many of the adult and young men's interpretations of their basketball experiences. The coaches, because they have played in racially hostile environments, understand the racial tensions that can arise and, therefore, are in a position to influence how the young men interpret similar situations. The young men's experiences, however, have occurred within a different context for interracial interaction, and therefore the players have their own interpretation of the relationship among race, social environment, and athletic ability. I demonstrate that the young men— rather than being swayed by conventional wisdom that grants superior athletic ability to blacks—indicate that although race may be a factor in athletic success, hard work is far more important.

I propose three reasons for the young men's alternative views that work against stereotypical assertions about the relationship between race and athletic ability: (1) the players interact with white athletes who share skills and abilities comparable to their own; (2) the players have been insulated from structural factors that raise racial distinctions to greater salience; and (3) the players have embraced a sense of meritocracy within their own athletic setting. In the end, the young men's competitive experiences with whites and others help to support their belief that with hard work they can make it to the next level. These perceptions are set within the context of the adult men's understandings of the racialized past politics of athletic participation for blacks in Northeast. These experiences form the foundation for my inquiry into race and basketball for the young men of Northeast.

Is It Your 'Hood or Your Race?

Public debate about the physical superiority of athletes based on racial categories has been ongoing. Despite the fact that race has been accepted by many as little more than a social construction, our belief in racial categories continues to have profound consequences for how we view ourselves and others.[4] For instance, the conclusions drawn by those who make arguments about the physical superiority of black athletes have influenced the self-image of many young black boys. The notion of black athletic superiority, coupled with the proliferation of successful black athletes, has conditioned many young men, in particular those individuals most disenfranchised from legitimate opportunity, to view sports as a viable means of escaping poverty.[5] Furthermore, individuals who associate a certain natural athletic ability to a particular racial group are likely to evaluate their own ability on the basis of such stereotypes.

The extent to which Americans use race as a proxy for athletic ability cannot be overstated. Many individuals view the black athlete as superior to other athletes. The overrepresentation of blacks in sports that require what many consider the most important athletic attributes—speed, leaping ability, and agility—reinforces the notion of black males as "natural" athletes.[6] The high representation of blacks in professional basketball and at the positions requiring attributes like speed in football impresses on many people the legitimacy of the natural black athlete. These frames of understanding have a subtle place in the minds of the Northeast Knights. For instance, in the following fieldnote, Mr. Thompson, a father of two of our former players, who acted as a conditioning coach over two seasons, questions the players' commitment to athletic success. Beyond his questions about desire for athletic success, he invokes race as part of the equation. Specifically, he questions the players' ability and desire vis-à-vis white athletes.

> I was waiting in the vestibule with B.T., Turo, David, and Pooty Cat. The guys were unwinding after riding all the way home from Nimrod County with little discussion. Nimrod had unexpectedly beaten us. We had the more talented team but did not play well enough to win. Mr. Thompson said, "It don't bother y'all to get your ass whipped?" He was obviously upset. All the players standing around me said, "Yeah."
>
> Mr. Thompson said to Turo, "I thought you said your senior class was

different." [He was referring to the fact that Turo, like seniors in each previous class, had vowed that they would be better than the class before them.]

Turo said, "It's still early in the season."

Mr. Thompson said, "Why don't you do something to make the season better? Why don't you have yourself in shooting practice tomorrow at 7:00 a.m.? I can't understand why the guys who are shooting half the shots are not even coming to shooting practice. You need to come to shooting practice. Will you be at shooting practice tomorrow?"

Turo didn't say anything. Mr. Thompson said, "You need to have your ass in practice." Turo still didn't respond. Mr. Thompson was becoming angrier as he began to realize the promise that we had failed to achieve. He asked the players, "Are y'all scared?"

"No," they replied in unison.

Mr. Thompson said, "Y'all get scared of playing them white boys just like you did in football?"

"What white boys?" Turo asked.

"The ones that beat y'all ass," replied Mr. Thompson. "You just got up there and got scared."

B.T. recalled, "Oh, yeah, he talking about West Farmington."

While all this was going on, I was thinking about intervening, but I decided against it. I thought that Mr. Thompson was being a little hard on the players. I turned off the gym lights and shut the door and we left.

Although Mr. Thompson questioned the general commitment of the players, his use of the phrase "y'all scared of playing them white boys" greatly shifted the emphasis of his critique of the players' efforts. By invoking race as a contributing factor to the players' poor performance, Mr. Thompson was calling into question not only the players' commitment but also their ability to face competition from whites. The insult in this statement is grounded in the taken-for-granted understanding that white athletes are less capable than black athletes. Thompson assumes that the stereotypical ability of black athletes, in and of itself, should bolster the players' confidence when competing against predominantly white teams. Yet he also insists that they must work. Thompson's challenge to the Northeast players is just one more suggestion to the players that black athletes are superior to white athletes and should therefore have little trouble prevailing.

Young men, like the Northeast Knights, are constantly bombarded with the rhetoric of black athletes as superior to white athletes. For instance, on June 10, 2004, Larry Bird, a white, former NBA and Hall of Fame player, made statements regarding the superiority of black athletes on an ESPN talk show. When asked whether the NBA lacked white superstars, Bird remarked,

> Well, I think so. . . . You know, when I played, you had me and Kevin [McHale] and some others throughout the league. I think it's good for a fan base because, as we all know, the majority of the fans are white America. And if you just had a couple of white guys in there, you might get them a little excited. But it is a black man's game, and it will be forever. I mean, the greatest athletes in the world are African-American.[7]

Bird subsequently added that during his playing days he found it "disrespectful" to him and his abilities when another white player was assigned to defend him. Bird's comments stand as just another affirmation to young males that blacks are indeed superior athletes.

Both Larry Bird's comments and Coach Thompson's criticisms of the Knights' performance raise an interesting question: do the young men themselves believe race to be a determining factor in athletic ability? During the interviews with the young men, I posed this question and an interrelated one. The first question was, "Does where an individual grows up determine whether he will be a good athlete?" This question attempts to explore the young men's understanding of the social processes involved in developing an individual's athletic ability. Their responses to this question were often related to the neighborhood social conditions that reflect social class and race. The second question was, "Does one's race matter as to whether an individual will be a good athlete?" This question attempts to understand the extent to which the young men emphasize race as key to athletic ability. Although these two questions were presented as distinct considerations, the players' responses were very much interrelated, given the fact that their neighborhood experience was also an exclusively black experience.[8] For many of the young men it was rare that they had an opportunity to personally assess whites' athletic ability prior to their own interracial competition with whites. Typically, this competition first occurred in racially integrated middle schools, where the young black men were in direct competition with whites for playing time on their middle school teams or in tournaments against white players from other schools.

In general, the players believed that one's neighborhood has some influence on becoming a good athlete but that one's race has little to do with the potential for an individual to become a good athlete. Still, the young men had nuanced perceptions of the impact of race and neighborhood on becoming a good athlete. The players' statements provide valuable insight. For instance, Danny, a frequently used substitute, shared the following:

> *May*: Does where you come from have anything to do with whether you are a good athlete or not? Like where you live? Where you grow up?
>
> *Danny*: It's got something to do with it. But just because you are from there [a particular neighborhood] don't mean you're automatically going to be good.
>
> *May*: Like, how do you mean when you say, "it has something to do with it"?
>
> *Danny*: Like, if somebody, like in your neighborhood—if everybody playing basketball, you're going to get up, you're going to want to play too. So you're going to do what's around you.
>
> *May*: Does your race matter about whether you will be a good athlete or not?
>
> *Danny*: Naw.
>
> *May*: Naw. You don't think so?
>
> *Danny*: No. [He shakes his head.]

Danny recognizes that one's social setting influences the frequency with which one is exposed to certain activities. In this case, basketball is a prominent activity for the young men in his neighborhood. When his peers play, Danny plays. He is, therefore, able to refine his skill as a player who can shoot and to maximize his own athletic ability through constant training. On the other hand, Danny suggests that race in and of itself has no impact on whether one becomes a good athlete. His belief is no doubt influenced by the fact that Danny played against white players during his time at Northeast High School and had an opportunity to witness that some of those white players were both skilled and outstanding athletes.

For instance, when we played North Farmington during Danny's senior year, two of the early baskets of the game for North Farmington were scored when one of their white players slam-dunked the basketball—generally considered the most athletic move in basketball. Later in that same game, the North Farmington team combined for two alley-oop slam-dunks. The slam-dunks in this game were defining moments of white male athletic ability for some of our players, and a secondary affirmation for others who had already become aware that "white men can jump."

It is easy to imagine the basketball courts in the hills of North Farmington filled with young white boys trying to develop their skills and athletic ability in much the same way that the young boys of Northeast spend their time on the playgrounds. The impact of the environment is not lost on the players, especially those players from areas where the leisure time they have is spent competing in sports. Cerico, a player who grew up in the densely populated housing project of Hillside, learned to deal with tough competition among other players. Because there was only one court to play on and the winning team remained on the court at the conclusion of each game, the games were intensely competitive. During Cerico's interview, he made the following observations when I asked whether social environment mattered:

> *Cerico*: Oh, yeah. 'Cause see, like, say you're playing in Hillside housing projects. Man, you going be more tougher and more—just more hard, man. Like, if you play that driveway ball, you be, like, you be out there by yourself, and your daddy just tell you to shoot. That ain't nothing. In Hillside you learn how it is [when you compete aggressively with others].
>
> *May*: Well, does whether someone is black, white, Chinese, Hispanic have anything to do with athletic ability?
>
> *Cerico*: Naw. If you can play, you can play, in my eyes. Honestly.

Cerico makes a distinction between the social environment of playing driveway ball and competing on the courts in Hillside. Cerico's use of the term "driveway ball" refers to the notion that suburban youths spend time shooting baskets in the solitude of their driveways. Conversely, true players spend time in competitive play on the playground, with the assumption being that such competition makes a better player.

Although Cerico concludes that one's race matters little as to whether one becomes a good athlete, I would argue that, to some degree, the social environments that produce good athletes are in fact racialized environments. Given the levels of segregation and the cultural attitudes developed in densely populated urban areas, where basketball is frequently played, players from these areas develop certain skills. The players that hail from these areas are disproportionately black. Thus, whereas some people attribute race as a biologically predetermining factor of athletic ability, I would argue that race as a social, rather than biological, construct has consequences that are significant as to whether individuals develop athletic ability. For instance, since there are far more blacks living in segregated and densely populated areas like Hillside than there are whites living in such areas, it is more likely that blacks are exposed to the kind of competitive playing environment that requires them to master control over their bodies in order to be successful. Thus, those athletes who spend time playing are developing reflexes and movements that enhance their physical abilities. The culture of competition in Hillside is one in which players emphasize aggressive aspects of the game and individualized showmanship. Indeed, it is such attributes that have come to be greatly appreciated by those who are spectators of professional basketball.

Unfortunately, the more time that players spend emphasizing these aspects of their game, the less time they spend developing fundamental skills like shooting. Some sports commentators have argued that because the media have highlighted the individualized showmanship—or, some would say, showboating—of athletic moves like the slam-dunk, aspects of playground basketball have undermined the sport itself. In fact, some have attributed the influx of foreign-born players into the NBA to the fact that they are attending basketball academies and learning fundamental skills, which make them more effective, albeit less entertaining, than basketball players from the United States.

Although most Northeast players believe that the social environment is key for whether an individual becomes a good athlete, some players believe that individual effort has a more profound effect on athletic outcomes. As Terry pointed out, "It's not necessarily where you grow up. It just depends on how hard you work at what you do. If you love what you do, you'll work at it. And eventually you'll get better."

Recall that Cerico commented that playing in Hillside would make one a better player than if one practiced alone in the driveway. He suggested that the social environment in which a player participates is essential to a player's success. Alternatively, Terry emphasized that individual desire and practice is an important determinant for athletic success. In Terry's way of thinking, a player who works at "driveway ball," although it is a solitary activity, can excel in basketball. Perhaps Terry's belief in such an approach is bolstered by the fact that he himself frequently worked in solitude and was able to become an outstanding two-sport athlete.

One of the key ideas that flow from the foregoing discussion is the extent to which players believe that one must work to achieve the goal of being a good athlete. For the players, the race of an individual has little to do with an individual's desire to work at being successful. Rather, the players generally believe that any individual who has achieved success as an athlete has had the drive, work ethic, and talent to achieve. The players' understandings of the relationships between hard work, social environment, and natural talent demonstrate a certain level of awareness. For this reason, many of the players are able to accept as a possibility the notion of naturally talented white athletes. Lionel, a starter during his senior year, gave the following example:

May: Do you think somebody's race has anything to do with whether they are considered a good athlete or not?

Lionel: Not necessarily—it's all on them. I mean, they say white boys can't jump. But I have seen some white boys that can jump! [I laugh.]

May: Name one? Who was that?

Lionel: I remember a couple of years ago, in my freshman year in high school, this white boy named John—this is when D. Benson was down here—he was playing on the varsity, but he didn't play because he had to transfer to Queens High School. 'Cause he was, like, he was going to get some time. He could jump. He was about 6'1", 6'2". He was gonna be D. Benson's back-up point guard.

Lionel makes the statement "it's all on them" to suggest two aspects of athletic ability. One aspect is the natural talent of an individual—the extent to which the individual is born with ability. The second is that the individual must take the time to develop that ability. Thus, it is "on them" as to whether they live up to their potential.

Initially, I was surprised by Lionel's remarks that he believed "white men could jump." When I asked him to name a player, my question was partly rhetorical and partly in jest. Since we only had one white player on the Northeast Knights during the time that Lionel played, I believed it would be difficult for Lionel to "name one." To my surprise, he identified John. Perhaps if Lionel had not remembered John, he still could have easily made reference to white players, like those slam-dunking white players from North Farmington, who would prove accurate examples of white males who were excellent athletes.

Although to some observers the players might seem to exhibit a naiveté regarding physiological differences between individuals and across groups, they exhibit an understanding of the complex ways in which natural ability and the nurturing of that ability are interrelated. Joco demonstrates this understanding:

> *Joco*: It doesn't matter where you from. If you got the talent, then it really doesn't matter. You got to use it.
> *May*: Where do you get the talent from?
> *Joco*: Hard work. Everybody has basic skills, but you got to work hard to get everything together.
> *May*: Do you think race has anything to do with whether you— somebody considers you a good athlete or not?
> *Joco*: In some cases—I figure some people think African Americans are just athletes anyway—in some cases, yeah.
> *May*: You said that people say African Americans are good athletes. I mean, so, do you ever play against any Chinese kids who [I begin to smile] were good athletes?
> *Joco*: Yeah. I have actually.
> *May*: What about whites? White kids?
> *Joco*: Yeah. They can play. If you got it, you got it.
> *May*: Is it skill or is it like natural ability—when you think about a good athlete?
> *Joco*: Uh, I guess natural ability. Those I've played against. Like, going to the park, they were good.

Joco's comments indicate a nuanced understanding of those with athletic ability. He suggests that everyone has "basic skills," or that they are born with certain abilities. These abilities, however, must be enhanced through hard work. Perhaps what is most interesting about Joco's comments is the extent to which he considers that natural ability runs throughout human populations and exists in various individuals across racial categories. For instance, he shares the conventional knowledge that "some people think African Americans are just athletes anyway." Here he suggests that this is not a personal belief of his but that his own beliefs are contrary to the notion of blacks as superior athletes. Joco's observations are made more compelling because he then goes on to give examples of having played with athletes from different racial and ethnic groups who he felt were naturally talented. For Joco, an individual's ability is something that he or she is born with, that exists throughout the human population, and that must be developed.

Whereas Joco rejects the notion that certain races are more likely to be good athletes than others, Tommy has a different take on the role of race in determining an athlete's abilities. Tommy's background is worth mentioning since it is different from the typical young man who competes for the Northeast Knights. Tommy and his brother David have lived with both parents since they were born, and their father played professional football for a few years. Tommy grew up playing sports at the recreation center and learned of his athletic ability at an early age. By high school not only did Tommy's basketball teammates recognize him as an excellent athlete, but his senior class at Northeast High School also voted him most athletic. Both Tommy and David experienced post-high-school athletic success (each went on to play college football at a major NCAA Division I university). Perhaps it is Tommy's middle-class family background that gives him a view that is more consistent with conventional wisdom about race and athletic ability. Tommy and David are the only two young men interviewed who stated definitively that race was significant as to whether a player would be considered a good athlete. Tommy provided the following view of race, genes, and social environment:

May: Do you think where you live or where you grow up has anything to do with whether you are going to be a good athlete or
not?
Tommy: Not really. 'Cause like, when I first started playing I was told
that the people from, like, Eastridge would be better [than people

from the middle-class neighborhood of Cedarton] because they were harder or whatever. You know, but I was just like . . .

May: They didn't know Tommy? [That is, they based their evaluation of his ability on neighborhood stereotypes.] [We laugh.]

Tommy: Naw.

May: What about, you think race has anything to do with whether somebody is a good athlete or not?

Tommy: Not necessarily. It's just, like, some of it you get from, like, just genes or whatever. Just being, like, a pure athlete, I think that's just genes pretty much.

May: You think particular races have a better or more of a chance of being pure athletes than other races?

Tommy: Yeah.

May: Like, so if you compared Asians and whites [we both laugh], you might say that Asians would be better players or better pure athletes than whites?

Tommy: I'd probably say it the other way around.

May: Yeah. What about blacks and whites?

Tommy: I would say blacks probably.

Although Tommy suggests that members of particular racial groups (for instance, whites) are better athletes than those of other racial groups (for instance, Asians), he is also aware that genes across racial groups are an important determinant as to whether an individual will be a pure athlete. It is conceivable, from Tommy's perspective, that individuals from various racial groups who are good athletes will have been born of parents who also were genetically more athletic than the average members of that racial group. Thus, those blacks who are pure athletes are born of parents who are also athletes, whereas those blacks who do not demonstrate athletic talent were not passed the genetic makeup to be pure athletes.

Interestingly, Tommy demonstrates a keen understanding of the racial hierarchy with regard to those athletes most frequently categorized as superior. His ranking of blacks over whites and whites over Asians reflects the social hierarchy of athleticism as it is understood generally. Perhaps his understanding of the politics of race in sports is grounded in the fact that his father was an excellent athlete throughout high school, college, and the professional ranks. It is likely that once Tommy had been identified as the son of Photon Colt, coaches, parents, and peers began dubbing him a natural athlete because his father had been a successful athlete. Furthermore, I speculate that since Tommy's youth, his father had exposed him, whether directly or indirectly, to stereotypical assertions about race, genes, and athletic ability. Thus, Tommy internalized these notions as explanations for why he at least felt that he was a better athlete than both his black and white peers. In a sense, his ability was predicated on the fact that he was born of a father who had demonstrated athleticism beyond what one might expect to be average or normal.

Whereas the players' perceptions of race and athletic ability are shaped by their participation in a contemporary context of sport, the perceptions of the adults involved with the Northeast Knights are grounded in experiences of more racially tumultuous times.

Confronting Racism

Big Harry, the father of Harry, one of our star players on the Northeast Knights, recalls playing football in high school against an all-white team in the 1970s. From my notes:

> Big Harry rode with us on the bus to the game. He is pretty talkative, so I was surprised that Coach Benson let him go with us. At any rate, on the way to the game, Big Harry began recounting his experience of playing football in one of the small white towns in the '70s. He said, "Man, let me tell you. I was playing football, and it used to be really bad. White folks would call you all kinds of stuff. Shit, the cheerleaders for the other school were calling you all types of N words. The fans were calling you all kinds of N words. They were something else. They would really be hostile toward you."

Big Harry's recollection is not unusual when one considers the social context of school desegregation in the South. With the busing of black students to predominantly white schools during the early 1970s, racial tensions were heightened to a fever pitch. Given the history of racial violence against blacks and the fact that there are still residual effects in some areas of Georgia today, one can easily imagine the level of intimidation that Big Harry might have endured during his participation in football games in rural parts of Georgia.[9]

Interestingly, Coach Odell Henry, who grew up in the Northeast area during the '80s and '90s, had similar recollections. During the 1994–95 basketball season, Coach Henry played high school basketball for Ford Heights in Northeast. During those years his team traveled to games in various rural areas of Northern Georgia. Coach Henry recalls a trip they took to North Farmington High School. Because this area is rural, it had been referred to by players and coaches as populated by "hillbillies"—a classist term with racial implications when used by blacks. Again from my notes:

> *Coach Henry had been listening to Big Harry's story about playing football in South Georgia. He then began to tell a story about playing in North Farmington. Coach Henry said, "We went up here to North Farmington in '94, '95. Shit, time we came in the door them white folks started calling us nigger. They would call you nigger when we went up to play. The fans and everyone else called you nigger. We went ahead and played the game, then we got the fuck up outta there. We didn't stop nowhere."*
>
> *Coach Frye agreed, "I went to scout a game up there recently, and they were acting that way. I was sitting on their side of the gym. But when they started hollering this I said to myself, 'Let me get back over to where I belong.' I got up and changed sides. I sat on the visitor's side."*

Although the commentary of the men might be perceived as an attempt to outboast one another in talk, the reality is that each recollection shared by the adults becomes part of an intertwined cluster of stories that fuse together in a collective memory of race and sport in Northeast. These stories are rarely challenged; there is a taken-for-granted understanding that this "shit happens." This taken-for-granted reality is reproduced in similar form through the generations.[10]

Even though Coach Frye and Coach Henry competed in sports a generation after Big Harry, they were still exposed to blatant racial comments from white spectators. Given the historical ties that certain racial epithets have to violence against blacks, these epithets are of real concern and are not taken lightly.

The fact that we, as coaches, had personal experience playing games in racially hostile places like North Farmington meant that we were in a position to help our players negotiate their experiences in a manner that might also help them to optimize their performance. Although I had never played at North Farmington, I had experienced similar environments while playing college basketball. It was one school in particular, Olivet Nazarene College in Kankakee, Illinois (seventy miles from Chicago), that seemed to have the most notorious reputation among our players and coaches for its racial hostility. When I had first heard about Olivet in 1985, our head coach was telling us in a pregame meeting, "It's a tough place to play. They don't really care about blacks." After the meeting I asked one of the black upperclassmen what Olivet was really like. He replied, "Man, they are racists at that place. Don't look for no calls. The fans yell all kinds of shit at you."

When we arrived at Olivet that evening, the gymnasium was packed with white fans that were energetic and vocal. As I recall, with the exception of one player, the Olivet team was all white. Although I do not recall hearing "niggers" or other racial epithets specifically, I interpreted the hostility with which the fans greeted us to be about much more than basketball. Maybe it was my white coach's saying "they really don't care about blacks" that had me predisposed to interpret the fans' behavior as racially motivated. Maybe it was my teammate's observation that "they are racists" that had me ready to look for racial hostility. Still, it felt like much more was going on than pure fan support. Perhaps, given what I had learned about Kankakee in general—my mother, for example, had referred to it as "Mississippi, Illinois," to connote the racist attitudes—and what I have experienced coaching since that time, it is difficult for me not to see the Olivet fans' hostility toward our team as racially motivated. The fans seemed to grasp onto the racial subtext of the game as a means for motivating their home team. I would argue that such a racial subtext is the basis on which many interpretive responses to interracial interactions are founded—in sports and in life generally.

The adults involved with the Northeast basketball program explicitly considered issues of race within the context of sports. These considerations flowed from past and present experiences. For instance, a key period of transformation in race relations in Northeast was the combining of Tuxton and Harriston high schools in 1971 to create Northeast High School. At that time residents and high school students were forced to confront direct competition between blacks and whites on the athletic playing field, among other places. This competition was exacerbated by the social constraints that had been placed on white and black interaction during Jim Crow segregation. Thus, with the emergence of integration, each athletic event involving whites and blacks had the potential to bring forth hostilities that re-asserted racial boundaries.

Big Harry's and the other coaches' recollections provide a context for understanding some of the adults' historical perceptions of whites in and around Northeast. Each successive generation seems to have dealt with mutations of the racial tension from the generation prior. Coach Henry's feelings of anxiety at being called a nigger in the 1990s confirmed his belief in racism. The young men that currently compete for the Northeast Knights must also confront racism within the context of the game. For instance, Cerico shared comments that identify the ongoing nature of racial antagonism that exists for the young men of the Northeast Knights. Cerico recounted an incident that occurred in 2001 during our game against North Farmington. His serendipitous disclosure was in response to my question about his own on-the-court behavior and whether he retaliates when he feels an opposing player has done something wrong to him.

> *May*: I mean, is there a difference between Cerico on the court and when he is Cerico just hanging out or whatever?
>
> *Cerico*: Oh, yeah. I think I act different. 'Cause on the court, man, it's just nothing but business. Man, I wanna win, that's all. Whatever it take, grabbing his jersey, pulling his shoes off, whatever.
>
> *May*: Anybody ever do something like that to you when you were playing?
>
> *Cerico*: Yeah. [I laugh.] I remember we played North Farmington. This white dude tripped me up, then he called me a nigger, man, May. God.
>
> *May*: What? [incredulously] When you was playing?
>
> *Cerico*: Yeah, we were playing. We was up in the tournament, too.
>
> *May*: [Questioning his seriousness] Wait.
>
> *Cerico*: Yeah, I swear. It was the tall dude. His name was Wyatt Jenkins . . .
>
> *May*: The one that was scoring all their points?
>
> *Cerico*: Yeah, the one that was scoring all the points. He tripped me up . . .
>
> *May*: He tripped you up and then called you a nigger?
>
> *Cerico*: Yeah. I had—I had to get him back. Do whatever it takes. I got an elbow in.
>
> *May*: I hadn't heard about that.

Cerico nonchalantly stated, "He tripped me up and called me a nigger." Such a casual disclosure to me suggests that racially charged incidents like this occur frequently but are rarely explicitly discussed by the Knights. It was only after I prodded Cerico to tell me about his own on-the-court attitude that this negative interracial experience came to light.

The frequency of such events is suggested by the fact that a few weeks earlier the Northeast Knights freshman team had gone to another school, Nimrod County, to play and had also received verbal harassment. Because of this racial antagonism, we had to have a police escort to Nimrod County. From my notes:

> We were headed to Nimrod County to play. The day before, Coach Henry had taken the freshmen up to Nimrod, and they beat the dickens out of Nimrod. Coach Henry told us that while he was there the referees had to stop the game and talk to the fans because the fans were shouting "nigger" at the Northeast Knight freshman players. These events from the day before prompted our principal to have a sheriff escort us all to the game. The girls' team had the escort there since they played before us. We had the escort coming back since we played last.

This incident suggests that racial antagonisms continue to be a part of the Northeast Knights' experiences, rather than some distant experiences that coaches recall from many years gone by. Given the fact that the Northeast Knights continue to play in predominantly white areas, the explicit statements like those of the fans from Nimrod County remind the players of the significance of race. However, even without such outward manifestations of racial antagonisms, the young men's understanding of the previous experiences of their coaches might still provide the subtext for negatively interpreting interracial encounters.

Beyond Taboo

Given the fact that so many of the players rarely suggested racial-group membership as a positive or negative indicator of athletic success, what have we garnered about the players' understanding about the relationship between race, social environment, and athletic ability?

John Entine, author of *Taboo: Why Black Athletes Dominate Sports and Why We Are Afraid to Talk about It*, observes that to most people who follow sports, it is clear that blacks are superior athletes and that this superiority is related to race and genes.[11] If we accept Entine's observation, then the Northeast Knights' evaluation of white athletes in comparison to black athletes is an anomaly. This raises the question of whether there is anything about the young men's experience at Northeast that inhibits them from identifying similar stereotypes about black males' athletic ability as compared with white males within their own competitive environment. Indeed, this is an interesting question, especially given the fact that these young men are cognizant of the significance of race in other areas of their lives.[12] I suggest the following three possible explanations for the players' perceptions about race and athletic ability: (1) the players interact with white athletes who share skills and abilities comparable to their own; (2) the players have been insulated from structural factors that raise racial distinctions to greater salience; and (3) the players have embraced a sense of meritocracy within their own athletic setting.

Most high school teams are composed of the best athletes within each school. Since the Knights do not compete at the elite level of high school basketball, they are exposed to white athletes who share comparable skills and abilities as their own. Specifically, Northeast High School players compete within a general pool of athletic talent where the subtle distinctions that make an athlete great are not present or yet identified. When the Knights compete against teams from North Farmington, Nimrod County, and Wilmington County, they are, for the most part, competing against white athletes who are good but not great. Given the players' own limited abilities and that of their white counterparts, the players may conclude that white males are as athletic as black males. The players are therefore evaluating athletic ability associated with race from the standpoint of their own participation and not from the grand scale used in general to evaluate elite athletes. Perhaps if the players were asked directly which athlete they thought was more athletic, a particular professional black athlete or a particular professional white athlete, they would select the black athlete. They might infer that professional black athletes are superior merely because they appear in the NBA in greater numbers.

A second explanation for the boys' perceptions of race and athletic ability is that although the Northeast Knights attend a racially mixed school, their limited interaction with whites within the school context does not permit them to assess the magnitude to which race plays out in broader society. Beyond their awareness that some whites might call them "nigger" and that there are limits on the level of association that they may have with whites, the players, like other blacks at Northeast, have not been exposed to the fullness of racial tension that experience grants. As teenagers, the players are in an idealistic stage of life—a stage in which race should not matter. This position helps to ground the young men's thoughts as to the importance of race for athletic ability. It is only after experiences that move beyond high school that the players might begin to get a sense of the complicated and pervasive nature of race within American culture. Thus, as the players make the transition into adulthood, one might expect that the influence of conventional wisdom might transform the young men's beliefs about race to include the notion of the superior black male athlete. That is, the more they become acclimated to the normative understandings of race, the more their views will become consistent with conventional wisdom about race and athletics.

The final explanation for the boys' perceptions is that the players have a belief, stemming from their idealism, in meritocracy. The players embrace the notion of equal opportunity. Their perceptions of the unlimited potential to become whatever one wishes are deeply entrenched in their minds; so too is the individualization of failure—that is, "you failed because you couldn't make it." The players' posture toward opportunity is embedded within the context of their own participation in basketball. Members of the Knights team come to understand that the coaches are constantly evaluating individual players and that those individuals who work hard and demonstrate ability are given the opportunity to play. This belief keeps the players thinking, "I know I'm going to have my chance one day," even among those who consistently have been marginal participants. The players' reliance on meritocracy is predictable, given Coach Benson's articulated belief that every player should be given an opportunity to perform. As the players see structural opportunities in practice, they come to perceive that those who are the best will indeed have an opportunity to demonstrate that ability.

Conclusion

The players and coaches of the Northeast Knights consider issues of race within the context of their sports experiences. Their perspectives on the significance of race in everyday life are grounded in their understanding of the historically racist social climate of places like Northeast. The coaches and players deconstruct their negative encounters with whites by using racial frames to explain the underlying source of conflict. Throughout my time with Coach Benson he maintained that underneath the surface of matters that involved blacks and whites, racial tension was a key subtext.

Although Coach Benson and the other coaches viewed race as the source of much conflict around sports, they rarely encouraged the young men of Northeast to focus on race as an impediment to their aspirations and achievement. Benson, in particular, would often emphasize that issues of race mattered little with respect to whether one was able to achieve. For Benson, individuals who become preoccupied with the motives of those acting to prevent success were wasting valuable time and energy—both important resources better used for actual competition. This perspective on how to deal with negative racial encounters is consistent with a key rationalization used by many blacks who choose to ignore racism and discrimination in order to focus their efforts on personal achievement. By focusing on the possibilities for success rather than the impediments of race, individuals avoid being derailed from their pursuits.

One underlying theme of the stories shared by coaches and players is that black men must compete, not only against the respective white teams or individuals within the playing context but also against negative historical conceptions of blacks more generally. From this standpoint, whites are perceived to enjoy a clear advantage over blacks because of the inequitable power dynamics rooted in whites' past oppressions of blacks.

The use of race as a framework for understanding negative encounters with whites raises an interesting question: to what extent are the players and coaches unnecessarily appropriating a racial framework to explain occurrences as "racial" that could just as easily be explained as everyday matters that affect individuals irrespective of race? For example, why is it that the Northeast Knights view their negative encounters with hostile fans from places like North Farmington—characterized as a white hillbilly town—as racists? What is the difference between hostile fans calling an opponent "nigger" as a means of disrupting concentration and hostile fans using other derogatory terms to unnerve their opponents?

The simple answer is that there is little difference with respect to fans' goals of affecting the visiting team's play. When one views the use of pejorative terms that have far-reaching historical implications, however, these terms have a far more profound impact on the psyche of the young black men and coaches who compete for teams like the Northeast Knights. It is clear to those involved that words like "nigger" were used as an expression of hate toward blacks. Furthermore, such words were historically supported by actual violent acts toward blacks. Thus, pejorative terms laden with historical meanings of hate transform the social context from one of an athletic competition to a symbolic battle over racial pride.

This transformation of a sporting event is consistent with the ways in which both whites and blacks transform generic conflict (i.e., conflict that would generally be considered negative by most anyone, irrespective of race) into a racialized conflict in which the stakes of respectability and honor are much higher. Within this context, not only are the players competing for the Northeast Knights, but once these racial lines are drawn, the players are also competing for the pride of blacks more broadly. Such a symbolic transformation of a sporting event is not surprising given that the Knights reside in an American social system built on conflict between racial and ethnic groups who are in competition for market goods and resources and who have limited means to attain those goods and resources. The impact of this social system is not always apparent to those in conflict.

Perhaps for the black athlete there is no context in which race has been of more salient importance than the discussions of blacks' purported superior athletic ability as compared to whites' ability. These discussions about blacks as superior athletes are undergirded by racist rhetoric that asserts that blacks are more impulsive and instinctual, and therefore less capable of rational thinking. Furthermore, these same notions inform both blacks' own boastful expressions of athletic success and whites' concessions to blacks for their purported athletic ability. It is this taken-for-granted notion that is the basis of conventional wisdom about the relationship between race and athletic ability. Yet the young men who compete for the Northeast Knights generally hold perceptions of athletic ability that run contrary to conventional wisdom that accords superior athletic ability to blacks.

The fact that the young men view sport as a level playing field becomes an impetus for their focus on basketball as a means of mobility. Within their own racially segregated communities the young men see that there are limits to the kinds of occupations that they can pursue as a means of social mobility. They see that people in their communities have gone to school and gotten an education only for the satisfaction of living in places from which the young men are trying to escape. The young men assess their situation in light of the idealized lifestyles of professional athletes and determine that playing basketball within their neighborhood environments can give them the best opportunity to move beyond where they live.

The Northeast players' communities are much like other densely populated, low-income, racially segregated urban areas throughout the United States. These disproportionately black areas are places where young men have ready mentors—those athletes who may have been successful high school athletes but have failed to move beyond—to direct them into sports. It is within their neighborhood contexts that the players believe they can develop the physical and mental toughness necessary for becoming a professional athlete. Furthermore, it is through their participation in high school athletics that the young men receive community support for their hard work. The young men derive a sense of autonomy from these experiences and charge forward in pursuit of social mobility through athletic participation.

5

Knight-Style Masculinity

Look at him. He's screaming like a little girl.

The game against our cross-town rival the Ford Heights Panthers was always an intense game. We would usually play them once early in December and then again in mid-January. And if both teams were pushing for the state playoffs, we'd end up playing them yet again for the regional playoffs. Still, no matter how either team played during the rest of the season, everyone looked forward to playing in "the big game." We played twenty-one times in my seven years at Northeast. We won eleven games and the Panthers won ten. Some of the games were close—two to four points. Others were blowouts.

Benson would always tell the players, "This game ain't no different than any other. All of our games are big games. Shit, I'm trying to win every one of them." But even the coaches treated this game differently. We would put on our Sunday's best suits, ties, and leather dress shoes for the game, and if we didn't have something stylish to wear, we'd go out and buy it—maybe just so we could hear the crowd hush and, "Ohhhh, they sharp," as four or five coaches entered the gym "dressed to the nines."

The players treated these games differently too. They would do all they could within the restrictions of high school basketball rules to set themselves apart from one another. Some of them would get the latest Nike sneakers and have them embellished with their name or number. Others would get fresh haircuts or newly braided cornrows—this meant that they likely waited in long lines at the barbershop or sat for a few hours as "the girl down the street" or some other female relative or friend braided their hair. Other players would enter the gymnasium with new headbands and wristbands worn in odd places like around the calf. Why? Because this was the game that "everybody and they momma" came to.

The fans would arrive early to the games. If you weren't there at least an hour and a half before the game, you weren't likely to get a seat. And if you got there less than thirty minutes before game time, you couldn't get in the door. There wasn't even standing room left by this time. The gym would seat about two thousand fans, but with the sardine rule in effect twenty-five hundred fans squeezed side by side. They were loud too. Not just cheering during the game, but arriving early so that they could get the attention of players during pregame warmups. You could hear various girlfriends, family members, and friends, dressed in their hippest outfits, calling out to individual players, "Calvin," "Pooty Cat," "Turo." The fans kept this up until the player acknowledged them with a subtle wave or head nod. The boys knew not to let Benson see them acknowledging the fans because by this time Benson would have already given his pregame speech and said, "Don't go out here waving to fans up in the stands and shit."

Fan-player interaction was one of Benson's biggest problems during this game. At halftime he might come in the locker room, whether we were winning or losing, and make reference to the fans: "Our problem is everybody playin' for the damn fans. Don't go back out here and play for the fans doing all that between-the-legs, behind-the-back, crossover stuff. They'll have your ass sitting next to me if you shoot 'cause they holler 'shoot,' or you start doing something you can't 'cause your uncle told you to."

But, Benson didn't mind much if the players "showed out" a little, just as long as we won the game. After all, he had grown up in the rivalry and knew how important it was to some people in Northeast. And players did show out a little because they knew that this game could make you a legend in the Northeast community.

One such game catapulted Calvin Cody to community stardom. It was the game when he became "the man." He was a freshman, and we were playing Ford Heights at their gym. We had lost quite a few good players to graduation the previous year, and we had a young team. The Panthers were a bit more experienced than we were and they had taller players, so the talk around Northeast was that we would be easily defeated by the Panthers. But once the game began a different story unfolded. The referee tossed the ball; we won the tip, scored the first basket, and never looked back. From that moment on we were in complete control. In the first five minutes we broke out to a 22–2 lead. Calvin Cody, who started in his first Knights-versus-

Panthers rivalry game, shot three deep three-point baskets in the first two minutes, and they all went *swish*. Each time he hit a basket our fans, sitting behind us, shouted, "Whoop!" We substituted the entire five players out of the game, and two nonstarters hit three-point baskets. The scoring blitz didn't stop until we played our twentieth Knight in the first quarter.

Although we maintained a comfortable eighteen point lead in the second quarter, tension went high when Lance, our starting center at 6'2", went up for a lay-up but collided with the 6'5", 240-pound Panther, Leo Scott. Leo grabbed Lance out of the air and threw him to the ground. They both landed on the court side by side.

Lance was a quiet but tough young man. He wasn't the kind of kid that spent a lot of time talking when a fight was about to ensue. He just fought. So it didn't surprise me that Lance didn't verbally protest the flagrant foul. He merely rolled over and shoved his elbow into Leo's neck as a message that he wasn't about to be "taken out." Leo pushed Lance up and then quickly stood to his feet. The referees, recognizing the intense nature of the rivalry and the possibility of more fights breaking out, separated the players instantly. Yet they didn't see one of the Ford Heights fans streaking across the court toward the players with his right hand clenched. Nor did they see that the entire Ford Heights team had jumped to their feet and started toward the cluster of players on the court. When our players saw the Ford Heights team move, they jumped from the bench. I quickly got to my feet. I turned toward our players and shouted, "Sit down. Don't nobody go on the court." Our players stopped. When I turned back to the court, I saw that the Ford Heights assistant coach had gotten their team under control, and the courtside security had grabbed the Panther fan and escorted him from the gym as he protested, "Man, Leo's my cousin. Don't nobody mess with my cousin like that."

The referees sent the players to their respective benches so they could officiate. When all was said and done, Leo was ejected for his flagrant foul, and Lance hit the awarded two free throws.

We finished the first half with only a ten-point lead but came back to the court with determination. We controlled the game in the second half, largely on the scoring of Calvin Cody. He stole several passes for lay-ups, hit a few more sweet jump shots, and scored on acrobatic moves to the basket. By the time we finished the game, we had won by twelve points and Calvin Cody finished with twenty-eight points.

Here he was a freshman, just out of middle school, playing against players bigger and stronger than he was. Scoring so many points in the big game was impressive. Most seniors, from either team, couldn't score twenty-eight points. As we walked to the locker room I could hear fans chatter: "Calvin Cody is going to be a great player," "That boy Calvin Cody can score," "Calvin is so cute." Calvin just smiled all the way to the locker room. He had become "the man" among men.

* * *

To be "the man among men" through athletic competition is one of the greatest accolades that a man can receive. Such endorsements can solidify a man's sense of masculinity. Among the young men of the Northeast Knights, descriptors like "crying like a girl," "being soft," "weak as water," "sweet," or "bitch-like" and their accompanying gestures are meant sometimes as lighthearted jokes and sometimes as serious insults. To convey signs of femininity—most notably through emotions or feelings—links the players to women rather than to masculine signifiers of toughness or stoicism linked to men.

As with any organization or institution, the Northeast Knights reflect how gender roles are understood in the United States. Men have long been cast into active roles, that is, as "doing things" and behaving in ways that produce material goods for the maintenance of society.[1] Conversely, women are passive, "have things done to them," and are viewed as nonproductive and emotional. Both men and women, through their everyday interactions, convey what is "proper" for a man and a woman to "do."[2] Although actual men and women challenge these stereotypical roles every day, these roles continue to be reproduced with women cast as passive and weak and men as strong and aggressive.[3]

These ideas are rooted in a belief that men—in particular, white men—are to be productive members in a society that emphasizes social mobility and material wealth.[4] A man must be economically independent from others.[5] More important, manhood in the United States requires that one not only establish economic independence but that one strives for economic dominance. Men have asserted dominance and power over women through such ideas about manhood.[6]

Like their white counterparts, African American men support ideas of enacting masculinity through economic independence. Yet these men are aware that they must also negotiate the constraints on their race within the context of a predominantly white world in which historically they have been excluded from participating in social, political, and economic institutions throughout the United States.[7] Despite historical limitations on their participation in broader institutions, African American men have adopted the acquisition of material wealth as an underlying principle for defining what it means to be a man.

Because masculinity is often related to one's economic independence in the United States, the young men view the acquisition of money and climbing the socioeconomic ladder as key ways of enacting masculinity. Within their own community context, however, the young men view these means of demonstrating masculinity as being limited to choices between hanging in the streets to "chase that paper" —make money—and "making it big" as an athlete. Most of the Northeast Knights believe that basketball can be a means to assert their masculinity and thereby can help them to achieve many of society's accolades: economic, sexual, and athletic success.

The young men view masculinity in nuanced ways that are exposed when the boys discuss and evaluate their own and one another's gendered behavior, sexuality, and relationships with girls. They encounter the kinds of complex situations, albeit on a smaller scale, that professional athletes themselves encounter. In such situations, the young men feel they must uphold the ideal of male dominance. I argue that for the Northeast Knights this sense of dominance is built on four underlying principles: (1) men should avoid effeminate behavior that could be mistaken as a sign of homosexuality; (2) men should pursue women as objects of sexual satisfaction; (3) men should demonstrate courage in the face of fear; and (4) men should pursue capital and status as a means of asserting power and dominance. These principles are in constant negotiation through the players' interactions with one another, the coaches, and the surrounding community.

Gendered Behavior and Sexuality

One evening when I was a teenager, my brother Tim and I sat in the dining room talking to Ellis, our father, who did not live with us. I decided to relax as we talked. I pulled my chair close to the table and rested my right elbow on the tabletop. My elbow remained on the table as I leaned forward and extended my forearm up so that I could rest my head on my hand. Instead of resting my chin in the palm of my hand, I flipped my wrist down and rested my chin on the back of my wrist. *Smack.* My father reached out and hit my hand with a force that caused me to lose balance and almost bump my head on the table. "What?" I said, startled from the swift and forceful blow.

"Don't ever let me see you do that again," he said.

"Do what? I was just resting my head on my hand."

"Don't ever let me see you flip your wrist like that."

"That's how I always hold my hand when I relax my head."

"Don't do it," he retorted. "Keep your wrist straight. Don't sit like some damn faggot. Where did you get that?"

"I don't know. I just sit like that."

"Only faggots or women flip their wrists like that. Like some damn sissy. I need to talk to your mother about that."

I sat up straight and wondered to myself what I had done wrong. I had failed to comprehend that a flipped wrist might be considered effeminate or, worse, might be taken as an indication of homosexuality. My father made all too clear to me that my behavior could be read in this way and that the consequences could be severe. According to child psychologists, by age three boys and girls have learned which activities, gestures, and behaviors are sex-appropriate.[8] Such expectations about the nature of masculinity—especially how men read and monitor one another's physical expressions—later helped me to understand the codes of masculinity among the Northeast Knights.

It is important to remember here that gender is itself a construction.[9] To say that a particular gesture—for example, a flipped wrist—is effeminate may work only to reaffirm traditional gender stereotypes about how men and women are expected to move and carry themselves. Still, because these stereotypes are so ingrained in our collective understanding, their use makes the examples that I present about behavior immediately comprehensible. My goal here is to reveal the characteristics that the young men and coaches take to be masculine or feminine and suggest how these characteristics are used as proxies for sexuality.

The young men of Northeast are cognizant of the importance that gestures and behavior have for staking claim to a masculine identity. For them, individuals need to be physically strong and aggressive.[10] Not meeting these rigid requirements could prove to be a problem.

Patrick, a 6'3" brown-skinned player, was one person who confronted the fact that his gestures, thought by the others to be "girly," tainted the masculine identity he sought to claim. His high-pitched voice and the fluid movement of his arms, including an occasional flipped wrist, was suggestive of a girl to many of the young men. Because of Patrick's mannerisms, the players teased him by referring to him as "Sweetness" or saying that he had "sugar" in his pants. Both vernacular terms have been used to suggest effeminate behavior reserved for gay men. Patrick and his mannerisms were the brunt of many jokes. This was especially the case when his effeminate gestures manifested themselves during an injury—a time when boys were expected to behave with stoicism and as little emotion as possible in the face of pain or injury, in other words, "like men." The oft-repeated "there's no crying in baseball" comes to mind and could just as easily be applied to any sport. The following is an example from my fieldnotes:

> Patrick jumped up and grabbed the ball but came down awkwardly on his right knee. When he hit the ground he let out a high-pitched shriek, and then he cried out, "Aaaahhh! My leg! My leg!" His appearance on the ground was exaggerated as he flailed around. The other players on our team watched as Patrick cried out from the injury. Patrick was finally able to stand to his feet after about a minute. It was then that his teammates started in on the jokes.
>
> "Look at him," Turo said to Lionel. "He's screaming like a little girl."
>
> "I see him. It's Sweetness," replied Lionel. They laughed.
>
> After the game was over the team got together and headed up to the cafeteria for lunch. On the walk to the cafeteria Turo went up to Lionel, who was walking a few steps in front of Patrick, and said, "What's this? What's this y'all?" He then jumped in the air and imitated Patrick landing on his right knee. He let out a shout and added some dramatic gestures. They were the kind of gestures that "damsels in distress" use. "Ahhhhh! My knee! My knee!" Arturo called out. The guys started laughing, and Lionel said, "That's Sweetness." The other players started making jokes, and soon there were players jumping around and flopping in the air to mock Patrick.

For the Northeast Knights, there were some exceptions to the expectation that boys act like men when injured—taken here to mean a young man's ability to demonstrate a stillness without verbal or physical acknowledgment of the pain.[11] Since the seriousness of an injury was not always immediately apparent, players and coaches might suspend their negative evaluation at the time of injury. Benson usually reserved his judgment and always asked players if they were okay.

Patrick did not immediately respond to Turo's joke. Turo had created a verbal landslide that drew the other players in. Patrick remained silent, with the exception of an occasional laugh. He was probably contemplating the times that he had successfully beaten Turo in other episodes of the team's ongoing game of verbal one-upmanship.[12]

In addition to their criticism of effeminate behavior, the young men view such behavior as prima facie evidence of a homosexual orientation. For instance, several players during interviews suggested that Patrick might be gay because of his effeminate gestures. One stated, "I used to think that Patrick was gay too. I ain't too much trust Patrick." These comments represent an antigay attitude consistent with blacks' general attitudes toward gays.[13] Although African Americans, as compared to whites, are slightly more likely to hold antigay attitudes toward gay men than whites have toward gay men, these differences disappear when the religiosity of the individual is held constant.[14] That is, those individuals who attend church regularly, irrespective of race, have more negative feelings toward gays than those who do not attend church.[15] Given the significance of religion, in particular, Christianity, for blacks in the South and for many of the young men of Northeast, I speculate that the young men of Northeast held more antigay attitudes than their black counterparts in other regions of the United States.[16] Thus, there is little surprise that Patrick's gestures, taken as an indication of homosexual behavior, might evoke his teammates' critical assessment and overt need to distance themselves from him and his behavior.

Yet Patrick's teammates also acknowledged Patrick as a high-status teammate because of one fact: he had a reputation for being able to "pull the girls"—that is, engage them in flirty conversation that is presumed to end in sexual encounters. Thus, in the young men's broad scheme of heterosexual, masculine identity, Patrick's ability to get the girls trumps his effeminate gestures and mannerisms.

If there were players who, in fact, engaged in homosexual behaviors or considered themselves gay, they did not acknowledge this to teammates. Surely it is because there is little tolerance for such behavior or identification in a setting where masculinity is marked by physical aggression and heterosexuality. The sharp resistance to homosexuality is evident in the words that Shamar shared in an interview:

> Naw. I don't mess with no gay people. 'Cause I'll beat somebody up. I don't like gay people. You know I ain't got nothing against them. But if they ever come up to me and, you know, talk to me the wrong way, I'ma be ready to fight. I might kill them. [He half smiles.]

Shamar's attitude is consistent with the ways that so many of the players think about gay people.[17] Given their general consensus about gays, there is little wonder that players engaged in all manner of face-work to avoid being labeled as gay.[18] This facework included physically fighting one's way out of such a reputation. Meshaq, one of the less-skilled players, used this approach.[19] Although he was 5'8" and slender, there was a powerful energy about Meshaq. He undertook all the conditioning and basketball drills with the fervor of a man dedicated to prove masculinity through speed, strength, and aggression. Still, his off-the-court gestures and high-pitched voice were even more flamboyant exhibits of effeminate behavior than Patrick's. Yet it was rare to hear his teammates suggest that he might be "sweet" or "soft." The reason becomes clear as Meshaq details in his interview how he had to fight to establish a heterosexual identity:

> *May*: Was there anybody on the team that they said was gay or anything like that?
>
> *Meshaq*: They probably thought I was gay. . . . Yeah, 'cause some of them say I sound like Michael Jackson. Then some of them say I had a little sweet tone in my voice.
>
> *May*: Yeah? Do you think that you make effeminate gestures or stuff that might make people think that you're gay?
>
> *Meshaq*: Naw, I don't think so. It's just probably my voice. 'Cause I've been dealing with that problem every since elementary.
>
> *May*: That people thought . . .
>
> *Meshaq*: Yeah. 'Cause I had got into a fight with one dude, and I got on top of him and started beating him. And this boy went back and told his sister—'cause this had happened in the bathroom—and said me and dude was doing something [as in a sexual act]. And we got in the fight, and we got suspended over the fight . . .
>
> *May*: But y'all were doing something together?

Meshaq: Yeah. But we had our clothes on. [His tone suggests that he thought the accusation was illogical.] That was the thing. And I was punching him in his face. [I laugh.] And so her little brother went back and told her—'cause I was going with the girl at the time. And so she started a rumor, and we broke up.

May: That you were gay?

Meshaq: Yeah. That was about my fourth- or fifth-grade year. And then she went to Northeast Middle and I went to William Ford [Middle School]. And I had to deal with that history out there, too. And it kinda stopped this year.

May: Just this year?

Meshaq: Yeah.

May: Before that it was going on even in your junior year?

Meshaq: Yeah.

May: Why do you think it stopped this year?

Meshaq: It got old to me. I don't know if it got old to them, and they stopped. Or they got tired of doing it or what.

May: So nobody on the basketball team ever said, "Meshaq you gay"?

Meshaq: Naw.

May: Well, I had never heard that either . . .

Meshaq: 'Cause they—they know not to. [He laughs.]

May: Why?

Meshaq: Because I won't threaten them, but, you know, they know I'll come back and get them though.

May: Oh, you'll beat somebody's ass basically is what you're saying? [We both laugh.]

Meshaq: Yeah.

Like Patrick, who was able to "pull the girls," Meshaq's ability to fight superseded the suggestion of homosexuality that his high-pitched voice and effeminate gestures were thought to convey. Meshaq and many of his teammates grew up in a rough neighborhood and were well aware of his neighborhood reputation as a fighter. In fact, in sixth grade he was assigned to a behavior class for difficult students. "I didn't see no reason for me to be in that class," Meshaq told me, "'cause most of the kids in there, they were straight-out criminals." Whether deserving or not, Meshaq was often in fights, usually because of teasing over his high-pitched voice. The teasing was enough to make him fighting mad, given the cultural expectations about masculinity.

The Knights' Status and Girls

Although high school basketball players do not have the status of professional or college basketball players, they still have considerable status within their schools.[20] For instance, right after graduating from high school LeBron James was the number-one draft pick in the 2003 NBA draft. James is an extreme example, but NBA and college scouts are very aware of the top high school (and middle school) players. During his senior year several of James's high school games were televised nationally. Although the young men who play for the Knights do not enjoy LeBron James's celebrity, they are well aware of how their status as a basketball player might influence their association with girls. The very fact that they compete, as Byron and Shamar indicate in the following excerpt from my fieldnotes, gives them access to girls, not only at their school but at schools nearby. The prospect of meeting girls is exciting for many of the players.[21]

> We had just finished practice and were about to leave the new gym. I stopped by the exit door on the upper level to talk to Byron and Shamar about the upcoming Forest County game.
>
> Byron said, "Forest County is the game."
>
> "Why?" I asked.
>
> "'Cause you can get a girl there," Shamar said, as he smiled.
>
> "Yeah," Byron added. "There are so many women at the game."
>
> "What?" I said with surprise.
>
> "For real, May," Shamar said. "You can get you so many women from there."
>
> I laughed at their excitement. As I walked away I said, "Y'all better be thinking about winning the game."
>
> Shamar said, "Don't worry, May. We gonna take care of business. Then we gonna take care of business." He smiled.

Indeed, the Forest County game was a big game for us, though we did not compete in their region or classification.[22] The game was irrelevant for making a successful bid for the state playoff championship; but from a social standpoint it was the second most popular game of the season. (The games with area rival Ford Heights were without a doubt the most popular.) This was because Forest County was geographically close to Northeast, a thirty-minute bus ride, and many of the residents from Northeast had relatives and friends in Forest County. More important, Saturday-night games at Forest County were a major social event for the largely black population. Entire families attended the games, and their players had local community superstar status. The teens dressed in the latest hip-hop fashions and were eager to attend the postgame party. The crowd was enthusiastic, and, as Byron and Shamar indicated, many teenage girls, sometimes with a young child in tow, came to watch the game and fawn over players from both teams.[23]

But "getting a girl" is often more complicated than just playing one game. Some players even point out that they "don't need basketball to get a girl" or that "basketball keeps you from having a girl because you're too busy." When I asked Shamar, one of the more popular players, "Does basketball help you get a girl?" his responses captured the complexity of the relationship between having status as a player and courting girls:

> In a way it do and a way it don't, 'cause everybody look at it like, you know, when you coming in the school, you really hear about the athletes. You know the people that play sports. And if you a big player in basketball, you know, the girls already talking about your name. Then, you know, them little young girls they come in there, "Oh, he playing varsity basketball." So they figure everybody like him.

Shamar is quick to point out that just playing basketball does not give you the golden key of access to girls. One might have status as a member of the Northeast Knights, but team status is less important than individual status on the team. And as noted previously, a player's status on the team is not strictly based on his athletic ability. Yet, as one player pointed out, being a member of the Knights can enhance a player's social status in school because being a Knight represents being a winner, and "everybody likes a winner." Even those marginal players that are members of the Knights have elevated status by their association with the Northeast Knights.

The players also recognize that girls' interests may be sparked by an individual player's spectacular play in a game, even if that player's off-the-court gestures are considered effeminate by his teammates. This is the case for Patrick, a nonstarter, whose gestures and movements were the subject of the boys' many jokes about sexuality and masculinity. Yet, according to Cerico, Patrick's slam-dunk during the Ford Heights game boosted his status with the girls. In effect, his dunk, an aggressive offensive move, was a statement of his masculinity—that is, an affirmation of his physical strength and athletic ability.

> *Cerico*: Let me tell you what you gotta do now, May. I'm for real now. Like Patrick. Remember when he dunked in the Ford Heights game, man? Patrick, he got—man, I know that boy . . .
> *May*: So when he got his dunk everybody [all the girls] was on him?
> *Cerico*: Trust me. Awe, man, that's all he had to do. He ain't gotta play no more. They gonna be like, "There's the boy that dunked right there."
> *May*: So when he did something spectacular on the court they gave him . . .
> *Cerico*: Yeah.
> *May*: So you think playing it can help you get girls . . .
> *Cerico*: Yeah, it can.

Many of the young men count on their status as a Knight to provide them with opportunities to enter into relationships with more than one young woman. They reason that they can have their "pick of the litter." The players' attitudes are like those professional players who have been involved in brief sexual encounters with a variety of women. For instance, the purported cavalier attitudes of players like former NBA All-Star Shawn Kemp, who allegedly fathered seven children out of wedlock from brief sexual encounters with seven different women, represent for the young men the vitality of such an attitude toward relationships with young women.[24] Indeed, most of the young men avoid exclusive relationships with girls. To many of the boys, having a single girlfriend would be counterproductive, since it would limit their opportunities to "play the field." In fact, the young men generally believe that being able to manage relationships with multiple girls is another mark of being a real man.

This belief positions young women as objects through which the young men may achieve their masculine identities. It is supported by a culture of misogyny that undergirds themes in the movies that the young men view and the music to which they listen. These movies, like *Two Can Play That Game* and *Breakin' All the Rules*, depict women as easily manipulated by men for sexual pleasure.[25] Similarly, the young men's affinity for gangsta rap exposes them to lyrics by rappers like T.I. and 50 Cent that denigrate women as "bitches" and "hos." Indeed, one of the more popular songs among the young men on the Northeast Knights team was 50 Cent's "P.I.M.P." from his *Get Rich or Die Tryin'* CD.[26] In the song, 50 Cent proclaims his ability to manipulate women for money and sex, while "a bitch can't get a dollar out of me." Thus, the young men receive messages from a variety of sources that portray women as sexual objects to be used by men for most any conceivable purpose.[27] Playing basketball for the Northeast Knights gives the boys status to leverage in their pursuit of girls.

Still, regardless of the status attained by participating on the team, there are some cases in which the players feel the Northeast Knights jersey cannot work its magic, even for players who are accomplished athletes. For instance, Terry was a well-known two-sport athlete, and despite his revelation to me that he wished to court girls, he had difficulty. As a starter for both basketball and football, he had established himself as "Mr. Knight." Perhaps his greatest defining characteristic was his size. He stood at 6'4" and carried 308 pounds; yet he was as agile and quick as someone half his size. His teddy-bear-like facial features and bright smile made him friendly and approachable. Underlying his imposing physical frame, however, was a person who demonstrated little self-confidence in social matters, especially with young women. If he pursued girls with the same level of confidence that he pursued quarterbacks on the gridiron or loose basketballs on the court, then he would have no problems, but this was not the case. He did not pursue girls in the same way that the other players did; thus, it was difficult for him to gain approval from the other young men because he could not "get the girls." Therefore, despite his other masculine attributes, he could not assert his heterosexuality and so, on some level, was not a "real" man.

Girls and Sex

What do the boys expect one another to "do" with those girls that they have pursued? Most expect to have sex, ranging from "messing around,"—that is, kissing and fondling—to "cutting" or "hitting"—sexual intercourse. The young men view sex as a natural part of a developing relationship and not as a special experience to wait for or hold off on.[28] In short, they and their friends want immediate sexual gratification. Further, most of the young men believe that the more women they have sex with, the more "manly" they are.[29]

Although the young men have the expectation that each will engage in sexual acts, few of them discuss the specifics of these acts with one another. In this regard, the Northeast players are like many other adolescent boys who avoid explicit discussion lest their limited knowledge about sex be exposed. Their inhibition in sharing facts about sex is rooted in male stereotypes that suggest men should be well informed, even expert, in all matters related to sex. Each young man should be able to say, "I already knew that," when presented with the details about sex. Such posturing by the young men suggests that they rarely engage in the exchange of meaningful information about sexual practices.

Still, there is pressure to provide at least cursory information about one's sex life. This information is important because it illustrates a young man's masculine identity to his peers. If a player does not pursue sexual encounters with a girl, then he is presumed to be "scared" —a quality that goes against standards of masculinity among the Northeast boys. For instance, Danny reveals the extent to which Arturo's fear of having sex with a girl spread throughout the school:

> *May*: Do they [his teammates] talk a lot about having sex, or whatever, or talking about what they should have done or what they could have done?
> *Danny*: Uh huh.
> *May*: Like, give me an example.
> *Danny*: Same old person, Turo. Some girl, she said, uh—I think he went to her house or something, and then he didn't do nothing with her and she was expecting him to do something with her. And then she told everybody. And when he came back to school, it was all over.
> *May*: They was lighting him up [teasing him]. I wonder why he didn't do nothing?
> *Danny*: [He laughs.] They say Turo is scary, I guess, I don't know.

The young men put social pressure on one another to avoid being scared in matters of sex. This pressure can have a profound mental effect on adolescents. For instance, one study found that one of the leading reasons that adolescents seek mental health services is due to pressures to participate in high-risk behaviors, particularly those related to sex.[30] Clearly, a peer group like the Northeast Knights police one another in standards of sexuality that make the young men aware that time with young women should be marked by some form of sexual encounter. If young men do not live up to this standard, then they risk being teased, embarrassed, or worse.

The boys' expectations get higher when the girl involved has a reputation for having sex with a variety of young men. I came to understand this during a prepractice discussion that I had while wrapping and taping players' ankles in the training room. Harry and Arturo talked to me about where they had partied over the previous weekend:

> "Where did y'all go?" I asked.
>
> "To The Place [a nightclub]," Turo replied.[31] "But I didn't go. I saw it was so many fights going on, I went right down to Rosewood," Turo added.
>
> "Rosewood is another club?" I asked.
>
> "Naw. I just know somebody that live there," Turo said.
>
> "The only reason I went into the club is 'cause I knew I could get in free," Harry said. He smiled and shook his head from side to side and said, "Boy, it was thick in there. After 11:30 you couldn't even walk. And they had the heat blasting." Harry turned to Turo and said, "When you went down to Rosewood was anybody there?"
>
> "Yeah," Turo replied. "It was a few girls and then the regular crew came down there. Sherry, Bettina . . ."
>
> "Bettina was down there?" Harry asked.
>
> "Yeah," Turo replied.
>
> "Who tried something?" Harry asked.
>
> "Nobody. She wasn't gone enough," Turo said.
>
> "Gone?" Harry said.
>
> "Yeah," Turo said. "Rich was trying to get her drunk, but she wasn't that drunk."
>
> "Man, nobody did nothing?" Harry asked in surprise.
>
> "Naw. I told you she wasn't gone enough," Turo replied.
>
> "Turo," I interjected, "Harry is trying to tell you she don't need to be drunk for you to do something."
>
> "That's right," Harry responded. "She would have started stripping her

clothes off for nothing. When she left Flatshoals [the housing project where she used to live] she started that."

In Harry's eyes, Turo had failed to take advantage of an opportunity to mess around with Bettina, a girl with a reputation for having casual sex. Harry looked shocked that Turo hadn't had sex with her, especially considering that a house party was supposed to be one of the easiest places to "hook up." In such a setting girls could more easily succumb to the pressure to mess around or do more.[32] So Turo had actually failed "big time" in Harry's eyes.

Many of the players were sexually experienced. In fact, thirteen of the eighteen players I interviewed claimed to have engaged in sexual intercourse. For most, they reported that sexual intercourse had occurred when they were around fifteen years old, although there was one as young as twelve. Much of what the players learned about sex was a product of their immediate environment. As Meshaq pointed out, "I learned a lot by just being around my peers." However, from what I observed, most of the sex talk among the boys was bravado that just reaffirmed male stereotypes of self-sufficiency and independence in matters related to sex.

Adolescents learn about the nature of sexual encounters from their peers and older classmates, members of their immediate and extended families, and members of their communities. Ideas about sex are also informed by ideas about race. For instance, given the fact that Northeast High School was once a racially segregated school for whites, the racial interaction between whites and blacks continues to be limited by a variety of social barriers. Black and white students often still live in segregated neighborhoods. Black residents live in places like Flatshoals, Hillside, and Eastridge that are urban and poor, while white students live in predominantly white affluent areas like Crossway. Living apart creates social distance among whites and blacks at school, often encouraging them to bypass social interaction with one another. Still, athletic status means that some of the Northeast Knights can transgress racial boundaries. Their celebrity status as athletes can also encourage interracial relationships.

Despite the small number of professional black athletes who have interracial marriages, these high-profile relationships, like those of former NBA All-Star and sports commentator Charles Barkley and current NBA All-Star Kobe Bryant, give the Northeast Knights examples of such relationships. Given the frequency with which these celebrity athletes are discussed in the media, their relationships, which may have been thought to be rare, are presented as quite common—so much so that players themselves can feel empowered to transgress social taboos against interracial relationships. The possibility of such relationships is yet another advantage of aspiring to a career in basketball—not for the sake of interracial dating per se but for the "freedom" that is accorded those who have athlete status to choose a mate. Some Northeast Knights, despite having grown up in segregated communities, decide to pursue encounters across racial boundaries.

Messing with White Girls

There are many stereotypes about relationships between white women and black men. One such stereotype is that white women are more than willing to share in covert intimacy and relationships with black men but are much less likely to have a public relationship. This stereotype is premised on the notion that the social cost of "dating" a black man is too high for both black men and white women to have publicly acknowledged relationships.[33] This notion is significant given that the nature of interracial relationships can be an indicator of racial tolerance.[34] That is, if family, friends, and peers of those dating accept overt interracial relationships as normative, then one might infer that there is greater racial tolerance in society for interaction between the races than there was in the past.[35] Irrespective of improved racial tolerance, the young men of Northeast continue to perceive the historical prohibitions against interracial relationships. The one clear exception for the young men of Northeast to the prevailing stereotypes of covert relationships is when the black male in the relationship is especially well known or is a financially viable professional athlete. None of the Northeast High School players fit the exceptional athlete status. Since there is social pressure against interracial dating, and blacks greatly outnumber whites at the high school, I began to wonder if any of the young men had actually explored sexual intimacy with their white female classmates. I wanted to know if the young men felt governed by historical social taboos against interracial dating and how they negotiated interracial relationships if they had them.

Cerico, a player who lived in the Hillside housing development, was the only player who had been publicly known to have a white girlfriend. Cerico and Amanda did not show public affection, but it was clear to the players and to others around the school that they were together. This raised the question of whether other players have interracial relationships that are less obvious than Cerico and Amanda's. When I asked Turo, the shy (or "scary") yet popular boy, he explained:

> I said, "Oh yeah, I think that Cerico was the only guy that had a white girl. Have you ever messed around with a white girl?"
> "Yeah. I messed around with Caroline Mitchell."
> "So you had sex with her?"
> "No, we just messed around."
> "Why didn't you have sex with her?"
> "Because I didn't put in my work."
> "What do you mean you didn't put in your work?"
> "I didn't spend the time. I was just talking to her."
> "Well, what did her parents have to say about you all? Did they know you were messing around?"
> "Didn't nobody know we messed around. When I did go over her parents' house, and that really wasn't that much, they weren't really friendly. At first her father, Mr. Mitchell, wouldn't even speak. I don't think they liked the idea of their daughter messing around with a black boy. He started to speak to me after a while when we kept playing basketball. [Caroline played basketball on the girls' team.] I wasn't the only one that messed with her."
> "Who else?"
> "Stromile Carrington. He used to mess with her."
> "Who else messed with white girls?"
> "Larique used to have one."
> "I know. Larique used to mess around with Rachel Heil. Did Larique have sex with Caroline also?"
> "I don't know."
> "Naw, you do know. What do you mean you don't know?"
> "Well, they say he had sex with her."

Although Turo was not a virgin, he did not have sex with Caroline because he "didn't put in work." To put in work is to do such things as spend time courting the girl at her home, meet her at her locker, or frequently call her on the telephone. Since Turo was less aggressive than his teammates when it came to girls, his "work" would be greater than that of players like Patrick or Larique—both of whom had reputations for aggressively trying to engage girls in sex. Interestingly, Turo was well aware of the extent to which he believed race to be a factor in the way Caroline's parents treated him. As Turo described, his status as merely a black boy was gradually transformed by his participation in athletics. Irrespective of the parents' motives for gradually accepting Turo, it is clear that basketball facilitated Turo's crossing racial lines that had been demarcated by social custom.

Approaching white girls is particularly more difficult for the boys than approaching black girls. The traditional black / white social boundaries at Northeast High School continue to have a profound influence on blacks' and whites' relationship choices. Yet several Knights muster the courage to engage in covert relationships with white girls. The boys and girls that have been willing to chance these encounters were part of a small nucleus of students that included girls on the girls' basketball team. These young men and women came into contact with one another daily. Thus, participation in basketball created the opportunity for players to date one another or make arrangements for social gatherings. This was frequently done without the scrutiny of parents or friends from the high school. Michelle Laughton, one of the former girls' basketball players whom I coached in my first year at Northeast, told me after she graduated that she had engaged in sexual intercourse with Larique while they were in high school. She had been able to conceal this fact from her parents. She then said,

> Mr. Mitchell, Caroline's father, had found out that I had been with Larique when I was in high school, and he told my dad, "You need to watch out for your daughter messing around with these black boys." What Mr. Mitchell don't know is, he better be worried about his own daughter, Caroline. He was up there worrying about me, and now his own daughter has messed around with a couple of those boys on the basketball team.

It is evident from Michelle's comments that racial tension continues to exist regarding interracial relationships. Further evidence of this tension can be found in Michelle's own post-high-school dating. After graduating from high school, Michelle dated a black male. Her parents attempted to prevent her from seeing him by sending her away to college. However, Michelle would often covertly return to Northeast to spend time with him. She ultimately gave birth to her boyfriend's son. Her family's worst nightmares had been realized. After a couple of years Michelle and her black boyfriend ended the relationship.

Many of the Northeast Knights understand the racial tension around interracial relationships like Michelle's. They have heard recollections from adults about the detrimental effects that an idle attraction to a white woman can produce. Indeed, most of the young men avoided approaching young white women because the real and symbolic threats to their lives lie just beneath the surface of their interracial interactions, as James suggests:

> *May*: You ever mess around with white girls?
>
> *James*: Nope, I never have.
>
> *May*: Any particular reason?
>
> *James*: Naw, I just never really actually talked to them like that. You don't really know what they going to do. You know what I'm saying? You have to slowly have to try to get it in there. [Conversation about sex.]
>
> *May*: Oh, how do you mean you don't know what they are going to do?
>
> *James*: White girls might call sexual harassment or something.

For James there is a cultural difference in how the girls might understand his advances. Given this cultural difference in interaction, James opts to avoid such interactions. Indeed, his avoidance is similar to the ways in which black men in the Jim Crow South avoided such interactions with white women for fear that they could lose their lives. This fear was legitimate given the fact that numerous black males were lynched on the mere supposition that they had looked at a white woman. Although James is not likely to receive the level of sanction that black males received in the early 1900s, he is well aware that there is a social cost to having interracial relationships and that misinterpretations can still happen.

Average players like James are less likely to attempt relationships with white young women, but the high-status athletes from Northeast are more likely to engage in sexual encounters across racial lines. Despite the fact that these young men have already had sexual intercourse, their encounters with their white classmates tend to be characterized as "messing around." For instance, when I asked Harry if he had ever had sex with a white girl, his response was, "I done played around with them but never cut one." Harry's response is consistent with yet another stereotype regarding the sexual practices of whites and blacks. Among some blacks, there is a popular perception that white women are more willing to engage in oral sex than are black women and, furthermore, that even if a white woman has never had sexual intercourse, she is still willing to perform oral sex. Beyond anecdotal evidence from black males, both athletes and nonathletes, there is limited research that confirms or disputes this stereotype.[36] Nevertheless, those Northeast Knights who have engaged in sexual encounters with white girls believe the stereotype.

The players' personal experience becomes further evidence for the stereotypes that they have heard about white women's willingness to perform oral sex. For instance, Pooty Cat revealed this stereotype to me when I asked him how he came to have oral sex with one of his white classmates. He said, "I just had heard that she did that, so it was kinda like I let her know that I wanted her to do that and she did." Pooty Cat probably approached the girl in the first place because he had heard that she was willing to perform oral sex. His teammate, Byron, another high-status player and starter, shared a similar story. However, he ended his story with, "May, I can't tell you all my secrets about how you get it done." For other high-status players like Shamar, Stromile, and Larique, who had "messed around" with white girls, the story was consistent. They engaged in covert sexual encounters with white girls, mostly limited to oral sex. Furthermore, only Cerico had ever had a serious relationship or feelings for a young white woman. Undoubtedly, the boys, like so many others, carry these stereotypes beyond the walls of Northeast and out into the world.

The young men's pursuits of encounters with white girls are like other men's aggressive pursuits of women as sexual objects. Indeed, this pursuit is a traditionally accepted means of asserting one's masculinity. As is shown in a variety of news stories about "groupies" on television or in sports magazines like *Sports Illustrated*, professional male athletes have an array of options for pursuing women. But regardless of the possible negative outcomes to which these options can lead for professional athletes—for example, out-of-wedlock births, contracting sexually transmitted diseases, and accusations of rape—the young men of the Northeast Knights believe that a career in sport provides vast opportunities for sexually exploiting women. The advantages and disadvantages of having these options are often the topic of adult commentary about girls and sex.

Adult Commentary about Girls and Sex

Beyond the personal consequences for the boys, intense relationships and sexual activity with girls can have a profound impact on the boys' concentration and focus on basketball. Coach Benson does not attempt to regulate the boys' relationships but often provides post-practice speeches that are a mixture of advice, directives, and criticism about relationships. As the head coach, one of his main concerns is to limit the distractions that the boys have during the season. But many of his speeches were not about the impact of relationships on basketball but about the kinds of aspirations the players should have for their relationships. For instance, in the following diatribe Benson shared his feelings about the overall state of some of the boys' relationships with girls:

> We had just finished practice, and we were about to get ready to leave. We went to the locker room, and Coach Benson started to talk. He said, "Y'all always spending time with your friends and girlfriends, and you don't do nothing but sit up there and talk about the same things all the time. You see them Monday through Friday, and you spend time with them all day long. Hell, some of you all spend more time with your girlfriends than you do your mother. Shit, you talk to the same girl all the time. Some of y'all need to quit talking to the same girl. You should get with Dr. May. He works at a university. He'll take you to meet some girls. Find you a girl that's going to be averaging 40K a year—averaging $40,000 a year. But some of you guys are so stuck on the girls you meet and talking the same thing. They ain't smart enough to talk about something else. See, y'all need to leave her alone because what's gonna happen is that she will mess around and get pregnant and have a retarded baby." At this point the entire team started laughing.
>
> After the laughter subsided Benson continued, "See, the baby will end up sitting in the room talking to the walls. And some of y'all girlfriends— this ain't nothing against anybody's girlfriend or anything—but some of y'all need to check your taste because it's in your mouth." The guys again

erupted with laughter. "Some of y'all date the girl who is the flavor of the month. Some kind of Lifesaver candy, green Lifesaver candy." The boys laughed again. "At least with some of you guys in a relationship the girl be telling you what to do. Shit, she be telling you 'tote this bag' or 'pick this up,' and you are always doing what she say do. She the strong one in the relationship." The guys kept laughing.

Implicit in Benson's statement is the belief that the boys are infatuated with a sexual relationship that has little substance. Benson's belief that the boys' relationships are too serious had been stressed to the young men many times. For instance, Coach Benson once commented to Ron, a starter, and his girlfriend, Jada, that they were acting like they were married. Jada replied in a serious tone, "I'm not worried about being married to Ron. We are already married in the eyes of God." In the fall of 2003 Jada became pregnant. I asked Ron what he intended to do now that he had an added responsibility. Ron said, "Coach, I'm still going to school. I got in, so I'm going." Ron left for college the following fall, but this did not negate the added stress that his girlfriend's pregnancy placed on him.

Benson indicates that such intense relationships could end in pregnancy and that there are certain consequences as a result. A player might end up with a "retarded baby." In telling this joke, Benson attempts to articulate the seriousness of young parenthood. His comments are grounded in his overall belief that the boys should grow and explore what the world has to offer before taking on the adult responsibilities that come with marriage and parenthood. They should be aspiring to do better educationally, socially, and athletically. He frequently reminded them, "You gotta get out of Northeast and see what else is out there." Still, underlying Benson's commentary is the belief that boys who get girls pregnant must also live up to that responsibility even though accepting it can jeopardize the young men's chances of mobility.

Despite providing the young men with useful insights about parental responsibility and the importance of having aspirations, in his postpractice speech Benson also reinforces misogynistic and sexist views about women. He refers to women as objects with limited intelligence because they "ain't smart enough to talk about something else." These comments reinforce negative attitudes about women.

Benson also characterizes young men as weak if they permit their girl-friends to "tell him what to do." Since the young men emphasize a masculinity that requires men to be mentally and physically strong, Benson's implicit message is that the young men must exercise domi-nance over women if they want to become men. Although Benson's messages may not be overt attempts to denigrate women, such com-mentary creates an environment within which the young men and adult men of Northeast can easily devalue women.

Given the fact that many of the players were sexually active and that a small number of them had intense relationships with girl-friends, coaches' commentary on these issues could provide a pool of information from which the players could draw. Still, the coaches could not live the players' lives for them. Nor could we rescue them from the consequences of their behavior. Indeed, part of becoming a man for the Northeast Knights was being able to negotiate relation-ships with women. Some players, especially those high-status players who had relationships with more than one girl, failed to effectively manage these relationships. The end result was that they "get caught up." Players were then confronted with the situation of having to "deal with their women." How well they were able to deal with their relationship is also a measure of masculinity for the young men. Like the examples of professional athletes' highly publicized incidents in-volving women—Kobe Bryant and Michael Jordan, for example, both reconciled their relationships with their wives after their private infi-delities became public—the young men of Northeast also must man-age their own incidents.

Getting Caught Up

As Shamar and Byron noted, games like the one against Forest County are especially exciting for the boys because they can meet "a lot of women" there. Since the culture of the Northeast Knights rarely supports boys' monogamous dating, especially when the boys are younger, some players attempt to covertly date more than one girl at a time. When they engage in this behavior, other players positively characterize them as "pimps" or "playas." For the Northeast Knights, the word "pimp" is figuratively used to describe someone who has a "stable" of girls. As one of the boys explained, "I was a pimp. This year I settled down with one girl." Similarly, a "playa" is someone who plays—who negotiates relationships with several girls at the same time. The boys use "pimp" and "playa" interchangeably within this context. Both terms are used to characterize boys who are presumed to be receiving some benefit, usually of a sexual nature, from manipulating relationships with more than one girl at a time. A "pimp" or "playa" has high status among the Northeast Knights. The player with this status is not just masculine, but he is "the man."

Maintaining his ability to be "the man," however, can be difficult and often leads to confrontations with girls over the issue of dating multiple partners. Being confronted is not problematic in and of itself; it is how the boy negotiates the confrontation with the girls that affirms his ability to "handle his business like a man." For instance, Calvin, a player who dated two girls at one time, recalled during his interview how he handled being "caught up." He described how two girls confronted him in the school cafeteria:

> *Calvin*: Man, they came in there when I was in there eating. I seen one of the girls come over there. She sat down and I looked up and I seen another girl and I said, "Oh, both of my girls in this lunch." So she came and sat right beside me, and I kept eating like I ain't see neither one of them. And then she was like, "Calvin you don't see me right here?" I was like, "Oh, yeah, I see you. What's up? I'm trying to eat, though, you know what I'm saying?" And then she was like, "I heard you go with this girl right here." [He gestures with his right thumb over his right shoulder.] I was like, "Who is that?" I was like, "Shhhhh. Whatever." I . . . threw my plate away and went outside, and they [the girls] started telling everybody to come outside. They was gonna confront me and everything. Then we got on the breezeway, and they was like, "Now tell me this. Which one you go with?" I was like, "I don't go with neither one of y'all." She was like, "You don't go with me? You just talked to me last night on the phone." I said, "I don't go with neither one of y'all," and I just walked off.
>
> *May*: They didn't get you, though?
>
> *Calvin*: Naw, they didn't get me. I got them.
>
> *May*: Oh, alright . . .

Calvin: They [his teammates] still talking about that today.

May: I thought they might have, like, jumped you and hit you upside your head [speaking in a high voice]: "I'll kill you."

Calvin: Naw. They didn't do nothing.

Calvin's teammates had told me this story about him being caught up. When they told the story they applauded the fact that even though the girls confronted Calvin, he escaped the event socially unscathed. In fact, Calvin's subsequent girlfriend was present when the incident in the cafeteria occurred, and she still gave him a chance to date her. Despite a few episodes of being "caught up," Calvin's good looks, sense of humor, and status as an outstanding basketball player continued to make him desirable to many girls.

Conclusion

On the Northeast Knights, a player who walks, talks, or cries "like a woman" may be considered male but not a "real man" because of his effeminate gestures. These gestures are considered to be a proxy for a homosexual identity, an identity that can be countered, however, if the young man effectively seeks out sexual relationships with women. This rigid heterosexual requirement as one basis of masculinity is thought to be the impetus behind black men's increased "down low" behavior. "Down low" or "D.L." behavior is the maintenance of a heterosexual public identity through, for instance, marriage and children, while maintaining extramarital sexual activity with men.[37] The young men of the Knights recognize the importance of demonstrating a heterosexual identity in support of masculinity.

Another key aspect of masculinity for the young men is that most respond with courage in the face of fear.[38] The young men employ the concept of acting courageously while facing daily the dangerous conditions in their communities. They exhibit the clear understanding that being aggressive and "fighting" for oneself is a requisite trait for survival as a man. The frequently quoted phrase "a scared man is a dead man" rings true in the experiences of the Northeast Knights. They have witnessed many of their peers lose their lives because they failed to address situations with the resolve and courage of a "real man." For the young men this courage is best exemplified in the life-styles of two well-known archetypes in their communities: drug-dealing "hustlas" and slam-dunking "hoopas." "Hustlas" demonstrate courage in their willingness to use violence in retaliation against any-one who attempts to interfere with their drug dealing. The "hoopas" demonstrate courage in physical confrontation on the court. Both of these archetypes are proximate icons for the freedom and power associated with material wealth in the 'hood. In the end, the players seek wealth by one of the most visibly traveled paths that they know. That path is hoopin'. Thus, basketball becomes not only a career pursuit for financial gain, status, and power, but it also becomes the center of many of the young men's masculine identities. Ultimately, though, the players' adoption of a masculine identity that is centered on the attainment of wealth through athletics has consequences for the young men's mobility.

6

Sportsmanship and the Need to Win

You out there to play hard and they out there to play hard. You trying to win just like they trying to win. So you gotta do whatever it take to win.

After working all summer on my basketball skills I was starting in one of my first games at Aurora University. I had been named the captain of the team. I felt that my energy and spirit were the intangibles that made me a real competitor. At one point during the game the opposing team took a shot. As I stepped in front of an opposing player to box him out I shouted, "Get off my back! Get off my back!" I eased into his body to seal him from the basket. The referee who was standing underneath the basket said to me, "Easy, number 12. Easy, number 12." The ball hit the rim and bounced high in the air. I pressed backward against the player's midsection and shouted, "Get off my back!" I jumped, grabbing the ball with two hands. When I came down with the ball the referee blew his whistle. I was relieved to think that I was finally being rewarded for my hard work and good rebound positioning. I thought, "Good, they got him for being on my back."

The referee calmly walked to the scorer's table and said, "Technical foul on number 12."[1] I was amazed. I had inside position, but I was given the technical foul because I had spoken to the other player. It took all that I could muster to keep from verbally exploding on the referee for what I believed to be an unfair call. Apparently, I was being penalized for playing in a manner that I had learned and that had become almost second nature. Talking and playing at the same time was all in the game. But the referee did not agree. To both the referee and outside observers, my behavior posed questions: Is he being a good sportsman or a bad sportsman with all that talk and aggressive play? Is his behavior even necessary in order to win? Or is it some alien form of "ghetto" ball infiltrating the confines of an official college game? Similar questions concerning sportsmanship may be asked of the young men's behavior for the Northeast Knights. Simply put, what is good and bad sportsmanship for the Knights?

Scholars and fans of sport have noted that notions of fair play and sportsmanship are increasingly being challenged because of an emphasis on "winning at all costs."[2] Not only has winning become the "all-consuming goal," but it has also become the standard by which athletes and coaches are consistently judged.[3] As sport sociologist Stanley Eitzen has noted, the pressure to win at all costs "pervades sport at *every* level and leads to cheating by coaches and athletes."[4] Youth sports, especially high school athletics, have become increasingly consumed by an attitude of winning with little regard for sportsmanship.[5] Most researchers attribute this decline in sportsmanship to a few reasons: the competitive context of traditional sport itself, the professionalization of coaches and the pressure on them to win, and the financial considerations for winning. Yet these researchers have given little consideration to how athletes and coaches alike understand notions of sportsmanship through the interrelated contexts of the game, the coaching style, and the everyday reality of the participants.[6] The popularity of competitive high school basketball compels us to consider how the Knights negotiate the interrelated contexts that influence sportsmanship.

In this chapter I demonstrate how the Knights' players and coaches mediate notions of sportsmanship through the contexts of the game, the coaches' philosophy regarding player conduct, and the everyday social reality of the athletes. The players' use of contexts—in particular, experiences from where they live and play—to define sportsmanlike behavior creates a dilemma as the young men must weigh the often-contradictory goals of winning against shifting definitions of sportsmanship. Although many other factors—including psychological ones—might also influence whether the Knights' players perform like sportsmen, my focus here is on the impact of social situations on individual conduct.

I argue that just as attitudes toward sportsmanship are contextual, so too are the young men's perceptions of opportunities for mobility. Again, the broader argument of this book is that players' aspirations for mobility have been influenced by mass media images of professional black athletes' success, the dangerous and desolate communities from which the young men hail, the young men's success within an average playing context, and the coaches' directives for the young men to work at playing sports beyond high school. The importance of contexts for how the young men think about sportsmanship represents a microcosm of the kinds of pressures they face as they contemplate the opportunities for mobility in the United States. Thus, by examining coaches' expectations, game context, community influence, and players' perceptions of sportsmanship we have an opportunity to closely examine the specific conditions under which players act.

A few definitions are in order. Although I recognize that ideas about sportsmanship are contextual, generally I consider sportsmanlike behavior to consist of "positive interaction with teammates, officials, coaches and opponents" including "providing verbal and/or nonverbal support, encouragement or praise, shaking hands, assisting someone who ha[s] fallen, or saying 'nice shot' or 'nice play.'"[7] Conversely, unsportsmanlike behaviors are "negative social interactions" including "arguing, retaliating, abusive language, and fighting or demonstrating displeasure with an official, opponent, teammate, or coach."[8]

Coaches' Expectations

The professionalization of high school sports has created a market for coaches who emphasize winning. High school sports are no longer merely for fostering school spirit, but they now generate income for schools. Coaches must now be certified in rules about player recruitment because of the high demand for premium athletes. In some instances, the notoriety of school teams and players—like LeBron James, who played for St. Vincent–St. Mary High School—provides schools with the opportunity for unparalleled media exposure, athletic equipment, and revenue from the sale of game tickets.

School administrators, fans, and parents expect players and coaches alike to put forth every effort to win.[9] Those coaches who survive the frequent hiring and firing of their colleagues have embraced the competitive spirit and have been able to motivate their players to victory. Coach Benson is one such coach. He often conveys his attitude about winning through recollections of his own personal experience. These recollections are important because they undergird his attitude about competing and help players develop a collective will focused on winning. Benson's use of such recollections is a frequent occurrence during the Knights' pregame Saturday-morning meetings. For example, in this excerpt from my fieldnotes he talks about his past experiences prior to our game with Willow Brook High School in Wilmington County:

> We had just finished our morning shoot-around and began to eat donuts and juice. Coach Benson called the team over to the bleachers and began talking generally about success and winning. He then said, "You see, gentlemen, when you win, all kind of things come your way. Everyone wants to be involved with a winner. See, some of these girls y'all chasing right now will come running to you when you win and keep winning." The players laughed as Benson continued, "That ain't the only thing. I remember when I was in college our basketball team was doing well. People would want to take you out to dinner and treat you. We used to go to the parties and get in free because we had established a reputation as winners. We'd be coming in the party and all the ladies would look at you and try to figure out how they can get to know you. So, gentlemen, winning will get you things and take you places you haven't even thought about."

Following the team's victory against Willow Brook, postgame events allowed Coach Benson to further convey his sentiment about winning with an added humorous twist:

> After we won the game we stopped at McDonalds in Wilmington County. While we were eating, three teenaged girls (all white) came in the restaurant. The girls were heavy and busty. They walked back to the restrooms. As soon as the players saw the young ladies enter they called out to one of the players on the team, "Hey Capleton. It's some girls in here you like." Even though Capleton is tall and slim, he likes "heavy girls." Anyway, Capleton walked to the back of the restaurant and started talking to them in his way. The rest of the team was looking from afar and making wisecracks like, "Capleton. Get 'em Capleton." The girls walked out of the back of the restaurant, and Capleton followed them. Everyone was laughing and joking because he was flirting with the girls pretty hard. Coach Benson even said, "Ain't a fat girl safe in this country with Capleton around."
> While we loaded up the bus, Capleton was still out in the parking lot talking to the girls. We finally got him on the bus, and the driver pulled out

of the driveway. The girls pulled in behind the bus and flashed their head-lights. The bus driver pulled out, and the girls followed us through the first turn. When we got on the expressway for our fifty-minute drive back to Northeast the girls continued following us. Coach Benson joked, "If they follow us all the way to Northeast we goin' have to call the police 'cause them girls are crazy."

The girls followed the bus for about twenty-five minutes, and the guys kept shouting, "They're following us!" Suddenly the girls pulled their car alongside the bus and turned on the interior light in their car. All three of them were in their bras. The players got extra loud and started shouting and pointing out the window. The girls got back behind the bus again. A few minutes later they pulled back alongside the bus and put the interior light on. This time the girls had taken off their bras and were showing their naked breast. The guys really started hooting up then. Finally, the girls got behind us again, flashed their lights, and then turned off at an exit. As the guys were laughing Coach Benson asked the bus driver to turn on the interior light so that he could make an announcement. When the driver turned on the light Coach Benson shouted, "Hey, hey. Listen." The players quieted down as Coach Benson said, "Now see, that's the kind of stuff that comes with winning." Everyone on the bus laughed.

Benson also conveys his sentiment for winning by occasionally paraphrasing the words of famous sports figures such as legendary football coach Vince Lombardi: "Like Vince Lombardi used to say, winning is not the most important thing, it's the only thing." Although Coach Benson's emphasis on winning may contradict his other explicitly stated goals of serving young men through athletics, winning remains the priority, as evident in some of his talk: "I don't care if it's five people out there on the floor in wheelchairs, you play to win," "If it's old folks from the nursing home and they step between these lines, then they're going to get their ass beat," and "You gotta do what it takes to win."

Benson's "You gotta do what it takes to win" attitude is not lost on the players, who put forth every effort to aggressively compete. The result is that players occasionally violate implicit and explicit standards of sportsmanship by "throwing an elbow," "talking trash," or giving their opponents a gratuitous "push" under the basket. Benson's leadership style helps create a moral atmosphere where players compromise levels of sportsmanship for victory. As D. Shields and his colleagues, writing in a special issue on sportsmanship, observed, the "moral atmosphere plays a significant role in mediating moral action in sport, and peers and the coach all play a prominent role in shaping the teams' collective norms" regarding fair play.[10] Although Benson's attitude contributes to his players' sportsmanship transgressions, his responses to his players' behaviors are at times contradictory. For instance, one moment he might tell a player to knock an opponent "the fuck over if he is in your way." The next moment he might admonish the same player for aggressive unsportsmanlike conduct that he himself previously encouraged. Such mixed messages mean that players are confronted with the sticky situation of choosing the appropriate behavior within the context of the game.

The Game

According to sport sociologist Stanley Eitzen, "Sport is not a pristine activity in a utopia but rather one that occurs in a society where only the fittest survive."[11] This suggests that the broader social context in which sports are played influences individuals' orientations toward sport. In the United States, the competitive atmosphere of everyday life has had a trickle-down effect on high school athletics. No longer are high school sports viewed solely as a means of providing extracurricular activities for students, but rather they are considered, among other things, as a means of generating income for the school, building school spirit, and producing competitive athletes for the college and professional ranks. These additional functions give added social pressure on high school athletics to be not just competitive but successful.

Beyond the added social pressure, high school sports like basketball are competitive in and of themselves. In basketball there are five players from each team working to score as many baskets as possible while preventing the opposing team from scoring. Basketball coaches and players both use terms like the "battle on the boards," "attacking the defense," or "pressuring the offense" to convey the combative nature of the sport. It is in the flow of competition, or "the heat of battle," that questions of sportsmanship arise. Players on the Northeast Knights, like many other high school athletes, are challenged to maintain the ideal of appropriate sportsmanlike decorum as they compete.

Game tension, however, can erode this ideal. For instance, one added tension for the Northeast Knights is playing games in Wilmington County, where racial tension becomes the backdrop for competing. The following excerpt from my fieldnotes narrates Northeast's game against Missionary High School in Wilmington County. The scene demonstrates how both the players' and coaches' attitudes and behavior about sportsmanship are affected by the context of playing in Wilmington County.

The game started well for us. We went up 14–9. Missionary's strategy was to match our platoon of players with a platoon of their own. Each time we substituted all five players off the floor they did the same. But instead of playing twenty guys last night, Benson decided that he would play a low-possessions game. He brought back most of the starters for the second quarter, and we held the ball in our triangle offense and scored. Then we ran a spread offense for two minutes, and the referee decided to call a traveling violation on Capleton. (This was a good call in my judgment. It was one of a few made by the officiating crew—composed of one African American and two white officials. I normally don't complain about officiating, but it seemed that the officials tried to do us in for real.)

On the last play of the half, Larique, one of our players, was shooting a jumpshot with five seconds left but was blatantly fouled. The defender grabbed his arm and pulled him to the ground so that he couldn't get the shot off, but the officials made no call. The ball was loose on the floor, and Sweet Pea, another one of our players, picked it up and hit the jump shot to end the half. We were up six points.

After Benson talked to the players for about two minutes at halftime we came back out to warm up. When we came out, there were no balls available for warmup. I finally got the assistant coach (who was white) to give us some balls. As he gave them to me to give to our players he said, "Just make sure your boys return our balls to the rack."

"They did the last time," I said.

"They had about eight balls and didn't return them," he said.

"No, they didn't have eight balls. They had four, and I'm the one that got them the first time. Is there a problem?" I asked.

The assistant coach rolled his eyes as he pulled the ball rack to the side. I asked, "Is that how you treat your guests?" He rolled his eyes again, and I walked away with the balls. At the end of the half I made sure that each of our guys that had balls went and returned the balls to him. (He seemed to be insinuating that our players would steal balls from the Missionary gymnasium. This disturbed me.)

After the half we came out ready to play. The officials, however, made a number of questionable calls against our players. You could see our players becoming more frustrated by the biased officiating. But how could you blame the players? (Self-control is subjective. I too was becoming frustrated. I wanted to verbally assault the referees on several occasions. I had to work hard to maintain my cool.) The African American official called a foul on Lewis, one of our players, and Capleton mumbled disagreement to himself. At that time one of the white officials overheard Capleton and gave him a technical foul for unsportsmanlike conduct.

Within that same play, Reginald, another one of our players, came and told me that the other white referee told him, "You better simmer down, Boy." (His use of the term "Boy" conjured up the racial prejudice of the "Old South.")[12] Missionary was given free throws and the ball back. Two minutes later the referees called a traveling violation on Larique. Larique was visibly frustrated. He walked over to the referee and handed him the ball. (Coach Benson, as part of his emphasis on sportsmanship, always instructs the players to just walk over and give the officials the basketball once a call has been made.) His motion was innocent at first and then right at the end of giving the official the ball he gave an ever-so-slight extra nudge to the ball. The official gave him a technical foul for unsportsmanlike conduct. Larique asked, "What did I do?" While the official went to the scorer's table to give the technical foul Benson went over and talked to the official. At that time, I pulled Larique and the rest of the players to the side and told them to get their heads back in the game. I added to Larique, "You did push the ball at the ref, and if I had been you I probably would have slung the thing into his face." The players laughed. This seemed to relax the team. The third quarter ended, and the game was tied at forty.

In the fourth quarter the game was a seesaw battle until we started running our spread offense (a long series of deliberate passing and cutting). We scored a few baskets and went up. The entire time we ran our spread offense the Missionary fans kept shouting, "Play fuckin' ball!" They booed us for holding the ball. In fact, when they started shouting obscenities I saw a couple with a young child get up and leave the game. With eight seconds left, we had a three-point lead, and Missionary got the ball and pushed it up the court and tried to hit a three-point basket. After the shot was missed Capleton slapped the ball out. Missionary called a timeout with 3.4 seconds left on the clock. The officials adjusted the time to five seconds. This was another highly frustrating occurrence. Missionary inbounded the ball but couldn't score. We won.

After the game, we had to usher players into the locker room because the Missionary crowd was hostile. When we got in the locker room I told Coach Benson, "I was so upset with the way the officials called the game, I wanted to fight one of the referees." Coach Benson said, "I'm telling you. The way they called the game will make you lose your religion out here." We huddled up in the locker room, and I said to the team, "That's the way you go into a hostile environment and kick some tail." We then chanted, "Knights." After we finished, T.J. said, "Coach May, tail? Tail? We fuckin' kicked some ass." I just smiled at him as the rest of the players laughed.

As we were leaving the locker room, there were still some of Missionary's fans in the gym hanging around, and they kept talking trash to our players. Coach Benson came out of the locker room and told the players, "Go to the bus, 'cause tonight is my night to smack the shit outta somebody. Y'all do it another night 'cause I'm smacking the shit outta somebody tonight if they wanna talk." Coach Benson kept telling our team to get on the bus. We got all the boys on the bus. Of course when they got on the bus they pulled down the windows and yelled stuff at the fans like, "You a faggot. I'll beat your punk ass." I pushed the windows up from the outside. At the same time Coach Benson was at the front of the bus yelling to the opposing fans, "Where are all the JV players? Hey JV players, y'all come up to the McDonald's up the road. I'm buying all of y'all a fuckin' happy meal. They got a JV special. It's a fuckin' happy meal." He got on the bus, and we went on to McDonalds.

The context of playing Missionary in their own gymnasium was layered with many factors that affected the conduct of the players and coaches alike. First, from past experience the players and coaches knew that it would be difficult to play schools like Missionary in Wilmington County. Historically, officials of the games in Wilmington County had given unfair treatment to the Northeast Knights because of the racial prejudice held by officials, fans, and teams from this mostly white region. Players readily recalled being called "nigger" and "boy" at Wilmington County games. At one Wilmington County school, the Knights had even been instructed to dress in a janitorial closet underneath the bleachers even though there was a locker room available. Thus, players and coaches had a higher level of awareness for inaccurate officiating and were poised to interpret such bad calls as racially biased.[13]

Second, Benson's own behavior was inconsistent with the emphasis he places on sportsmanship. He derided the other team and its players, and his behavior provided another challenge to notions of sportsmanship for the players. Finally, the fans' hostility created a perceived threat to the players. The players responded to this threat using the repertoire of defensive strategies that they have developed in the context of their own community environment—an environment that poses challenges to everyday survival. This community context helps the players frame their behavior in sports.

Fighting to Survive

The majority of players on the Northeast basketball team are from housing developments that surround Northeast High School. In their community the young men learn that those who are willing to defend themselves physically are the ones who survive. According to one player, "You gotta be willing to fight to survive. If somebody attacks you, then you gotta get them back." This attitude is consistent with the way in which men of many cultures have addressed their need to survive. But the frequency with which the young men from Northeast confront aggressive behavior is what gives the community considerable influence on players' behavior. The players' retaliatory behavior that disregards standards of sportsmanship may manifest itself on the court or in a related manner off the court.

> We were playing our intracity rival, Ford Heights. We were up by four points with forty-four seconds left in the game. Capleton jumped high for the defensive rebound. After he pulled the rebound down he saw Larique running down the court, so he threw him the ball. Larique ran down the court, caught the ball, and got up as high as he could to shoot the lay-up. At the same time Larique was shooting the lay-up, one of the opposing players ran down the court full speed and jumped right into Larique when he was at the highest point of his jump. Larique hit his head against the backboard, his feet hit the mat under the basket, and then his head hit the ground. Our entire bench jumped up to take the floor. I jumped up because the foul was essentially a "take-out foul" (a foul intended to injure a player). I moved a few

steps from the bench and turned around and told all of our players to sit down. It was tripped out because guys that don't ever want to do much fighting or anything were pretty upset. The game was held up fifteen minutes while Larique lay on the ground. During this time, Troy, one of our hotheads (a player eager to fight), just kept getting upset and moving around and staring at the other team's bench because he wanted to go after the guy that knocked Larique down. I had to grab him by his jersey and tell him to sit down. I then pulled him and Lance, another aggressive player, to the side and said, "Y'all can't lose control now. Y'all know who these guys are. If it is that serious you will have the opportunity in a more conducive setting to take care of them." (All of this to mean, if you want to get them, you have to get them at another moment. I was banking on the fact that once that emotion died down then the urge to do something violent would also die). I asked Lance to try and keep Troy under control.

While Benson was tending to Larique I kept talking to the players. Coach Benson returned to the bench and started talking about what we had to do to finish off the game. Troy was still a little out of control, and finally his former football coach came down out of the stands and took him into our locker room.

The paramedics arrived, and they stabilized Larique's neck and transported him to the hospital. . . . Also, during the time Larique was down I pulled Coach Benson to the side and said, "I think we better not even go shake hands today. We better just let the coaches shake hands, and we should send the team to the locker room." Coach Benson said, "Okay, let's do that." As Larique was removed the fans clapped. The game resumed. . . . We eventually won the game. Coach Benson said after the game, "Damn. We always gotta pay such a high price for a win."

Game over, night over? No. Benson and I went to the hospital to check on Larique and his family after the game. When we arrived at the hospital there were about thirty friends and family waiting to see Larique. As coaches, we got to go back first. When we saw him he was shuttering and shaking. His mother kept trying to comfort him, and he kept saying, "Momma, my head hurts so bad. Make it stop, Momma." Tears started rising up in his eyes. I asked him had they tried to give him anything. He said no. They had given him a CAT scan to check for internal damage. He had a big fat hickie on his head but remained conscious. I went back out into the lobby and sat down. Coach Benson came out a little later and said, "I can't hardly stand to see him like that." I sat talking to another player's father, and then Coach Benson went back into Larique's room.

While I sat in the lobby, David, the young man from the Ford Heights team who had fouled Larique, arrived at the hospital. Of course our two hotheads, Lance and Troy, were also present. One of the ladies who was waiting to see Larique turned to me and asked, "Are you one of the Northeast Coaches?"

"Yeah," I said.

"Well you better go and get your players 'cause they out here trying to get after that boy who knocked Larique down," she said. Right after she said this someone else told me that Mr. Hunt, our statistician, had sent David home. Luckily for all the young men, Mr. Hunt, who has worked with a lot of the kids from all over Northeast, saw David first and told him it would just be better if he went home. So he left. . . . Larique ultimately overcame his concussion to play three games later and help Northeast secure a position in the state tournament.

The Northeast players' desire to retaliate is partly conditioned by their community's normative expectation that one retaliate when attacked. Although the players never attacked the player from Ford Heights, they stood ready to transcend normative standards of sportsmanship should the need arise to defend themselves.

Players' Perceptions and Situational Sportsmanship

As suggested previously, sportsmanship is characterized by notions of civility and is "a matter of being good (character) and doing right (action) in sports."[14] Based on this characterization, the athletes who compete for the Northeast Knights evaluate sportsmanship as good or bad contingent on the shifting contexts of the game. The young men view some aggressive physical play—often a measure of sportsmanship—as appropriate or justified on the basis of preceding events that have occurred in the game. In most cases, the players see intense physical response as justified retaliation for a prior act of aggression by an opponent. At some level, behavior that might otherwise be considered unsportsmanlike is permissible, even desirable. Coach Benson, as head coach of the Knights, has the primary responsibility for imparting standards of good sportsmanship to the young men. The players' interview responses regarding Coach Benson's teachings on good sportsmanship are at best marked by ambivalence.

For the Northeast Knights, like other high school basketball teams, actual games provide the social space within which the young men enact sportsmanlike behavior. This space and the behavior within it, however, are controlled by a number of elements, including referees. For instance, Joco recognizes that certain behavior, as interpreted by referees, might be costly to the team. He therefore restricts his own behavior based on what he believes the referees will allow. Still, he understands that, irrespective of the referees, he must respond to an opposing player's act of aggression with his own aggression.

May: When you lost your cool, how come you didn't demonstrate it?

Joco: For one thing, the referees are a little picky. You know, they like picking on us anyway, so I let it ride. Wasn't too much I could do about it. It was over and done with. You can't force the issue. You force the issue, then it would cost you the game.

May: Did you think that anybody ever did anything to you when you were playing, like from the opposing team, that would upset you?

Joco: Oh, all the time. Tug on your shorts, step on your feet, hold you, grab you. Talk to you and everything. [He laughs.]

May: You ever do anything to get them back, or did you ever say anything?

Joco: Yeah.

May: Yeah? Like what?

Joco: I might hold him, step on his feet so he can't go nowhere, shoot him a bow [swing an elbow to the player's body].

May: Now, do you think that was good sportsmanship?

Joco: Naw. But it's all in the game. I mean, everybody does it. There's nobody out there that doesn't. It's like intimidation, you know what I'm saying?

May: You think Coach Benson tried to teach you good sportsmanship?

Joco: Yeah.

May: Okay. Was there any time he didn't try to teach you good sportsmanship?

Joco: Naw. It was like, if you out on the court, you gotta stand up for yourself, you know?

May: Yeah. Can you think of an example of when he tried to teach you good sportsmanship—what would he say or do?

Joco: Like for instance, if you going for a loose ball, and y'all both hit,

collide or whatever, you going be a little angry, and you be like,
"Man, what are you doing? Chill out." You know, help your teammate up, give him a handshake, pat him or whatever, good job,
good play or whatever, keep going.

May: Any time you thought he tried to do anything that wasn't—say
or instruct you to do anything that wasn't good sportsmanship?

Joco: Naw, nothing I can think of. Naw.

Joco concedes that certain behavior is considered bad sportsmanship
but believes that bad sportsmanship is part of the game. It is part of
the intimidation that one uses to command a mental edge over one's
opponent. Furthermore, behaviors like "shooting a bow" or "tugging
jerseys" are part of "standing up for yourself," such that one player's
aggressive act against another player begets retaliation. Although Joco
suggests that certain behavior is unsportsmanlike, he feels that Benson
teaches young men good sportsmanship.

Contributing to whether players believe certain behavior is good
or bad sportsmanship is the extent to which they experience a shift
in their own personality when they step on the court. For most of
the players, their on-the-court demeanor is much more aggressive
than their off-the-court demeanor. This aggressive personality may be
intensified based on the opponents' responses to the player. For instance, starting players, like Harry, are most often the target of aggressive play by other teams.

May: Do you think you conduct yourself on the court the same way
you do off?

Harry: Naw.

May: Tell me what's different about it?

Harry: 'Cause on the court I'm playing to win. Off, I just be shy and
don't talk to people.

May: You don't talk a lot when you're on the court either?

Harry: It depends. Like if the team we playing against start running
they mouth, I'll get started.

May: You ever been grabbed before, poked, or elbowed?

Harry: Have I? [He says this like he is asking me rhetorically, "Are
you serious?"] Uh hum.

May: You ever do anything back?

Harry: Yeah.

May: Yeah. You think that's bad sportsmanship?

Harry: No.

May: You think Coach Benson teaches sportsmanship?

Harry: Yeah.

May: How so? Give me an example?

Harry: Say, if I knock a player down, then he say I should pick them up and ask him is he alright.

May: Do you think he teaches you anything that's not sportsmanship?

Harry: Yep. [We both laugh.]

May: Like what?

Harry: Just like when he said, "Somebody hit you, hit them back. Get them at a good time. Don't get them in the open."

Although Joco and Harry both believe that a retaliatory act of aggression toward one's opponent is part of the game, Harry does not see his conduct as bad sportsmanship. Still, both Harry and Joco are willing to participate in these acts of aggression to the extent that it will help them win. Within the context of winning, this behavior is most acceptable. Since Coach Benson trained both Harry and Joco as to what constitutes good sportsmanship, it is interesting that Harry believes that Coach Benson's directives concerning sportsmanship are both good and bad, whereas Joco acknowledges learning that throwing elbows is part of the game but sees it as bad sportsmanship. In reality, it does not matter that Joco views rough behavior as part of the game and Harry views it as bad sportsmanship. The central point is that both have an understanding that, good or bad, rough play is part of the game.

The ambiguity of Coach Benson's instructions about sportsmanship is easily gleaned from the comments made by Danny. In fact, Danny points out that Coach Benson's comments are not made with the intent for players to actually act on them but rather to feel supported by them.

May: Do you think that Coach Benson taught good sportsmanship, or what did you think about that?

Danny: Good sportsmanship?

May: Yeah.

Danny: Sometimes. Other times he'd tell you to slap somebody in the face.

May: [I laugh.] So it was kinda mixed?

Danny: Yeah.

May: Can you think of an example when he told you something that was good sportsmanship—to do something that was good sportsmanship?

Danny: Oh, like when the referee make a bad call. He said just give them the ball and go back down court and don't say nothing to them.

May: What about when he'd tell you to do something that didn't seem like good sportsmanship?

Danny: It was funny, but I didn't really think about doing it. [Pause] 'Cause I'm not that type person that just goin' hit nobody anyway.

Deciding what qualifies as good or bad sportsmanship is difficult when the coach's own standards constantly change. Here, Danny seems unconcerned with Coach Benson's admonishments and even views Coach Benson's statements of action as funny rather than as something that he should respond to in actuality.

As Danny points out, Coach Benson's directives are frequently viewed as a source of comic relief, although few players ever laugh directly at Coach Benson's order to "knock the shit out of him." For instance, James describes his perception of Coach Benson's commentary regarding sportsmanlike behavior:

> *May*: Did he teach you anything that was bad sportsmanship?
>
> *James*: A little. But as far as, like, talking a little, it's like one play you might get, like—he might—you might get bowed in your chest, and Benson would probably say something like, "Next time you come back down you bow him right in the mouth." I think he really did that just as a joke.
>
> *May*: As a joke?
>
> *James*: Yeah.

James perceives Benson's statements as a joke, but I would suggest that these statements are Benson's way of demonstrating empathy with the young man who has just suffered a certain level of physical aggression. Benson's "Next time you come back down you bow him" is his way of acknowledging that he has witnessed the opposing player's unfair act. Ironically, Coach Benson's statements to the players seem to reduce the probability that the Northeast player will retaliate. In fact, for the short period of time that Coach Benson has the player's attention, the player is afforded a brief moment to cool down and refocus on the game at hand rather than finding a way to retaliate against the culprit. In short, Benson's remarks help to defuse the possibility of heightening the aggression on the court.

Benson seems more concerned with conveying an overall aggressive attitude that he expects the young men to adopt. This aggressive attitude is consistent with the overall notions of masculinity that they construct through interaction with one another. Essentially, the sport of basketball requires players to exhibit a certain level of aggressiveness in order to be successful. Where there is physical contact involved, there is the potential for heightened conflict. Thus, there is a thin line between Coach Benson's desire to have the players play at the maximum level of aggressiveness allowed for any one game and the expectation that players act according to standards of sportsmanship taken to be understood by those who compete in basketball games. This thin line means that players must reconcile their behavior with the expectations of the referees and coaches.

By its nature, officiating is always subjective, and the players must make adjustments to the level of verbal and physical aggression that seems permissible. If one of the players crosses the line in the eyes of the referee, it can hurt the team's chances of winning, possibly even cost the team the game. Still, players know that they sometimes have to push the boundaries of sportsmanship if they are to be successful.

Calvin is a case in point. Calvin consistently suffered injuries at the hands of opposing teams. He had injuries to his ankles, thumb, and head. At various times throughout his career, Calvin missed several consecutive games due to injury and played many games with lingering injuries. Calvin clearly understood the consequences of competitive physical play. This outlook allowed him to endure physical punishment without losing focus during games.

> *May*: How do you have a positive attitude when so much other stuff is going on? With people poking you [he laughs] and elbowing you and . . .

Calvin: I just let whatever happen happen, you know, and try to work through it. You know what I'm saying? Like, say somebody shoot a bow in the game, I might try to do it back to them, but later in the game . . .

May: You think Coach Benson taught you good sportsmanship?

Calvin: Well, yeah. Yeah, I would say that.

May: Tell me what's a good example of how he taught you good sportsmanship?

Calvin: You know, he like said, "This game is not for suckers," or whatever. [I laugh.] You know what I mean? I mean, you out there to play hard, and they out there to play hard. You trying to win just like they trying to win, so you gotta do whatever it take to win.

May: Right. Is that good sportsmanship though?

Calvin: Yep. I mean, say he [the opponent] go up, you might knock him out the air, and he'll [Coach Benson] tell you to pick him up and ask him if he alright. You know what I'm saying?

May: Oh, okay. But you can still knock them out the air, but just pick him up?

Calvin: [He laughs.] You can, if you going for the ball. [I laugh.] You know what I'm saying? If you going to foul somebody, you got to foul them hard.

May: Yeah. Over your career now, you have taken a few injuries, but did you think those times that you got hurt were times when people were really trying to do something to you?

Calvin: Well.

May: Like, when we played North Farmington? [Calvin sustained a head injury that had him removed from the game. He ultimately missed four games.]

Calvin: Yeah.

May: The time you got hurt, did you think . . .

Calvin: I thought so for a minute. But then, like days later, I was like, ssshhh, they was trying to win the game like we was trying to win the game.

May: What about against Ford Heights? [Calvin was going for a lay-up when one of the Ford Heights players appeared out of position to take the offensive foul underneath the basket. Calvin sustained a wrist injury on this play.]

Calvin: I thought the same thing. A lot of people say he did it on purpose but . . .

May: Do you know him?

Calvin: Yeah, I know Bryan.

May: Yeah.

Calvin: Me and him played on an AAU team [a summer club team]
one time one year.

May: Oh, with Stevens [another Ford Heights player]?

Calvin: Yeah.

Calvin's positive attitude to such physical play that could easily be
construed as bad sportsmanship is noteworthy. Calvin attributes the
opposing players' motives as strictly an attempt to win the game and
not necessarily as bad sportsmanship. As Calvin points out, "you trying to win just like they trying to win." As long as the injuries from
intense physical competition come within this context, then Calvin
finds the behavior acceptable. Of course, a desire to win and unsportsmanlike play are not mutually exclusive; but this is Calvin's rationalization.

Perspective is important here. As Calvin points out, when an injury occurs as the result of rough play during the game, his immediate
response is to interpret the aggressive act as the opposing player's intention to harm him. Yet, upon further reflection, typically after the
game, Calvin comes to the conclusion that the opponent is merely
competing aggressively in order to win. This further supports the
coaches' admonitions not to act out in the heat of the moment but to
wait for another time to act. Clearly, Coach Benson is pivotal in assuaging the intensity with which players might respond when they are victims of aggressive play. The coaches can provide a calming voice to
players who might otherwise become carried away in the intensity of
the game. Ironically, these same coaches can drive players to become
more aggressive and might encourage them to intentionally act to
harm another player. Yet most players understand the context within
which the coach gives these directives and therefore are less likely to
take them as serious admonitions to harm an opposing player.

Since many of the players recognize aggressive play that borders
on unsportsmanlike behavior as part of the game, the young men typically are able to control their emotions without assistance from their

coaches. In fact, very few physical altercations result from aggressive play or talk during games. Several considerations deter players from initiating on-the-court fights. These include referees, the penalty of being ejected from a game for fighting, and possible punishment from school administration. These considerations are frequently interdependent, but they may be brought to bear separately. The referee's failure to punish a player for aggressive play does not negate the possibility that the school will administer separate and distinct punishment for the player. For instance, the referees may not penalize a player who ends up in a skirmish during the game, but school officials might later institute their own punishment. This happened in the case of Smitty J, who was not ejected during a skirmish with another player from Ford Heights. However, Dr. Morris, Northeast High School's principal, later suspended Smitty J for one game.

Indeed, I only witnessed one physical altercation involving our players during the time that I coached at Northeast High School. This incident occurred during a summer tournament. Oddly enough, it involved Calvin, the player who most frequently endured rough physical play and trash talk.

> *May*: Alright, the last thing was when we were in the Run and Shoot [a summer league] that year. Tell me what you remember about that, 'cause I don't remember the same thing.
> *Calvin*: Which one? When we had got to fighting that year?
> *May*: Yeah.
> *Calvin*: Oh, ssshhh. It all started because of Lavelier. They was at the free-throw line, and I'm sitting there, and Lavelier talking trash to the dude [the opposing team's player], and I start laughing. He [Lavelier] was like, "Ain't that right, C?" And I start laughing, you know what I'm saying? So I guess I'm the smallest one, he [the opposing player] going to pick me out the crowd. [Lavelier is 6'2" and Calvin is 5'11".] So one time I went down and got fouled. I was at the free-throw line, and I felt somebody come past my ear. So I turned around and threw the ball at him, and I rushed him, then I seen everybody come off the bench . . .
> *May*: I had my daughter with me. She and I were on the floor, and I was like, "Y'all break it up, break it up, break it up."[15]
> *Calvin*: [He laughs.] All I know I seen was Big Terry and Philip was

over there stumping on somebody's head. [He laughs.] That was
the year right there.

Team fights are perhaps the most severe example of unsportsmanlike
conduct. Such fights indicate a loss of control on a grander scale than
just one or two players. Calvin's description of the physical altercation
stands as another example of the importance of context. Calvin took
the opposing player's graze across his face as a violation of sportsmanship. As onlookers, we perceived Calvin's response as an appropriate retaliation.

Calvin's retelling of the events is like that of many of his teammates who retell stories in which they acted in response to some unsportsmanlike behavior that they believed warranted a reaction. The
players' behaviors in these recollections are consistent with those of
professional players like Ron Artest of the NBA's Indiana Pacers and
Rasheed Wallace of the Detroit Pistons, who have been shown on television throwing punches, choking opponents, or performing other
acts considered unsportsmanlike. In an incident that brought much
negative attention to the NBA, Ron Artest ran into the stands and
punched a fan that he believed tossed a soft drink at him. Although
these behaviors might seem unjustified, it is difficult for an outside
observer to gauge such acts when players are responding to acts by
others.

Conclusion

Some people might suggest that the newfound emphasis on winning
in youth sport has been responsible for the deterioration of sportsmanship among teams like the Knights. But in viewing the historically
competitive attitudes of Americans, it is clear that winning has been a
longstanding tradition. In fact, the competitive ideal of winning at all
costs has been the basis on which capitalist countries like the United
States have been built. It is no surprise, then, that our sport, including
youth sport, would manifest the contradictions between fair play and
all-out victory.

Perhaps what has most contributed to the contradictions between
sportsmanship and winning has been the greater emphasis on the material rewards that we give to the victor. Winners are given status and

wealth, while losers are little recognized. Still, we push for an ideal of sportsmanship and fair play in competition even though much contradicts this ideal. How can we suggest to youth that they compete fairly and with a decorum of sportsmanship when there are countless examples of misconduct throughout all realms of everyday life? High-profile incidents of competitive misconduct in school, business, and sport reaffirm to youth the importance of "doing whatever it takes to win."

Like the players' perceptions of sportsmanship, their views of opportunity for social mobility are nestled within contexts of everyday lives. Within their communities, athletics is emphasized as a way to surmount the difficult odds with which the young men are faced against achieving a better life. The frequent presentation of black professional athletes' "rags-to-riches" stories on television introduces and reflects the ideology of the American Dream. This ideology suggests that those individuals who work hard and effectively compete within their chosen fields of endeavor are those individuals who become successful. Given the multitude of former athletes and the appreciation for athletic success within their communities, it becomes easy to understand how the young men choose sports as a means of mobility. These players live in communities in which former athletes—albeit perceived as failures within the broader context of athletic success— have indispensable expertise to share with aspiring young athletes. This guidance reaffirms the desirability of hoop dreams for young men like the Northeast Knights.

7

The Dirty Trick

It was difficult for me to think about my own culpability in encouraging black males to pursue an elusive hoop dream.

It was nearing the end of my fifth season coaching the Northeast
Knights, and Shamar was pissed. We had played sixteen games, and
with each game his playing time had dwindled away. He was frustrated because he had hoped before the season started that he would
be a major contributor to our team during the season. He had even
talked casually about the possibility of playing college basketball the
following year. Shamar had impressed all the coaches throughout his
career because he was a natural leader, a hard worker, and a competitor, and he showed tenacity unparalleled by most of his teammates.
Still, during his senior season we were reminded with each game that
it didn't matter how much character Shamar demonstrated, his size, at
5'4", and his low weight made him too small to be consistently effective against guards several inches taller, bigger, and stronger. For this
reason Shamar spent most of his senior season watching younger
players on the Knights play in front of him.

Despite being frustrated, Shamar began each game with the hope
that he would get more playing time and an opportunity to contribute
to the team's play. He was upbeat before each game, and this was important, because although Shamar didn't play much, his teammates
listened to him and were inspired by him.

Since we were entering a key regular-season region game against
Daleton High School, we would need all the help we could get, especially Shamar's inspiration. If we could defeat Daleton, we would be
in first place in the region and in excellent position to make the state
playoffs. The importance of the game was reiterated to the players
when Benson, before the players even dressed, had a long talk with

the young men about playing hard for the team and stepping up and taking a leadership role.

"Always work hard gentlemen," Benson said. " 'Cause you don't know how good you can be. And if your teammate needs help, then someone has got to step up and take a leadership role. It's time for us to prove how good we can be. Now get dressed, and let's get ready to play."

As the shortest player on our team, Shamar led the team out for pregame warmup. On this night Shamar led the other players onto the floor with his usual enthusiasm; the atmosphere in the gym was electric—like a state playoff game. This was the first game that we had our pep band playing live music throughout the game. They were drumming up rhythmic beats with the precision and expertise of a big-time college pep band. But the band also had an adverse effect. Halfway through warmups Shamar complained to me that his head was hurting.

"May, those drums are loud," Shamar said.

I wasn't surprised because I could feel the tension in my own head each time the drum majors pounded the drums.

"My head is killing me," Shamar said as he covered his ears with both hands.

"Go into the hallway and get away from the band," I said. The other players continued to warm up as Shamar walked through the double doors into the hallway. I followed him.

Shamar leaned against the wall, slid to the floor, and remained squatting there with both hands holding his head.

"Are you alright?" I asked.

"No, May. My head, my head," Shamar said.

"Does it feel like a headache or something else?"

"No. It's throbbing all over."

I opened the double door and called to another player, "Go and get Mr. Thompson and Mr. Gaines." They were two volunteers that had helped the team out all season in various capacities. When they got to me I said, "Can y'all take Shamar to see the trainer? He says that his head is killing him."

It was unusual to see Shamar being helped through the gym. He was small but tough, and he had what we like to call "heart." If there was something bothering him and we could see it, then there was something really wrong with him. As he was led across the gym and into the training room in our locker room I was worried that our players might be distracted by his absence.

I went back on the court and supervised our team warmup. A few minutes later Mr. Thompson came to me and said, "Shamar had a migraine headache, and the trainer gave him some pain reliever. They had to tape cardboard over the glass door inside the training room because Shamar said the lights in the locker room were making his head hurt worse."

"Alright, thanks," I said.

As I stood contemplating what Shamar's absence could mean for how I substituted players into the game, the horn sounded. It was time for us to play.

The Devils of Daleton High School had taller but less-experienced players. They were a team made up of talented sophomores that had good basketball skills but had not yet learned to make good court decisions. Their inexperience showed early in the game when Calvin Cody, now a senior, started the game off fast with a couple of steals and quick lay-ups. Calvin led a total team defensive effort that was impressive. We didn't let the Daleton Devils get the ball across the half court much in the first quarter, and we kept the ball away from their two post players who outsized our players by four to five inches.

Still, I could sense that with each passing minute the Devils seemed to mature exponentially. By the beginning of the second quarter Daleton stopped making stupid mistakes and started getting the ball inside to their better players. Not only did they start scoring more, but they also found a way to keep Calvin Cody, our leading scorer, away from the ball. The half ended with the Devils leading by six points.

As usual Benson was upset with our mistakes, but he had his attention diverted as we passed the training room where Shamar was lying.

"May, go in there and check on Shamar for me," Benson said.

"Alright," I said.

The other players continued into the locker room, and I could hear Benson fussing at them as I walked into the training room to check on Shamar.

Shamar was now awake, but his eyes were still sensitive to the light as he sat up.

"May, what made me fall asleep?" he asked.

"Your headache and that pain killer the trainer gave you," I replied.

"How are we doing?"

"We're down six points."

As the players scurried past the training room to go back on the court I helped Shamar stand to his feet. He was still groggy, and he squinted from the bright light emanating from the locker room. He got his bearings after gaining control of his wobbly legs and stood on his small feet. He hardly seemed like the courageous, full-spirited person that I had coached for three years now. I held Shamar under his arm and walked him out the double doors back into the gym. We made it to the bench, and I sat him next to Benson as the other players warmed up for the second half.

"You okay, Shamar?" Benson asked.

"Yeah," Shamar said.

"Well, just sit right there. Take your time. You'll be alright."

I had no intention of using Shamar in the game. I was just glad that he was back on the bench because his presence would provide encouragement to his teammates.

The horn sounded.

In the first few minutes of the third quarter, we looked like a different team. Calvin Cody scored baskets in our well-executed offense, and we played defense with tenacity. But even with all our great team play in the third quarter we couldn't shake the upstart Daleton Devils. At the end of the third quarter, the game was tied.

From the outset of the fourth quarter we exchanged crucial baskets with Daleton, and the game was nip and tuck. Shamar was beginning to feel better as the effects of the medication wore off—he started to cheer for his teammates and shout instructions. The game was so close that neither team could amass a lead greater than four points in the fourth quarter. We would score, and then the Devils would score. We had Calvin Cody to carry us, and they relied on a young flashy guard to help carry them.

With sixteen seconds left one of Daleton's guards took a short jumpshot in the lane, but it bounced off the goal, and Ron, a Knight about 6'2", grabbed the rebound with the time running.

15, 14, 13.

Ron handed the ball to Calvin, who was experienced enough to know that he didn't have to rush the play. He let the traffic clear and then dribbled the ball upcourt. Shamar was cheering him on, "Come on C! Come on C!"

12 . . .

I shouted, "Benson, tell Calvin to dribble the clock down to seven seconds and then call a timeout!"

11, 10 . . .

Benson, without hesitation, said to Calvin, "We're going to run the clock down to seven seconds and then call a timeout." Calvin dribbled the clock down. "Timeout," he shouted with seven seconds left. We used a thirty-second timeout.

When Calvin and the other players came over to the bench, Benson said, "We got to score here."

I was about to interrupt Benson, and then I stopped. Benson looked at me and said, "No coach. Go ahead."

I stepped into the center of the huddle and said, "Run your line into three. Take the ball out and get it to Pooty Cat, and then run it to Calvin."

Shamar, in his usual enthusiastic voiced, turned to Calvin and said, "Come on C. You got him."

"Now Pooty Cat," Benson interrupted, "if Calvin isn't open, don't try to force it to him. Just dribble to the basket."

We got the ball into Pooty Cat, but the Devils wouldn't let us get it to Calvin. Pooty Cat took an off-balance shot, and the horn sounded. He missed the shot. Overtime!

In the overtime, there was more close-game drama that ended in a tie, and before we knew it we had to play a second overtime. By this second overtime Shamar was intently watching the game and cheering his teammates. No one could tell that he had suffered from a migraine headache earlier.

The Devils won the jump ball, and the second overtime started the way the first one had. We exchanged several baskets with the Devils, and the game remained close the entire first three minutes, but by the last minute of overtime, Calvin seemed to have decided that he just wanted the game to be over. On our next possession he drove to the basket hard and shot a lay-up as he was fouled. The ball rolled around the rim and then dropped straight through the net. Calvin walked to the free-throw line and very coolly hit the free throw. We were up three. On the next possession the Devils went inside and scored to cut the lead to one point. We still had the lead, but we had a big problem.

Calvin was showing his trademark limp that appeared right before his legs cramped. On the inbound Calvin started bringing the ball up the court then suddenly stopped and shouted to the referee, "Timeout! Timeout!"

The referee signaled us for the timeout, and Calvin sat on the floor as the cramps moved up his calves to his thighs. Mr. Thompson went out to the court and started massaging Calvin's legs, and Benson and I contemplated whom we would substitute for Calvin.

We were both hesitant to send in a young player because each time we did, we lost ground. This would be an important possession for us because there were only thirty seconds left in the game. We had to go with someone with experience. I walked up to Benson and said "Benson we can go with Ricky or . . ."

"Shit, let's go with one of these younger guys," Benson interrupted. I really couldn't blame Benson for his decision because I wasn't confident that Ricky, also a senior, could get the job done. Ricky had been having a bad game. Although I had lost confidence in Ricky during the game, I did have more confidence in Shamar than a younger player.

"What about Shamar?" I said. Benson looked at me, then looked at Shamar. Shamar didn't hesitate. He stood from the bench and began to pull off his warmup jacket as Benson replied, "Alright."

When we inbounded the ball, Shamar brought the ball up and passed it through our offense. We took a quick shot and missed. The Devils ran the ball up the court and with eleven seconds left scored and took the lead by one point with seven seconds left.

Thinking quickly, Shamar shouted to Pooty Cat, "Take the ball out quick, Cat. Take it out, Cat."

Pooty Cat threw the ball to Shamar.

7, 6, . . .

Shamar dribbled the ball up the court at top speed, weaving in and out of traffic with his little quick feet. He showed no signs of relenting.

5, 4 . . .

Shamar stopped in the middle of the lane and pulled up a midrange jumpshot. I held my breath as I watched the shot hit the back of the rim.

3, 2 . . .

Time seemed to stop as B.T. sprinted after Shamar's missed shot and grabbed the rebound. He then went right back up and shot the ball off the glass.

1, 0.

The horn sounded, the ball went through the net, and the referee shouted, "Basket good." Our players charged the floor and tackled B.T. I looked for Shamar in the crowd of Knights celebrating. I was proud of him. He had stood up and shown leadership.

I found Shamar in the crowd, gave him a high-five, and said, "You can help us with your fire and desire. That's what you bring to this team. You have to remember that even when you get frustrated about playing."

"Yeah," said Shamar. He had a tear forming in his eye. "I'll re-member that."

I reached back and tapped his head then backside to acknowledge what he had done. Few people watching the game would know that Shamar had been struggling through the fact that he wasn't playing much this season as a senior. Nor would they know that he had a migraine and was knocked out for the first half of the game. But, like other "Rudyesque" or "Hoosieresque" stories in which the smaller, persistent opponent defeats the bigger and more talented opponent by sheer force of will, Shamar reminded us all of what could be done with grit and perseverance. Moments like this fueled some of the young men's sense that they could be successful in basketball beyond high school and against long odds.

Living through the Hoop and Constructing Aspirations for Hoopin'

The young men have shared with us in their own words the benefits of participating in high school basketball. They have told stories of how basketball has kept them out of street life, given them greater status within their communities, created opportunities for interracial relationships, helped them to become men, and generally improved their overall quality of life. Yet, despite these benefits, there is a by-product of their participation in high school basketball that casts a shadow on the value of this experience for the young men beyond their years at Northeast High School.

I discovered a troubling phenomenon during my exit interviews with the players. Many of them, although they had not even been re-cruited to play college basketball, believed that they had the oppor-tunity to play in college. At least eleven of the eighteen players I in-terviewed had aspirations for competitive basketball beyond high school, and some saw professional basketball as a real possibility. The sincerity with which they espoused, "I'll play in college," was trou-bling indeed. They believed they could be "walk-ons" and simply be-come members of a college basketball team.[1] I was astonished. It was difficult for me to conceive that a player like Pooty Cat, standing at 5'5", believed that he could effectively compete with taller, more athletic, and more skilled players. Furthermore, despite not being re-cruited to play, these players generally believed that if a college coach got one look at their ability, then the coach would give the players an opportunity to play college basketball. The commonplace acceptance of this notion meant that several Northeast players, beyond those whom I interviewed, asked me to help them put together highlight videotapes to send to colleges in the hope of securing a scholarship. In reality, college coaches rarely use these videotapes to evaluate poten-tial college players.

Not only did some of the players believe they could play beyond high school, but some also considered themselves capable of playing professionally. For instance, Cerico—a 6'3", 200-pound occasional starter for us—demonstrated this notion in his response to my ques-tion as to whether he was capable of playing professional basketball:

> Yeah. I got the skills. Like what all them folks [substitute players] do-ing on the bench, man? I don't understand that. They supposed to be professional players. I know I'm better than some of them.

Cerico's statement indicates the extent to which some players believe that their aspirations for professional athletics are legitimate. It also re-veals the extent to which some players might fail to consider struc-tural impediments to their aspirations. The young men dream of play-ing but don't realize the odds are heavily stacked against their pursuit.

What are those odds? As has become familiar to many people through such films as *Hoop Dreams*, high school athletics are glorified in many ways as a means for obtaining a college education on an ath-letic scholarship, yet few young men with such aspirations will make it to the college ranks.[2] According to sociologist Wilbert Leonard's analysis of high school and college participation rates for basketball, the chances of an individual advancing to the next level of competition are remote. For instance, Leonard analyzed participation data for 2001 from the National Collegiate Athletic Association and from the National Federation of State High School Associations. He found that, of the 530,068 high school players, only 13,365 went on to compete at the college level. In other words, there was .03 probability that high school players would move on to compete in college basketball. Additionally, of the 530,068 high school basketball players, only 405 players advanced to the professional level. This is a measly .001 probability.[3]

The number of professional basketball players that compete today has increased since the late 1990s, yet the probability that high school athletes will transition to the professional ranks remains very low.[4] Because the number of high school players competing has also grown significantly, it is more difficult today for high school players to transition to the professional ranks than in 2001. Despite the reduced probability of transitioning to the next level of competition, the greatest number of high school basketball players selected directly from high school in the first round of the NBA draft occurred in 2004.

In 2006, the NBA, citing the unusually high number of young men attempting the leap from high school to professional basketball, instituted an age limit of nineteen years to prevent the influx of underprepared high school players who somehow believe that they had the skills and ability to enter the NBA draft and become successful NBA players. In fact, there had been several high school players that made the leap to the professional ranks, but only a few had success. Players like Kevin Garnett, Kobe Bryant, and LeBron James represent those players enjoying the greatest success from going professional after high school. Yet far more prevalent than these rare success stories are the cases of players who have had less noteworthy professional careers—like Thomas Hamilton, a former high school prep star. Hamilton, at 7'2", 330 pounds, was a virtual giant in a sport that has long recognized the advantages of being tall, but he had very little success, playing just two NBA seasons. Examples of players that have made it professionally do not begin to account for the far greater number of players that have failed to make it to the professional ranks at all.

If there are so many stories of failed athletes, why do young men like Cerico and other members of the Northeast Knights accept athletics as a way up the ladder? It would seem that average players like those on the Knights would understand that those who "make it" are exceptional. Yet many of the young men with whom I worked failed to comprehend the special talents of those who continued playing basketball beyond high school. I speculate that the Knights' aspirations of hoop dreams are not unusual but, rather, widely held by a vast majority of average players, especially young black male players.[5] These aspirations for athletic success are a manifestation of what I call the "dirty trick"—the often-affirmed notion that athletics is a viable means of social mobility. Why would these young men believe in this hoop dream? I believe there are four main reasons.

First, the media, be it television programs like *NBA's Inside Stuff* or MTV's *Cribs*, suggest to average players the viability of athletic success as a means of mobility or "coming up." Profiles of the lifestyles of professional black athletes who come from places much like those where the Knights live are highly suggestive, even inspirational, for these young men. The young men often make comments like, "I'm going play pro like Vince Carter when I finish school" or "I want to drive a Bentley like Allen Iverson," suggesting knowledge of the lives, career paths, and playing experiences of these professional athletes.[6]

Second, the communities in which the young men have grown up support success through stereotypical means for black males. For those young men who seek mobility, the perceptions of opportunity are limited by the deleterious conditions of their communities, where the allure of a lifestyle of fast money, drug sales, and criminal violence is readily glorified. Faced with these challenges, the young men look for other paths that are considered viable by others within their communities. They seek to "make it to the league" or "get a record deal." Many figures within their communities support these aspirations.

Third, the young men compete with other average players, providing them with an unrealistic measure of their skill; with only limited success they can readily overestimate their abilities. The young men are blinded to the extensive pool of quality athletes who will be competing for the few opportunities for social mobility through basketball. Although the players see former players within their own communities who have failed to achieve their hoop dreams, they, like so many other average players chasing hoop dreams, continue to rely on their own individual drive, hard work, and performance within game contexts as a means of distinguishing themselves from those who have tried to become college and professional athletes but have failed. In this regard players for the Northeast Knights have grasped onto the rhetoric of individualism consistent throughout stories of success for those individuals who have become star players.

Finally, the coaches, myself included, encourage the young men to pursue hoop dreams. The immediate benefit for coaches is that the players commit to developing their skills, working hard to develop what they believe is necessary for playing basketball at the next level. This hard work has immediate benefits to the team and their coaches. Better players produce a better team for a coach who is constantly under pressure from parents, the school, and the community to win.

Mass-Media Depictions

On a broad level, mass-media depictions of black athletes playing with their toys of consumption paint desirable pictures of success for many young black men. Although these depictions are not explicit calls for the young men to invest their time in trying to achieve the dream of playing basketball at the professional level, these are pictures of men that also hail from communities like Flat Shoals, Hillside, and Eastridge. In theory, these professional players stand as exemplars of what can be done if the young men would focus their energy and just work harder to achieve athletic success.

Interestingly, media accounts of successful professional basketball players are typically predicated on the fact that the player has struggled through some social or economic limitations. Very few black males who are professional basketball players have been identified as products of uncomplicated middle-class family backgrounds. Whether this is a true representation of those players in the NBA is a question to be pursued empirically. Perhaps a comparative analysis of individual professional players' backgrounds might reveal that the majority of professional players are from traditional two-parent, middle-class family backgrounds with few complications. Still, I would contend that the games and the players often are made more interesting to a broader audience with dramatic side stories about players' off-the-court behaviors involving sex, violence, and crime. The general viewing audience's preoccupation with such matters makes controversial athletic figures or "bad boy" athletes more entertaining than run-of-the-mill professional athletes. Thus, this small population of players becomes the face of basketball. In fact, the stars of the NBA are generally players who are represented as having come from a troubled past. These professional players are frequently those with whom many of the Northeast Knights identify.

For instance, Allen Iverson, the All-Star guard for the Denver Nuggets and league Most Valuable Player in 2001, was selected by several of the Northeast Knights as their favorite athlete. Iverson's biography includes being arrested, charged, and convicted of brutally attacking patrons in a bowling alley melee in Virginia while he was in high school.[7] The conviction was later overturned, but Iverson, since becoming a professional basketball player, has continued to have trouble follow him, with arrests on marijuana charges in 1997 and a 2002 arrest in connection with assault, weapons charges, and making terroristic threats.[8] These charges were also later dropped. For the Northeast Knights who view Iverson with esteem, it is Iverson's skills as a basketball player, his relatively small stature at six feet, and his notoriety for off-the-court incidents that make him an attractive icon. To the young men, Iverson represents a gifted athlete who has attained wealth but maintained his "street" identity. According to Shamar, this means that Iverson "ain't never backed down."

The success of players like Iverson fuels the aspirations of young men who already believe they have the bare essentials for athletic success. Although these young men recognize that physical attributes like height might limit opportunities for participation in the future, most of the young men consistently reported to me that the main things that separate those who achieve the status of a professional player and those who fail is hard work and desire. For instance, Danny's response to my inquiry about what one needed to do to become a professional player indicates the importance he places on hard work:

> Just make yourself better. Work out or practice at whatever you need
> to practice at. If you wanna do it. It all depends on if you wanna do it.

For Danny, it is up to the individual if they wish to pursue athletic competition beyond high school. Like Danny, Calvin also believes in hard work but notes the importance of the right mental attitude:

I think—I don't know how many [players are trying to play in college and go pro]—but I think it's a lot of people out there. They just
ain't got the head to keep going.

These young men give little consideration to structural factors
that might limit success but, rather, focus on what individuals can do
to achieve their athletic aspirations. Perhaps the young men's focus
on individual effort is based on the emphasis of individual accounta-
bility in our society. The young men reason that if the professional
players they see on television are able to overcome desolate social conditions to achieve athletic success, then they too might achieve success
through their own hard work. It is easy to understand why the NBA,
made up of nearly 80 percent black players, suggests to the young
men, who wake up each day to difficult situations in their own communities, the viability of pursuing social mobility through sports.

Community Influences

The kinds of communities from which many of the Northeast Knights
hail are well known. Blacks, who have been disproportionately represented among the urban poor, have been bound to places like Flat
Shoals, Hillside, and Eastridge through a mixture of social forces like
racial discrimination and residential segregation.[9] The generational
and cyclical impact of poverty on black families from densely populated, highly concentrated, and socially isolated poor, urban areas
has been documented by social scientists.[10] The nature of such communities is that few residents within them experience social mobility. Not only are the residents cut off from economic opportunity,
but because they are socially isolated from populations of people who
are part of the mainstream, they are also separated from social resources that could help them in their quest for social mobility. Thus,
for individuals living in such communities, there are very few illustra-
tions of life beyond their economically and socially depleted communities.

Coach Benson serves as one example of an individual within the
community who is socially connected to the mainstream. His legitimacy as an educator and as a community member allows him to

bridge the gap, for many of the young men, between their community environment and opportunities in the social world beyond. However, given the number of young men who Benson himself has claimed to have lost, it is clear that his impact on the negative effects of the community is only significant for a select group of young men coming from the desolate areas of Northeast. Still, Benson maintains a level of optimism for helping as many young men as possible.

As indicated previously, the media images of successful black athletes, absent alternative ideas of "making it," become paragons of accomplishment for the young men. Furthermore, the young men from Northeast are preoccupied with media representations within the local context of Northeast. For instance, when the local newspaper selects all-star teams for various sports in the area, the players take note. They also follow the newspaper's weekly feature stories that include color photographs of local high school sports figures. The media exposure of local athletes carries with it a notoriety that many of the Northeast players both overtly and covertly aspire to attain for themselves. Coach Benson acknowledges the young men's success by posting the pictures or news clippings on the walls in the entrance to the team locker room. As players enter the locker room and pass the postings one can hear players mumbling phrases like "I'm gonna get my picture up on the wall too."

In addition to the attention given the athletes by the local media, players' peers and other community members give recognition to successful local athletes. As many of the players have suggested, their ability to avoid some of the delinquent activities thrust upon others growing up in their communities is partly based on the respect they are accorded because of their participation in the Northeast Knights basketball program. Beyond the recognition of athletic success by the players' peers, adult community members view athletics with pride and therefore give local athletes additional support and encouragement. Thus, in a practical sense, the young men's participation with the Northeast Knights provides them with opportunities for mobility or, at a minimum, safe passage through the streets of places like Flat Shoals, Hillside, and Eastridge. The positive feedback given to players by the community regarding athletic pursuits helps to reaffirm to the players the viability of athletic pursuits for enjoying a successful and fulfilling life.

Self-Conceptions and Competitive Context

The community's support as motivation for players' aspirations to pursue an athletic career appears secondary to the players' own self-conceptions of their athletic ability. When they were younger, as middle school players, many of the Northeast Knights watched as older generations of varsity players performed on the court. In a sense, these older generations of Knights became role models of athletic success for the younger players. Young players internalized the work and drive of the older players and emulated it. As the young players moved on to high school, they began to understand the virtue of their own athletic ability on the court. Players and coaches alike have recognized this kind of rising confidence as necessary for success on the court at the varsity level. It is understood that in order for a player to be successful at the varsity level, he must have a positive self-conception of his own ability.[11] The importance of confidence is not lost on Coach Benson, who has aptly stated, "You get confidence from beating people's ass!" This self-conception is initially heightened through successful competition with one's peers in the freshman and sophomore years. However, players' enhanced self-conceptions are developed most through athletic competition with other schools' varsity players.

As the Northeast Knights compete against other schools and have success, individual players begin to develop more confidence. Although this heightened positive self-evaluation has instrumental use within the context of competitive athletics in high school, it can complicate young men's abilities to evaluate more objectively their preparedness to compete in broader contexts. In this sense, there are two key aspects of team competitive play that players seem to omit in their evaluation of their own ability.

First, players from Northeast, like so many other athletes in collegiate and professional sports, frequently focus on their individual contributions over those of the team. Thus, the Northeast players, in their evaluation of their own ability, may inadequately consider the extent to which their individual success is predicated on their teammates' efforts. Indeed, Coach Benson is well aware of the ways in which individuals begin to think about their own contributions over the team. He is quick to point out to the team, after an excellent individual performance by a player, "He can't get anywhere without the rest of us."

The second weakness of the players' evaluations of their individual performance is their limited understanding of the universe in which they compete. Among players from other schools in the region of Wilmington County, the players of Northeast are highly competitive. But the region in which the Knights play does not represent the elite level of basketball being played throughout various parts of the state. The elite level of high school basketball is considered to be players who compete for Amateur Athletic Union (AAU) club teams or those who are invited to High School All America camps, which are sponsored by athletic-apparel manufacturers like Nike, Adidas, and Reebok. Over the seven years that I was with Northeast, we only had three players who were of the ability to compete in AAU. Each competed on teams at the younger levels but ultimately were edged out at the higher, more competitive age groups like sixteen-year-olds and over. Thus, most of the Northeast players have little experience with elite basketball. Essentially, they examine their individual success in the Wilmington County region and then extrapolate that success across the vast numbers of high school basketball players throughout the state and country. Such a projection leads players to falsely reason that they are among the best athletes competing in basketball. For instance, Pooty Cat talks about the transformation of players from high school to college and then to professional in light of his own ability. His positive evaluation of himself and players his size is derived from his success against mediocre talent at the high school level.

> I'm gonna try to take it to the next level and play after that. . . . They [colleges] might look for a player with speed, got good defense, so you might not be tall enough to play the position you want to play. But, uh, you might play point guard. Well, you might play shooting guard, and if you go to the pros, they end up turning you to a point guard because of your height.

Pooty Cat believes that irrespective of his size, if he has other physical attributes like speed, he can make it playing basketball beyond high school. He transforms his success against his peers in the Northeast Knights' region to the possibility of playing for a college team.

In addition to the Knights' comparisons of their abilities to other players throughout the state, they also frequently compare their own playing style and moves with some of their favorite professional players. In their minds they see themselves as capable of playing like NBA stars because their moves, mimicked from star players, are effective at the level on which the high school players compete. For instance, during a Northeast Knights team tape-review session, the team watched video of one of our games as Harry, our starting guard, was about to begin an offensive move. As the film pictured Harry dribbling the ball, Harry shouts, "Watch this crossover like Iverson. Watch it, watch it. Got him. Iverson!" His teammates shouted in support of Harry's move on the film. Such comparative statements evidence players' affirmations that they are capable of making moves like the professionals. During his interview, Harry reaffirmed confidence in his ability vis-à-vis Allen Iverson:

> *May*: Now, you are looking at Iverson and you see him doing things out there on the court. Is there anything that he can do that you would like to be able to do?
> *Harry*: I can do.
> *May*: You can do?
> *Harry*: Yeah.
> *May*: Okay. Name something you do that he does.
> *Harry*: Crossover. I can jump like him, and I can shoot.

Like Harry, B.T. shares a similar evaluation of his skills in comparison to one of his favorite players, Kobe Bryant:

> I can play like him. Like, uh, on his fadeaway, he'll get that separation by giving a fake, a juke left, and then he'll fade to the right. Or he'll, uh, you know, take that hop but don't walk with it and just take one more step and just lay it up. I think I got a nice game like Kobe. They're [NBA players] just a little taller.

Although it may appear irrational for the young men to equate their own playing ability with professional players, I contend that it would be difficult to find current professional players who themselves had not imagined that they too were capable of the skills demonstrated by the professional athletes whom they watched in their youth. This initial belief that "I can play like" a particular professional player becomes part of the continued drive to play professionally.

Coaches' Influence

The job of a coach is to motivate players to give their best effort. Good coaches are experts at conjuring up the right balance between intrinsic and extrinsic motivations for players' participation. Intrinsic motivations are those motivations predicated on some internal stimulation that an athlete might receive from participating in the activity (e.g., feelings of autonomy, competence, and relatedness). Extrinsic motivations are predicated on external rewards that the athlete receives for successful participation (e.g., awards, recognition, and support).[12] As I discovered during the interviews with players, some players desired to play both college and professional basketball. These desires lead the young men to latch onto the words of encouragement from coaches. With statements like "some of y'all could play at the next level, but you gotta work harder" echoing in their ears, players give maximum effort in practice and games. Unfortunately, most of these athletes do not possess the requisite natural ability or height to be successful at the next level. Still, these average players have to be motivated by coaches in order to create the intrateam competition necessary for producing a winning team.

As an assistant coach and a sociologist with full understanding of the low probability of athletic success beyond high school, it was difficult for me to think about my own culpability in encouraging young black males to pursue an elusive hoop dream.[13] At first, I found myself remaining silent when players asked me, "Coach May, what do I have to work on to play in college?" Over time, I looked at the young men, some of whom were frail and uncoordinated, and realized that many of them were merely seeking a measure of hope for their futures. All around them was failure, and they wanted more from life than failure but did not know how to get it. I soon learned to offer the young men general encouragement like, "Work on your jump shot. You gotta be a better shooter to play at the next level." I knew that most of the players I gave this answer to could never become the kind of athlete that competed at the next level. Yet I, like the other coaches, purposely gave them hope.

The coaches' intentional misleading of the members of the Northeast Knights begs the question: If the Northeast coaches understood the limited opportunity for athletic success beyond high school for many of these young men, why did they insist on setting the players up for failure? More pointedly, why did we not encourage the young men to focus on their education? After all, the coaches were black men who had attended school and had successful careers. The answers to these questions are both simple and complex. First, from a practical standpoint, coaches had their own self-serving need for players to be dedicated to the sport and all that it encompassed. There was constant pressure on us to succeed. We had pressure from parents wanting their young men to have athletic careers beyond high school, from the Northeast community that wanted to be represented well in athletics when we played schools from other areas, and from the school administration that recognized the school pride that a winning team could generate. We understood that our ability to manipulate our players to give their best effort to win meant that we got to keep our jobs. Indeed, at the end of the day, no one cared how many lives we positively influenced when we were losing games. Winning is the American way, and people expected us to win.

Beyond our need for success, I also believe that there is another more profound reason for our complicity. Through the ups and downs of the seasons and dealing with the difficult lives of our players, we came to understand that most of the young men with whom we worked were at a critical juncture in their lives. For many of the young men, the years that they had endured poverty, troubled families, apathetic teachers, and communities filled with nihilism and pessimism were taking a toll on them. More important, it was clear to us that basketball was key to their salvation.

This point was made most clear to me when, just two weeks after basketball season, Vinny, one of our players, was suspended three times from school. During the season, I had considered Vinny an extreme discipline problem and at one point contemplated resigning my coaching responsibilities because of the continued conflict I had with Vinny. One day during the season I had given Vinny a directive, and he began to complain. I approached him, and he put his hand up and said, "You better get out my face. You better get out my face." I looked at Benson, hoping for intervention because I felt the urge to physically attack Vinny. None was forthcoming. Before I made the mistake of hitting Vinny, I turned for the gym exit and left practice early. When I met with Coach Benson the next day to explain my position he let me speak, then he said, "Coach, I understand what you are saying, but you just can't give up on the kid like that. You have to remember that we are not working with all the parts. For some of the kids we are working with, we are the only structure they have." Benson reminded me that we were there to give the young men a chance. If we gave up on them, then they would likely fail. When Vinny and I met the next day, he was apologetic, and we had no further conflicts.

Many observers might suggest that if we really wanted to give the players a chance, our primary goal as coaches should have been to focus the young men's aspirations on academic success. But, for these young men, who had been given little chance from early on in their lives, basketball was the only carrot that we could hold out. Their education had already done them a disservice. Many of the players had been passed along to each successive grade with gradually fewer basic skills for success at the next grade level. Mr. Hunt, our statistician, also worked at Northeast Middle School and knew well the challenges that elementary and middle school teachers in Northeast faced with educating the young men prior to their matriculation into high school. Limited resources, lack of parental support, and apathy were all issues teachers had to contend with as they tried to provide a basic education to the youths. At the same time, the young men, as they grew older, became less and less enthusiastic about education as a way out of their desolate communities. Thus, the possibility of moving up the socioeconomic ladder through athletics was nearly the last option for these young men. They could still believe in the possibility of success and take pride in their own hard work and dedication to basketball. Basketball was rewarding in ways that other aspects of life had not been. So we consciously perpetrated the dirty trick.

There is, however, an important irony: by immersing the young men in basketball, their aspirations for post-high-school athletic success helped them to focus on, at minimum, high school graduation. It was Coach Benson's hope that by helping the young men focus on basketball, and providing them with the necessary support and structure (e.g., mandatory two-hour-a-day study hall), they might get out of Northeast and survive the lure of the streets. Although this might mean that some young men would leave Northeast High School disillusioned about their prospects for playing basketball, they would have nevertheless graduated high school, which is no small achievement. Furthermore, in their efforts to participate in basketball beyond high school the young men might find other endeavors to undertake. Indeed, this was the case for many of the young men who graduated from Northeast High School.

In my seven years at Northeast I learned that some of the young men who had told me that they had hoped to play college and professional basketball left Northeast and tried out for college teams but were cut. In fact, of the eleven players who wished to continue playing nine tried out, but none was successful. But in going away to college, irrespective of the quality of education being provided there, the young men discovered alternatives to basketball. Several of the young men attended local community colleges with limited resources. Others had the opportunity to attend small state schools or a historically black college or university. In some instances, these institutions amounted to little more than an extension of the high school experience given the low quality of the technology and instruction being provided. Still, players began learning trades and technical skills. At the time of this writing, it is too early to know how many of the young men will escape the pull of the streets in Northeast, but I am hopeful that some will.

Some of those players who did not go away to college sought work in various local service and manufacturing industries like the local Boys and Girls Club or TCC manufacturers, a local company that produces electrical transformers. Although these young men had been misled about the promise of basketball, that deception gave them mobility and goals that they might never have imagined if they had remained mired in the deleterious conditions of their communities. Yes, some failed, but some succeeded as they modified their aspirations from having post-high-school athletic careers.

Dirty Tricks and the American Way

There is a popular critique made by those who question the viability of encouraging young black males to seek athletic success. This critique is often posed as the following: Why are so many black males attempting to become athletes? They have a greater chance of becoming a brain surgeon than becoming a professional athlete.[14] This statement is premised on the notion that there are fewer employment opportunities for professional athletes than there are for brain surgeons. This idea, on its face, might well be true from a purely statistical probability standpoint.

However, the reality is different for the young men of the Northeast Knights. If one takes into account the fact that these young men are beginning their lives cut off from the educational and financial resources necessary for becoming a successful brain surgeon, then the odds against such success grow steeper. If one also considers the probability that these young men might meet with racial discrimination that hinders the acquisition of essential skills for becoming a brain surgeon, then the odds grow steeper still.[15] Furthermore, if one considers the fact that these young men do not share social networks with individuals who have knowledge of the proper steps for becoming a brain surgeon, then the odds against their success grow even steeper. Thus, if it can be argued that players like those from Northeast only have "a chance in hell" of becoming a professional athlete, then I suggest that their structural starting point means that they only have "a chance in two hells" of becoming brain surgeons. Although this example is extreme, it is useful for demonstrating the different positions from which various individuals may start their quest for the same goal. Furthermore, it demonstrates the patent inequality in our social system.

The deceptions committed by the coaches, who have the knowledge of the unlikely odds of young men becoming professional athletes, are no different than those perpetrated by various individuals and groups within our broader social system. For instance, our American ethos, rooted in capitalism, teaches us to strive for prominence and success because the market opportunity for us to do so is open to all. We are told by individuals within various American institutions that "you can be anything you want to be." The pervasiveness of this idea can be gleaned in most any kindergarten classroom in the country. When students are asked what they wish to become there is little doubt that at least one student will echo the phrase "I want to become the president of the United States." Although this may be an unrealistic aspiration for a particular student, it is supported as a real possibility. Indeed, we are encouraged to "dream big" and "reach for the stars."

Perhaps parents are the greatest supporters of our "big dreams."

They are often in the best position to know the limits of their children's abilities, and yet they support their children's far-fetched aspirations. An excellent example is the parent who supports the child who has aspirations for musical success, despite the fact that the parent recognizes early on that the child lacks musical talent. Indeed, we consider this parent to be a good parent for supporting the child's endeavors. At some point, however, the child will encounter failure regarding his or her aspirations. What happens when this occurs?

With big dreams comes the possibility of big failures. But our system has a way of dealing with these failures. We are taught that our failure to succeed in our life goals is due to some shortcomings that we have as individuals. "You didn't do it because you weren't able to." Although this may be true to some extent, we often simply internalize our failures in a way that does not question the role of the broader social forces at work contributing to our failure. In fact, as we move through various stages of our lives and fail to achieve our goals, many of us become less critical of the structural obstacles that might block our achievement. We simply learn to modify our aspirations. We turn inward, critique ourselves, and then "lower the bar." This modification of aspirations is a testament to the stability of our social system. This system is predicated on the very real human need for hope. We must have hope for things to come in order to have the will to live. So powerful is this notion that few of us need more than one or two real examples of rags-to-riches stories to become committed to our aspirations, no matter how difficult their achievement might seem. Thus, it is in this context that run-of-the-mill players, like those who compete for the Northeast Knights, can easily aspire to become professional athletes against what seem to others to be impossible odds.

Throughout this book, I have examined the ways in which young men live their lives through basketball. I have attempted to demonstrate how the sports context in which the young men operate reflects various aspects of broader society. For instance, I have exposed the extent to which "dirty tricks" are part and parcel of a social system that effectively supports many of the most difficult aspirations to achieve —one of which is aspiring to play professional basketball. It is my hope that by exposing these "tricks" that I have given those individuals who choose to "aim high" in their goals the opportunity to enter the metaphorical game with full awareness of the tension between individual effort and structural barriers. Thus, just as players competing in team sports learn that there is no "I" in team, so too can other individuals learn that there is no singular "I" in their achievements and failures. In reality, there is a structural "we" over which the "I" has little control.

Epilogue

The Death of Calvin Cody

In the end that is all we could have ever done.

It was February 8, 2006, at about 7:30 p.m., and I had just finished playing basketball at Texas A&M University's student recreation center. I was sitting in my car with the engine running. I removed my cell phone from my bag and placed it in my lap. As I pulled out of the parking lot onto the street I noticed that I had a text message. I flipped open my cell phone to find a message from Tchaka, one of my former Northeast High School players. Tchaka had graduated from Northeast in 1999, gone on to college, and was now in his second year of law school. We had kept in touch with each other over the years, but several months had passed since I had last talked to him. As I held the car in the road I managed to read the following text message: "Did you hear what happened to Calvin Cody?"

I wasn't sure what to think about the message. I steadied my car and typed my reply to Tchaka: "No. What happened?"

As I waited for Tchaka's response I began to recall how Calvin had survived his adolescent years in Eastridge, graduated from high school, and went on to play basketball at a small college in Georgia. The last time I had seen Calvin was during his winter break from school, when he came for a visit to the high school. On his visit we laughed and joked, and he told me how excited he was to be playing college basketball. I could still hear his enthusiastic shout of "May Dog"—my nickname among the players—echo in my ears. My thoughts then slipped further back to his high school career. I thought about what a great kid Calvin had been for me to coach. Calvin was the kind of young man to whom special things should happen. He worked hard, developed his skills through individual practice, did whatever coaches asked him to, and was generally pleasant to all those with whom he came into contact. He was well liked by players, coaches, teachers, and people from the community. My recollections of Calvin were interrupted when my phone vibrated.

I flipped open my phone and read Tchaka's reply: "Calvin shot and killed himself."

I partially bowed my head and shook it from side to side. I couldn't believe it. How could someone who had survived the temptation of drugs and the neighborhood violence of Eastridge choose to take his own life? I took a deep breath and replied to Tchaka, "What happened?" Even as I typed the message I couldn't believe that I was asking this question about Calvin Cody. For me, Calvin represented all that was good about Coach Benson's efforts and the Northeast Knights. Calvin had succeeded because he was determined, and basketball provided the social space in which he could succeed. He had been "saved" by his involvement in basketball. But had he really survived? I began to wonder if somehow Calvin's family history had caught up to him in the form of foul play. Did someone shoot him and make it look like suicide? Did he, after years of avoiding the drugs and violence, decide that he should get involved? Something wasn't right. There had to be some other explanation for his death because Calvin was too good a kid, too happy, too motivated to commit suicide.

Tchaka replied back, "I'm in class right now. Call Mr. Hunt. He can tell you."

"Thanks for letting me know," I typed back.

"I had to. I knew you coached him," Tchaka replied.

I called Sammy Hunt, team statistician, but was instantly forwarded to Hunt's message box.

I left a message: "Hey, Hunt. I have heard some disturbing news about Calvin, and I want to know if it is true or not. Please call me back when you get this message. May."

As I ended the call an eerie feeling came over me while I navigated the dark highway road. I began to accept that Calvin Cody indeed was gone. In a fit of mixed emotions—anger, frustration, sadness—I banged the steering wheel of my car several times with my open hand.

"Fuck!" I yelled.

With each successive strike to the steering wheel I let go of the confused mix of emotions: "Fuck, fuck, fuck, fuck."

I began to think, why this kid? Why that way? I had many questions that could not be answered. I frantically called other coaches from the Northeast coaching staff, but no one answered their phones. This was a sure sign that Calvin Cody was gone.

* * *

Later that evening Hunt returned my call. Hunt had been Calvin's mentor from middle school through high school.

"Hi, Reuben. I got your message," he said.

"So, Hunt, is it true? What happened?" I asked.

"Calvin shot himself yesterday," he said stoically. Despite his calm tone, I knew Hunt was hurting. He and Calvin had developed a close bond, spending many hours together getting Calvin's schoolwork done, traveling to and from basketball practice and games, and sharing the pains and joys of life. During my interview with Calvin after his senior year of basketball, Calvin told me how important Hunt had been to helping him get through school.

"Are you alright?" I asked Hunt.

"Yes," he replied. "I'm okay right now. This morning I couldn't make it to work. I got up and started on my way, but when I got to the school and entered the building it hit me. My principal saw me and told me to go home. I was a mess this morning. But I'm doing a little better now."

"Well, what happened?" I asked cautiously.

Hunt took a deep breath and began, "Last night we had our playoff game against Norton. We won the game and qualified for the state playoffs. After we got back to the school I dropped the kids off and went by my classroom to do some work for about twenty minutes. On my way back home I got a call from Ken Rowe (a twenty-year-old cousin of Coach Benson). Ken told me that Calvin had shot himself and told me to go over to the hospital. When I got to the hospital, Benson was in the turnaround leaving with Calvin's father in the car. Benson stuck his hand out the window as I approached his car and then put his hand to his face and started crying, 'He's gone.'"

"Damn," I said. "Hunt, why? Why did he do it?"

"Well, you know Calvin had been complaining about pain in his chest. So on Tuesday he was on the phone talking to his friend Terrence, and Terrence said that Calvin was on the phone complaining about the pain in his chest. Calvin's girlfriend had just left him too, so

I think he was depressed about that. And he hadn't made it back to school for whatever reason. But he was on the phone with Terrence, and Terrence said something to him, but Calvin didn't answer. Then all of a sudden Terrence heard a single gun shot. He hung up the phone and drove over to Calvin's apartment. He found Calvin on the ground with a single shot in his heart. Calvin was still alive, so Terrence called an ambulance. They got him to the hospital but couldn't save him."

"Are we sure there wasn't any foul play?" I asked.

"As they do all cases, the police are investigating his death," said Hunt. "But he was in a lot of pain. The doctors had told him that he would have to have corrective surgery for his heart."

Apparently, Calvin was experiencing pain from a heart ailment that he had as a young man. In all the time that I had coached Calvin, I had never known him to complain about pain in his chest. Perhaps he was in pain when he played and just didn't say anything. Calvin was the kind of kid that wouldn't complain.

"I just don't understand," I said to Hunt.

"I didn't even know he had a gun," Hunt replied. "The last time I saw him he was doing alright."

"When is the funeral?"

"They don't know yet."

"Well, please let me know. I'm going to do whatever I can to make it."

"Take care."

"You too."

* * *

I made the trip to Northeast to attend the funeral. The service was held at St. Ezekiel Baptist Church—six blocks from Calvin's grandmother's house in Eastridge. The church usually held about four hundred churchgoers, but on this day it seemed to overflow with many more people packed in the pews and standing along the walls in the church.

The visitors were directed to stand as the procession of family members entered the church to view Calvin's body for the last time. Calvin had a huge family. There were about sixty members in all. Calvin's grandmother, a short, heavy woman, who appeared to suffer from both her health ailments and the pain of having lost one of her

favorite grandchildren, had to be helped down the aisle. Walking behind her were young men whom I had coached when they were in the
ninth grade a few years before but hadn't even realized that they were
Calvin's cousins. Standing prominently among Calvin's kinfolk was
Coach Benson, Calvin's uncle. Benson moved at a steady pace behind
his younger brother, Nathan, Calvin's father. For the first time I could
see the likeness between the two brothers.

I felt sympathy for Benson because I knew that he and Calvin had
been close. As I stood watching the family enter the church, I recalled
the only time that I had ever seen Benson show an attitude during a
game other than his dogged tenacity, competitive intensity, or cutting
humor. We were playing a competitive regional game against North
Farmington when Calvin went up for a lay-up and was struck by an
opposing player. Calvin sustained a neck and head injury and lay still
on the gym floor. Benson, who had gone to evaluate Calvin's injury,
was overwhelmed by the appearance of Calvin lying immobile on the
floor. He sat on the floor next to Calvin and began rocking back and
forth with tears welling up in his eyes. Although Benson might have
been Calvin's high school basketball coach, it was clear that Benson
was Calvin's uncle first and foremost.

When the family took their seats at the funeral I looked around
the church, and judging from the wide variety of people represented, I
couldn't help but believe that Calvin had been an inspiration to many
people. As I listened to the speakers recall their fond memories of Calvin, I couldn't hold back my tears anymore. Dr. Elizabeth Morris, the
principal of Northeast High School, spoke of how good a kid Calvin
had been and how good a basketball player he was. She said that he
was the kind of kid that didn't disappoint because he had promised
her that he would graduate from high school. She felt that Calvin had
shown perseverance in earning a "real" diploma from Northeast High
School when so many other young people were merely receiving cer-
tificates of attendance—a piece of paper that simply stated that the
student had attended high school.

Mr. Hunt stepped to the microphone next, struggling a great deal
to gather his composure. Once he began to speak of Calvin, however, he seemed calm. Hunt spoke about meeting Calvin in the sixth
grade and seeing Calvin's love for basketball even then. Calvin would
beg Hunt to open the gym so he could shoot baskets no matter how
late they had worked. Hunt also talked about how Calvin could be a

stubborn kid. He gave the example of how Calvin, after making one of the top AAU (Amateur Athletic Union) club teams in the state of Georgia, didn't want to play AAU basketball because he didn't want to travel three hours just to go to practice.

Then Ms. Linden, Calvin's favorite high school teacher, talked about how hard Calvin had worked. She shared a wonderful story about how her husband and his friend had played and beaten Calvin and Shamar in a game of basketball, but that the two men secretly suspected that Calvin and Shamar had let them win. She talked about how Calvin was a caring individual who, when her husband had fallen from a ladder working on the house, drove her husband to the hospital emergency room.

The last of the nonclergy to speak was Coach Benson. His presence was noteworthy because he was the only African American and only family member to speak at the funeral. He struggled as he began by saying, "You all have to understand this is a very difficult time for our family. This is the second nephew that I have lost in the last eighteen months." (His nephew had been gunned down in a neighborhood altercation.) Benson then began to describe how each person's life was made up of chapters and that those chapters are all little histories that come together. "People might say all the good things about my nephew because they each had a chapter with Calvin. But Calvin was a special kid to me because he understood the importance of family."

Finally, Rev. Reed, an African American pastor of Calvin's home church, St. Mark's, gave a fiery eulogy. He talked about sharing with his twenty-year-old daughter his own confusion about what to say at Calvin's funeral. He then talked about Calvin accepting Christ in his life and joining the church. He reminded the mourners, "Y'all need to follow Calvin's example and become Christians! His short life should remind young people to think about the things they are doing in their lives and try to get themselves together."

As each of the speakers at Calvin's funeral shared stories of their own relationships with Calvin, I reflected on all that I had done and become as a part of the Northeast Knights. I thought about the way that Calvin's life had become intertwined with mine through basketball. In a way, I too had been "saved." My salvation came in the form of basketball, which took me from a mundane life disconnected from others to one of deep connection to young men in a spiritual way. Calvin's life also represented to me the difficulties faced by so many young black men whose lives end in violent death. Although the official cause of Calvin's death was ruled a suicide, I was reminded that the threat of violent death remains close at hand for these young men.

* * *

After the funeral I went outside and talked to Benson for the first time since I had left Northeast eight months earlier. When he saw me he smiled and said, "Yo, man, what's up?"

We shook hands and embraced as he continued, "I'm glad you made it back. Get your gear together 'cause we are putting the band back together. We're going go out here and get us a region championship." Since I had worked with Benson for seven years I had a sense of what he meant. He wanted me to join the team for the game against Ford Heights that afternoon. It was as if I had never left the Knights. I had mixed emotions because in one sense I was proud to have had such an esteemed position that I would be invited back without hesitation, but at the same time I thought that my presence might be a distraction to some of the young men on the team who were not familiar with me.

"Okay," I said. "I'm going to ride over there with y'all."

"Alright," Benson replied.

As I stepped away from Benson many people greeted him and offered their condolences. I watched Benson greet others, and I could see the slow transition of Benson from a man who suffered the pain of having to bury his second nephew to tragedy in less than two years to a man becoming ever more focused on the task at hand—the chance to beat Ford Heights for the first time in three tries that year to win a region championship. His thoughts of basketball would spare him some pain from the hurt of that day. He too had been "saved" by basketball.

* * *

I met Coach Milton Frye, one of the assistants, outside the church, and his wife drove us to the Northeast High School gymnasium. One of the former Northeast High School athletes who had become a sports star, Troy Wilson, now a professional football player, had purchased for his little brother, Eric—a sophomore on the Knights basketball team—and each player on the basketball team a new pair of Air Jordans for the region championship game against Ford Heights. I watched Troy standing outside his red Hummer in front of the gym handing out the new shoes to players as drizzle began to fall from the sky. I couldn't help but think about how Troy's success against very long odds helped to fuel the idea for so many of the young men that they too could really be professional athletes like Troy.

When I walked into the gym I saw Coach David Shore. He had left the funeral early to prepare uniforms for the game. We greeted each other, and then he invited me to have a slice of pizza, our tradi-tional pregame meal. I grabbed a slice of pepperoni pizza and sat on the bleachers. All these pregame activities were so familiar to me. I ate the pizza, and the room-temperature, greasy mass went down heavily on my stomach. As I sat on the bleachers and the players moved in and out of the locker room getting dressed for the game, I began to feel the little nervous tension that I used to feel before each game. But this time was different. I hadn't coached in a full season, and I knew very little about the Ford Heights Panthers.

All the players were present except Michael Hammond. Ham-mond was about 6'0" and 190 pounds and had become a star in much the same way that Calvin Cody had early in his career. Like Calvin, Michael had performed well in his freshman year and went on to be the leading scorer for the Knights in his sophomore and junior years. He was now a senior and continued to lead the team in scoring. He was a big part of the reason why that year the Northeast Knights had made it to the region championship game. In just an hour or so the Knights—my Knights, as I couldn't help but still feel a part of the team—would be competing to be named the best of twelve teams in the region.

Michael Hammond was late to meet the bus because he had ig-nored Coach Benson's suggestion to go to the gym directly after the funeral. Instead, Michael attended Calvin's burial with the rest of the Hammond family. I really couldn't blame him. Calvin Cody had lived right up the street, and Hammond grew up watching him through middle school and high school. Calvin was like a mentor to Michael, and Michael viewed Calvin as a model of success.

Benson, who had also attended the burial, arrived at the gym a few minutes before our scheduled departure. Michael jogged in a minute or so after Benson and then went into the locker room and changed into his uniform quickly. Benson instructed the other players to begin loading the bus, and Hammond trotted out of the gym and onto the bus a few minutes later.

Before I got on the bus Coach Frye said, "May, we saved you your seat." I climbed up the steps to the yellow school bus and found my usual seat on the left-hand side of the bus, third seat back. It was unusual that the other assistant coach, Odell Henry, was absent. He used to sit in the seat in front of mine, but as I had learned earlier he and his fiancée were getting married that day. It was a wedding plan that they had initiated well before they could have known of Calvin's passing or the day of the region championship. Coach Henry's absence did not bother Benson, who once said, "Life has to go on even in death. Shit, funerals are for people that are living. The dead don't hear a damn thing. They're dead."

On the twenty-minute ride to Ford Heights, the players talked softly about whatever was on their minds. This was unusual because as a rule Benson demanded silence on the bus ride before each game. He had established this rule as a way to get the young men focused on the game at hand, but this day was unique. These players, most of whom had just attended the funeral, were being asked to play a basketball game under emotionally draining circumstances. Calvin was a community hero and had touched all of their lives in some way, so there was a feeling of sadness and unrest that was almost palpable on the bus, the tension perhaps needing to be released by the soft banter among the boys.

Shamar, who had played for Coach Benson a few years earlier and graduated from high school, was now an assistant coach. He had attained para-professional status at the high school and worked as a teacher's assistant. Since Shamar was still very close in age to the players, he sat in the back of the bus. No doubt this seating assignment was Coach Benson's way of more effectively monitoring the behavior of Vinny and Travis, two players who were a bit more impulsive and difficult to manage than those players that had played during my time at Northeast. In fact, Vinny was the same player with whom I had a conflict during my last season officially coaching the Northeast Knights.

* * *

When we arrived at Ford Heights High School, we entered the gym through the pass gate. I walked in with the team without being questioned, but it felt odd because I still felt a bit like an outsider. Once inside Coach Frye gave me a black cotton sweatband with a white vinyl number 5 pressed on it. He said, "Here you go, May. We all got one for Calvin." We were commemorating Calvin Cody's life with his high school number. The players entered the locker room as the coaches stood outside watching the girls' region championship.

After a few minutes I walked into the locker room to see how the players were doing. When I walked in, Vinny said, "What's up, May?" He walked up to me and held out his hand. We gripped hands and pulled each other in and embraced. I said, "What's up, Vinny?"

"We gonna get this win," he replied.

Vinny was only about 5'7", but he had well-defined muscles and weighed about 180 pounds. He was pretty aggressive in most matters, and that is what made him a good basketball player. He wasn't afraid to compete with anyone, no matter how big. Because he greeted me so pleasantly, it was hard for me to believe he was the same kid that had challenged my authority almost a year earlier, when he told me, "Get out my face."

The rest of the players were bouncing basketballs off the walls and stretching. Not much was different to me; the players were getting prepared, and the coaches were getting prepared. I had a chance to talk to Shay-Daddy, the nickname I had given Shamar when he played for Northeast a few years before. I shouted, "Shay-Daddy, where you at? What's up?"

One of the players shouted, "He really is 'Shay-Daddy' now."

"What?"

"He is Shay-Daddy now. His girl is about to have a baby."

"Yeah. I got my girl pregnant," Shamar said as he stuck his head out from behind the row of lockers.

I didn't know exactly what to say. I just said, "Well that's a lot of responsibility." Shamar looked a bit frustrated, as if he had been reminded of this fact on several occasions. He said, "I know."

"You can handle it," I said.

"I have to," Shamar said.

I didn't pursue further conversation with Shamar because he and Calvin had been real close. They were homeboys who had played together, and I could tell that Shamar was a bit distracted by the enormity of burying a friend his own age.

I looked around the locker room a bit more, and then I went back outside and found Benson watching the last few minutes of the girls' championship game.

"Benson?"

"Yeah, coach."

"I don't want to be too much of a distraction, but is it alright if I sit on the bench? I don't want to get in the way or anything."

"Shit, man. You're alright. You can't do anything but help us."

"But I haven't seen Ford Heights play or anything."

"You've seen them play before. They do the same shit," Benson said emphatically.

There it was again. Benson was giving me confidence in the way he had so many other times. I followed Benson and the other coaches back into the locker room for the pregame talk. Benson's speech was short. He told the players, "There's really nothing to say, gentlemen. We've played them before, and we know exactly what they are going to do. We have to do what it takes to win. Play as hard as you can. Coach Frye, you have anything to say?"

"Yeah," Frye replied, "let's get this one for Calvin."

"May," Benson said, "do you have anything?"

"No," I said, "just play hard."

We huddled together and put our hands in the center of the circle and began reciting the Lord's Prayer. "Our Father . . ." As we recited the prayer I felt that it had more importance to me on this particular day. I had been reminded, through Calvin's death, how fragile life was, and this made my need for the presence of God a material one. I suspect that the other coaches and players felt this added significance as we spoke in collective unison through every verse, "Amen."

After we finished Vinny stepped up and said, "Knights on three: 1-2-3."

"Knights!" we echoed.

The players got prepared to enter the gym for warmups, and Coach Frye shouted, "We came to get a region championship. Don't forget to hold your hand high to the sky when you come out. Remember Calvin. This is for Calvin."

All the players held up their right hands, adorned in black wristbands with the number 5 displayed prominently. They took the floor as our fans on the south side of the gym erupted in cheers. I walked out with the other coaches and sat on the bench. All the things that I used to do, like get water, collect balls, monitor team warmup, and evaluate the opponent, all seemed foreign to me. There were other coaches doing that now. I sat on the bench as much a spectator as the fan in the stands. I turned to Benson on the bench and said, "Is there anything in particular you want me to look for or do?" I was searching for my significance on the team bench.

"Just tell me what you see," Benson said.

"Alright," I said. *This shouldn't be hard*, I thought. *I got this.*

But when the horn sounded and it was time to begin, I still found it hard to believe that I was back coaching. It was a lot different coaching competitive boys' high school basketball than it was coaching nine-year-old girls in recreational basketball like I had been doing for the last few weeks back in Texas. Teenage boys respected you and responded when you spoke to them forcefully, but little girls would become frightened and think you were a mean man if you spoke to them that way. These boys were competing for a championship and had pride and masculinity riding on the game. For the girls I coached, they simply were abiding by the main precept of the recreation league, "to have fun." There were rules for the boys, but those who were successful had learned to push the limits of those rules, whereas the girls played by rules that were enforced by referees and coaches alike with few modifications. Finally, the boys played at a speed seemingly ten times as fast as those little girls.

The public-address announcer introduced the starting lineup for each team. When he announced the last of our starters, "Michael Hammond," I noticed that Michael was not wearing his typical number 22 jersey. He had worn 22 for the previous three years in both football and basketball. For this game, however, he was wearing Calvin Cody's number 5 jersey—a jersey that had been worn by many other very good guards at Northeast High School. Michael was dedicating this game to Calvin Cody in his own way. They had grown up in the same neighborhood, played well at the same high school, and had hopes and dreams that would take them beyond Northeast—a dream now over for Calvin Cody.

In the first quarter we played flat, and Ford Heights ran out to an eleven-point lead. Midway through the first quarter Coach Frye, now in my former role as first assistant coach, said to Benson, "Coach, we better call a timeout."

Benson called the timeout, and he brought the guys over and told them to sit down. Frye and Benson stepped into the huddle.

"Gentlemen, just settle down," Benson said.

"Relax and get the rhythm of the game. We have played them many times before," Frye added.

"Y'all alright," Benson concluded.

When Benson and Frye were finished I stepped in the huddle and shouted, "Guys, the main problem is that five people ain't playing defense. Five people ain't playing defense. That's the main problem." The players looked at me intensely as I spoke. I was surprised to see that I was still able to command attention from the young men, even those whom I had only seen playing for the junior varsity team in the previous year. In fact, their attentiveness to my directives helped to renew my own confidence—a confidence that had eroded each day I was away from coaching high school boys.

After the timeout, the players seemed to have more energy. They played better defense and started passing the ball to one another. They were able to cut the lead down to five points by the end of the first quarter. Ford Heights led 20–15. The players walked back to the bench for the quarter break, and Frye turned to me and said, "May, you got something?"

"Give me a little time, Frye," I said. "It's coming back slowly."

"Alright," Frye said.

The second quarter started, and I began to see plays as they were unfolding and to think of strategies. I felt like I was in tune with the game. Our players were playing hard, but it was clear that the emotional drain from Calvin's funeral was having an impact on their focus. We went into halftime down 52–43. Benson did not even take the guys back to the locker room. We just sat on the steps inside the gym corridor.

Benson said, "Guys, you got to play together. We already know the kid number 3 is going to take the three-point shot. And you know that kid B.K. is just going to dribble right around the screen and shoot the shot in the seam."

"Benson," I said, "what's happening is that when they send a man through, our guy on the back side is sliding with him, so when B.K. dribbles up top there is no one there. We have to step up over the top."

"Coach," Benson said, "come right here and show them what you are talking about. Some of these younger guys won't understand." Benson then stepped up, and I explained using him for demonstration.

After I finished demonstrating Benson turned to Coach Frye and said, "You got anything?"

"Yeah," Frye replied. "We gotta rebound better. We can't play scared by the basket."

"Alright," Benson said, "go out there and shoot." The guys jogged back to the court to warm up for the second half.

In the second half we started off playing sluggishly again. The Panthers scored baskets over us and around us as if we really didn't want to play. We hung in the game for a little bit, but by the time the third quarter was over the Panthers had us down by eighteen points.

In the fourth quarter we began chipping away at the lead, but we weren't getting any closer than fourteen points. The fans seemed to believe that the game was over. We weren't playing well, and we didn't seem to have the ability to score in order to get the job done. I was even beginning to feel as though things couldn't get better. I looked at Frye, and he looked frustrated. Frye wanted to win a region championship not only for the sake of being a champion but also because he had coached Calvin Cody in the sixth, seventh, and eighth grades, and he wanted to win this game as a tribute to Cody's memory. With four minutes left Benson called a timeout and then began talking calmly to the players.

Hammond wasn't having his best game in Calvin's jersey, and the other players were frustrated. Vinny in particular really wanted to win the game. He was from Eastridge like Hammond and Calvin, and he was trying to get the job done but felt his teammates weren't always passing him the ball. In the timeout, something happened that I would never have believed if I had not been standing in the huddle. Fred, a guard that played sometimes with Vinny, said, "Man, we are trying to win, and Vinny needs to pass the ball to the open man." Vinny got upset when he heard Fred's complaint since he felt that he actually wasn't getting the ball enough to score.

In the blink of an eye Vinny took the water bottle that he had been drinking from and violently hurled it three seats away and hit Fred in the face. I stepped back in disbelief as the full water bottle hit Fred above the right eyebrow and rolled onto the court. I was thinking, "What the fuck?" but remembered of how troubled Vinny was. He was in behavioral classes in school because he had violent impulses that I had not witnessed to this extent. For some reason, I believed Vinny was doing better given my initial interaction with him in the locker room. But I had forgotten that "the heat of the battle" could transform any man, especially a young man like Vinny who was already on the edge.

Coach Frye grabbed Vinny by the arm and took him to the end of the bench, and Benson stepped into the huddle and said, "You see, he is just trying to win. He's just upset because he is trying to win, and he wants his teammates to help him." Benson transformed a possibly volatile situation into motivation for his players. He spoke in a calm voice. I thought this was unusual because Benson had always been a fiery coach. Coach Frye later told me that Benson had taken this approach because the team was really young and inexperienced and because his own verbal responses only pushed Vinny and Travis to act more erratically.

When the horn sounded, Benson replaced Vinny in the lineup to give him an opportunity to cool down. The players went out and played a little better, but we were still down by eight points with ninety seconds left in the game.

Benson looked at Vinny and said, "Are you ready?"

Vinny was sitting calmly and said, "Yeah."

Benson held Vinny by the shoulder and told him, "You gotta shoot now." He moved Vinny toward the scorer's table and got him in the game. At this time Fred was still on the floor, and his bruised ego from having been hit in the face with the water bottle seemed to have been healed by the return of Vinny. He and Vinny played together as if all was forgiven. I think all the players on the team realized how "off" Vinny was, and they knew that Benson wouldn't send him away, not only because Vinny was a good basketball player but also because Benson just didn't turn kids away. They knew they had to learn to work with Vinny, just as Vinny knew he had to learn to work with them.

With time running down, our team played tough defense, and Vinny hit a deep three-point basket. Seconds later we got another stop, and Vinny came down and got a pass from Fred and hit another deep three-point basket. The energy from the crowd was growing because with each effort on our part, the possibility for our success improved. On the next play, Vinny stole the ball from the Ford Heights guard and made the lay-up. The crowd erupted. I was energized by Vinny's effort. In forty-five seconds Vinny had scored eight points and tied the game at 86. We forced Ford Heights to take one more bad shot. We came down with the rebound, advanced the ball up the court, and ran our spread offense.

Fred threw the ball to Michael Hammond, a player who could be trusted to score or get to the free-throw line in a tight game. With seventeen seconds left Hammond drove to the basket and pulled up a running jump shot. *Swish.* We went up by two points, 88–86. When Ford Heights got the ball inbounds, Ben Carson, not realizing that we had a two-point lead, fouled Ford Heights' best free-throw shooter with seconds left.

"Dammit," Benson shouted.

"No, no, Ben, no," Frye shouted.

The coaches couldn't believe it. I knew Carson felt bad after he realized his mistake. Coach Benson called a thirty-second timeout to develop a strategy. As Carson came off the floor I walked up to him and hugged him and said, "That's alright. You didn't know. You didn't know. We got this."

Benson pulled the guys together and said, "If he misses the second free throw, we gotta get the rebound. If you can't grab the rebound, slap it back down the court, but don't let them rebound that ball and put it in. If it goes through the basket, get it out of the net quickly. Get the ball to Hammond or Vinny." He pointed to Hammond and Vinny and said, "Y'all don't even look back. Go straight down the court and try to score."

"Coach," I said. "We better run our press breaker. You know they are going to come with the press." The press breaker was an offense developed to move the ball down the floor against a team's full-court pressure.

Benson paused for a minute then said, "Run your press breaker."

The horn sounded, and the players returned to the court. The best free-throw shooter for Ford Heights stepped to the free-throw line. The fans for both teams seemed to be in silent anticipation as the shooter lined up the shot and easily sank the first free throw. As he prepared to shoot the second one I just kept thinking, *please let him miss it.* The Panther stepped to the line and knocked down the free throw just like Benson had predicted. After the ball went through the net our players panicked. Instead of calmly setting up our press-break play, one of the least adept passers on the team inbounded the ball. Worse than that, he couldn't get the ball to Hammond or Vinny. Instead he threw the ball in to Ben Carson. Carson was capable but was not as confident as Hammond or Vinny. Carson dribbled the ball nervously from side to side as seconds ticked down.

6, 5, 4, 3 . . .

Carson got just across half court with two seconds left and had to heave up a deep three-point shot that hit the back of the rim and bounced up and away from the basket. He missed. 2, 1, 0.

The horn sounded. Overtime.

There was a great deal of excitement flowing through the crowd. We had shown so much fight getting back into the game that I guess the energy was too intense for some fans. The police had to grab a twenty-something-year-old Ford Heights fan and escort him out of the gym for screaming and pointing at a Northeast fan. As the police were escorting the man from the gym, one of the Ford Heights players suddenly ran across the floor and out of the gym behind the fan being escorted by the police. It turned out that the ejected fan was his older brother.

We had about three minutes to prepare our strategy. We kept our players on the bench while the referees sorted out how the player would be handled for his infraction—I couldn't help but think of Ron Artest, former player for the NBA's Indiana Pacers, who ran into the stands and struck a fan. (Artest received the harshest penalty ever leveled by the NBA by getting a seventy-three-game suspension that ended his play for that year.) When the referees came to the scorer's table they had ejected the Ford Heights player from the game. He wouldn't be able to play in the overtime, and he would also have to serve a two-game suspension as mandated by the Georgia High School Association's rules. He wasn't a key player, but he had played well as a role player. The Panther head coach protested the officials' decision but quickly relented. He was well aware that his player had committed an inexcusable infraction.

Once the overtime started the crowd channeled its focus on the game again. The overtime was tight also, but the Panthers were able to take a three-point lead, 98–95, with eighteen seconds left. Vinny worked his magic once more. He shot a deep three-point shot. *Swish.* We tied the game at 98, and neither team was able to score in the remaining time. I was exhausted at the end of the first overtime but began to think that it was our destiny to win this game. Frye had explained to me that both of the previous games between Ford Heights and Northeast had ended in buzzer-beater defeats for Northeast.

We started our second overtime, and the crowd was buzzing. We continued to fight, but the Panthers pushed their lead up to six points, 108–102, with two minutes left. We just didn't have anything left. The lead was insurmountable for us this time. Vinny and Hammond both took shots to try to pull us closer, but the emotional stress that they had been under after the events of the day had taken its toll. We were only able to score two more points. As the clock ran down to zero, the final score on the scoreboard was Panthers 108, Knights 104. It had been a double-overtime thriller.

The tournament officials immediately announced us as region runner-up and gave us the trophy. They then presented the Ford Heights Panthers with their first-place trophy. As the Panthers smiled and took pictures at half court, Vinny began to cry. Dr. Morris, the Northeast High School principal, walked to our bench and told all the young men, "Hold your heads up. You have nothing to be ashamed of." But Vinny kept his head low and continued crying. He seemed to be hurt more than any other player. Mr. Hunt, who had served as a source of support for many of the young men in the past, including Calvin Cody, told Vinny, "Hold your head up. You played well. I couldn't be more proud of you than I am today." Vinny continued crying as we walked back up to the locker room. I couldn't help but feel sorry for Vinny. He had been greatly invested in winning the game. It was hard to believe that this sniffling boy had been the violently aggressive young man who had thrown a water bottle at his teammate.

In the locker room Benson simply said, "Gentlemen, we had a chance to win the game but didn't. It's too bad we had to lose after all we've been through. Now just go home and get your rest. We got to play next week in the state playoffs. Shit, if you ain't ready to play, you just need to stay your ass here next week." The state tournament would be single-game elimination.

"Knights on three: 1, 2, 3," Hammond said.

"Knights," we echoed.

Although we had failed to defeat Ford Heights for the region championship, many people had described the game as the best double-overtime thriller to be played in the area. It was particularly special for me to sit on the bench and to encourage and watch the young men who had not more than a few hours before attended a funeral to bury Calvin Cody.

* * *

On my flight home I contemplated whether the other coaches and I had done all we could have done for Calvin. We had encouraged him to play basketball. We had given him a place to be someone through athletics in middle school and high school. I suspect, however, that it was Calvin's investment in basketball and ultimately the prospect that he could no longer compete because of his heart problems that drove him to take his own life. I was left wondering if we had as coaches helped him escape to a better place. Had our "dirty trick" worked?

When I shared my thoughts with my wife she said, "You know you all might have been the only reason that Calvin lasted as long as he did." In my grief I hadn't looked at it that way. I reflected on my wife's words and thought about Calvin's interview with me some three years earlier. He told me that playing basketball had helped him stay out of trouble. It was then that I realized that indeed we had given Calvin Cody a chance. In the end that is all we could do.

My experience with the Northeast Knights has taught me that basketball offers young black men like Calvin—who see so clearly the reality that their opportunities are constrained by their race and by where they live, go to school, and grow up—a chance to hope for better in spite of their dismal starting point. These young men should no more be derided than any of us who invest our lives in long-shot dreams. After all, such dreams are conceived in a society that says to all, "you all can achieve whatever you want if you work for it." The sad reality is that young black men continue to be disproportionately blocked from achieving alternatives to hoop dreams.

Methodological Appendix

The primary methodological approach I used for collecting data for this study is ethnography, sometimes referred to as participant observation. Ethnography is the study of groups and individuals through direct participation and observation. In this approach, the researcher becomes a participant in the subjects' activities in order to learn the nuances of the social life in which the subjects are engaged.[1] The researcher, typically over months and years of study, records written fieldnotes from his or her experiences. These fieldnotes become the basis on which the researcher structures an argument about how some aspect of social life functions for those individuals who take part in the activities.

Sociologists have used ethnography as an effective means of exploring a variety of activities, behaviors, and lifestyles.[2] The primary advantage of ethnography is that it permits the researcher to learn firsthand about his or her subjects. The researcher learns details about human behavior and theorizes categorical relationships based on that understanding. Although this approach permits the researcher to acquire in-depth knowledge about the social phenomena under study, the main disadvantage of this approach is that the researcher's presence may alter the subjects' behavior. Furthermore, since the data is based on what the researcher observes, it is limited by the researcher's own subjective perceptions.[3] Despite these disadvantages, ethnography continues to be recognized as a valuable research approach for understanding social life in ways that other approaches cannot.

In addition to ethnography, I used tape-recorded interviews to supplement data gathered through participant observation. These open-ended interviews permit the researcher to capture the experiences of the subject in the subject's own words.[4] The respondents can be directed to elaborate their experiences in a way that helps to clarify the meanings that they give to their experiences.

I have drawn on data collected through participant observation and interviews to explore the Northeast Knights. In the remainder of this appendix I describe the specific process used in this study for (1) collecting data, (2) analyzing data, and (3) developing my approach to representing the lives of the young and adult men of the Northeast Knights. I will share the nuances of how I arrived at my research question, how I managed my role as coach-researcher, how I conducted interviews, and why I chose to write in a reflexive manner. This information will give the reader a clear understanding of the overall project.

Data Collection

When I began to work with the boys' team in 1998 I became curious as to why so many of the young men were so interested in playing basketball. After my second year of coaching, and rereading my personal journal entries from previous years of coaching, I noted the consistent ways in which basketball was central to the lives of many of the young men. Something significant was clearly going on. I decided to formally study the young men who played for the Northeast Knights. I approached Coach Benson to see if I could begin to formally study the young men of Northeast, including interviewing them about their basketball careers. Benson provided encouragement, and I received approval for the project. For the next five years I kept detailed field-notes.

I began taking more notes on the young men's interactions with coaches, parents, referees, school officials, and players from other schools. I began to document the activities that took place on the bus, in the locker room, in practice, and before and after games. I wrote notes on parental interaction with coaches, players, and booster-club members. In addition to taking elaborate fieldnotes, I also retained copies of school documents regarding the team and its activities.

My fieldnotes contained various bits of information about players and coaches. From time to time I would jokingly remind the players and coaches that "I'm gonna put that in my book." At other times the players and coaches would jokingly comment, "I don't wanna read about that shit in your book" or "May, you need to put this in your book" or "That's what you need to write your book about." For the most part, however, we rarely discussed my research. We were all preoccupied with basketball. Indeed, my preoccupation with basketball required me to demonstrate a great deal of discipline when it was time to write fieldnotes, a practice that proved especially difficult after completing full days of a physically and emotionally draining activity like coaching basketball. Fortunately, after writing daily for so many years, I had developed the necessary stamina for taking such notes.

In spring 2001, after my third year of coaching the Knights, I conducted my first round of in-depth exit interviews. (There were six interviews in 2001, five in 2002, and eight in 2003.) I selected senior boys who had completed their final season for the Northeast Knights. I tried to interview each senior player, but for various reasons I was only able to interview about 75 percent of those players who graduated from 2001 to 2003. I selected senior basketball players for a number of reasons. First, they were able to consent to their own interview since all those whom I interviewed were eighteen or nineteen years old. Second, these young men would be more open to criticizing coaches without fear of repercussions. Indeed, the ease with which the young men questioned me about some of my perspectives on coaching during their interviews was interesting. Finally, these young men's basketball careers had been decided for the most part, and they could better reflect on their past experiences. They knew whether or not they would be playing basketball beyond high school. During these interviews I learned of many of their enduring aspirations to play basketball despite the fact that they had not received scholarship offers from colleges. In fact, not one of the eighteen young men I interviewed had received scholarship offers for basketball.

The interviews were conducted in my office at the university where I worked. I usually drove the young men to my office after they were dismissed from school. Discussions that took place on the ride to and from the interview were also documented in my fieldnotes. Upon arriving at my office I offered the player a soft drink before we started the interview. I then explained the study and had the player complete the necessary human-subject forms that authorized their consent to be interviewed. I also informed the respondents that they could choose not to answer any question and that they also could terminate the interview at any time and request the audiocassette of the interview.

I conducted one interview per day, each lasting an average of about an hour and fifteen minutes. I tape-recorded all the interviews. During the interview I asked the young men a variety of questions

including questions about their backgrounds, families, sports participation, sources of support and encouragement, friends, media, professional athletes, role models, extracurricular activities, academics, future sport orientation, and their greatest memories from sport participation. I used follow-up questions to get the respondents to clarify
particular points. About midway through, each interview usually took
on the character of an easy-flowing conversation given my familiarity
with each respondent. This is when I usually asked questions about
more sensitive issues like drug and alcohol use and sexuality.

Once I completed my questions, I kept the tape recorder running
and invited the young men to ask me any questions or share anything they thought was important. This invitation was significant. The
players easily shared their disappointment about some of my and the
other coaches' performance. They criticized us for particular losses,
team policies, or game strategy. In short, the young men took the opportunity to be forthright. Yet also consistent was the general high
regard with which the young men spoke of Coach Benson. They felt
he cared about them as individuals. After the collection of interview
data in the spring, I spent the summer months transcribing each set of
interviews. I began data analysis after the first set of interviews was
completed.

Data Analysis

The data for this study were analyzed using a grounded theory approach.[5] Central steps in this approach to data analysis include the
comparison of data, the creation of analytical categories, and the development of theory from this process of comparison.[6] While in the
field I began coding my observations into thematic categories.[7] These
categories emerged from my rereading of fieldnotes from the previous
year. I gave these categories particular consideration in subsequent
years of the study given their initial presence. For instance, early in
the study I noted the fluctuating notion of sportsmanship in competitive play for the young men. Thus, in subsequent coding of data I
was careful to note incidents in which questions of sportsmanship
were addressed. I was able to develop my own initial thoughts about
sportsmanship, which I then incorporated into the interview guide.
During the interviews I probed the players about sportsmanship. The

conclusions drawn from this process of continuously collecting, coding, and analyzing data are reported in chapter 6. I followed a similar process as other significant categories emerged from the data.

To further develop interview questions for analysis I incorporated ideas generated from fieldnotes, previous interviews, and literature in the sociology of sport.[8] I was able to make comparisons across individual respondents' interviews because I had used the same interview guide for each player's interview. Although there was some variation in interview questions because of the open-ended nature of the interviews and the refinement of the interview instrument, I still investigated core topical matters in all the interviews. For instance, I was able to make a comparison of all eighteen respondents' answers to the question, Does where an individual grows up determine whether he will become a good athlete? By analyzing the respondents' answers to this question along with their responses regarding race and athletic ability, I was able to theorize about how the young men understood the relationships among sport, social environment, race, and athletic ability. These findings are discussed in chapter 4.

During the collection, coding, and analysis of the data, prominent themes emerged around players' aspirations, their ideas about mobility, their connection to their communities, and their adoption of mass-media images in everyday discourse. It was on these conceptual pillars that I built the central argument to this book regarding the players' focus on athletics as a means of achieving mobility. Although there were a variety of topics that could have been shaped to make theoretical statements about the young men's participation in basketball, I chose aspirations and mobility because of their relevance beyond the world of the Northeast Knights. After arriving at the central topic for consideration, I was then confronted with the complex matter of determining how I would represent to others what I had learned about the young men of the Northeast Knights.

Representation

Ethnographers are presented with the difficult situation of deciding how they will represent their subjects to others who are not privy to the context in which the research is conducted. This situation is made more difficult by the fact that the data from which the ethnographer is drawing is typically a complex, amorphous mass of events or incidents that may or may not have direct relevance to the ethnographer's narrowly defined research question. Furthermore, mainstream conventions in social science writing require the ethnographer to speak with a level of certainty and "objectivity" that is often challenged by the fluctuating behavior of participants in the field and by the researcher's own subjective perceptions. I grappled with these complexities in deciding how I would tell the story of the Northeast Knights.

Perhaps the most transparent method that the ethnographer can employ to represent the subjects is to bare all by presenting fieldnotes in their entirety.[9] In such proposed writings the ethnographer's thoughts and impressions about the subjects, findings, and theory would then be on full display for the readers. This, however, is an impractical approach given the shear volume of fieldnotes produced in most ethnographic research endeavors. More important, unedited fieldnotes frequently diverge into "irrelevant" matters that fail to serve the interest of presenting categorical ideas with some measure of generalizability.[10] In this regard, baring all would fail to meet at least one convention for social science writing. Thus, the ethnographer must make choices about who is represented and how.

In making choices about how others will be represented, ethnographers must negotiate their own power. For instance, at the outset of writing *Living Through the Hoop* I recognized the disparity in power that I had over the representation of the young men of the Northeast Knights. They had no "voice" in the matter. My solution was simple. In my first draft of this book, I attempted to give all the individual coaches and young men an opportunity to speak. This produced a 130,000-word document in which a majority of the more than sixty players I encountered in my seven years were permitted to speak. It was clear after feedback from other readers that this polyphonic approach to writing the manuscript was overwhelming. Most readers preferred the assurance of conceptual simplicity to the replication of everyday life complexity. Ultimately, I decided to write a reflexive ethnography—one in which the ethnographer speaks openly about the complex relationship between ethnographer, informants, and the field.[11]

My motivation for presenting the narrative of the Northeast Knights in a reflexive manner was centered on three ideas: (1) I believed that my experiences, as a coach of the Northeast Knights, were interconnected with the young men's experiences in such a way that "their" story was "our" story—a story I was qualified to tell; (2) I wished to expose my own background as a way of setting in relief the ways in which structural positions from which individuals start toward mobility affects their chances for success; and (3) I wanted to bring to the fore my own responsibility in the ethical dilemma of encouraging the young men to pursue mobility through athletics.

First, I wanted to tell the story from the perspective of an individual who was an active participant on the team. Initially, I had joined the boys' basketball team at Northeast High School without the intention of conducting research. Instead, I sought to enjoy the experience of coaching and bonding with young and adult men like myself. I was drawn into the team for the love of the game. Therefore, as I contemplated the final write-up of the book, I believed that I could be true to the spirit of the Northeast Knights by centering the narrative on my voice. I based this belief on the idea that once a researcher takes on a "membership role," "the researchers' own perspectives, experiences, and emotions become equally important to the accounts gathered from others, instead of serving as an important, but secondary, enhancement."[12] I believed my life was deeply connected to the other participants.[13] Thus, I believed that I could represent the Northeast Knights well given my relationship to the team's coaches and players.

The second idea that influenced my decision to write the book in a reflexive manner was my belief that by sharing some of my own experiences of pursuing the hoop dream, I could set into relief the lives of the young men at Northeast. I believed that if I had been presented with "choices" similar to the ones the players were faced with, then I might well have been consumed by the idea of mobility through athletics. In fact, had my mother not experienced social mobility early in my childhood, I would have lived in communities beset with conditions similar to those experienced daily by many of the Northeast Knights. Because my family moved up the socioeconomic ladder— largely due to my mother's dogged pursuit and her good fortune to have the assistance of a few "facilitators" from outside the community who directed her path in a focused manner—I was not left to believe that athletics were my last or only hope of climbing out of the ghetto.

Despite these differences, I still identified greatly with the stereotypical association of African American males as athletes. I too had pursued basketball at Aurora University as a sophomore. The only playing experience I had at that time was in middle school; yet I believed that I had a chance to play college basketball. Was I that much different from the young men of Northeast who had similar athletic dreams even though they had not been offered scholarships to play college basketball?

I remember when I decided to play college basketball. My mother was adamantly against this pursuit. When I telephoned her to let her know that I was going to go out for the team she said, "Son, you don't need to play basketball. You have much better things to do than chase a basketball up and down the court." I could see her logic given my first year of academic probation. But my mother failed to understand the attraction of basketball. In retrospect, I was very much like many of the young men of Northeast, except I had been consistently exposed to viable alternatives for mobility other than athletics from a younger age. I made my choices with knowledge about the world that differed from those of the young men of the Northeast Knights.

The third idea motivating my decision to write the book reflexively was my desire to expose my own culpability as a participant within an oppressive structure that influenced young men to pursue mobility through athletics against great odds. I had knowledge of the limited opportunity for mobility through athletics, yet I reinforced this possibility to young men who I believed were merely seeking a measure of hope. I had become swept away in the compelling powers of the structure. I would have a chance to reflect on my contradictory behavior in a very public way through my writings. For me, the story of the Northeast Knights as told from a reflexive perspective is about much more than young men and basketball, but about how institutions limit our view of the world and our perceptions of choice. Furthermore, it is about how even those who are well aware of the long odds can still be compelled to pursue big dreams.

Although my decision to write reflexively might be problematic for some readers, I believe that I have made these choices with a clear understanding of the limits and advantages of ethnography. Indeed, there is no perfect way to share all that one has learned about a particular social world or how the researcher has influenced that social world. In the end, the reader will have to evaluate whether I have satisfactorily achieved my goals.

Notes

Notes to the Preface

1. See Reuben A. Buford May, *Talking at Trena's: Everyday Conversations in an African American Tavern* (New York: NYU Press, 2001).

2. In Georgia, coaches are permitted to coach their teams in summer tournaments and camps in June and July. This is not a permissible practice in some other states.

3. Although there have been books that examine the exploits of high school basketball teams over a season (for instance, Paul Bates's *Vicarious Thrills*, Bill Reynolds's *Fall River Dreams*, Thomas Dygard's *Tournament Upstart*, and Ira Berkow's *The DuSable Panthers*), none of these books constitutes an in-depth sociological examination of a high school basketball team over time. This omission is surprising, given that high school basketball teams have been popular for their production of players drafted directly into the National Basketball Association (NBA), the world's most renowned professional basketball league. Furthermore, the experiences of these players around issues of race, culture, and class continue to be subjects of much popular commentary and debate. Thus, this book injects an analysis of empirical data into the largely impressionistic debate about the role of sports in the lives of black men. Like Todd Boyd and Kenneth L. Shropshire's *Basketball Jones* and Darcy Frey's *The Last Shot*, this book confronts the contradictory issues of black male athletes' participation in sports.

4. See Patricia A. Adler and Peter Adler, *Membership Roles in Field Research* (Newbury Park, CA: Sage, 1987), 34.

5. See Michelle Fine and Lori Weis, "Writing the 'Wrongs' of Fieldwork," *Qualitative Inquiry* 2 (1996): 263.

6. Although some scholars have criticized various forms of reflexive ethnography as self-indulgent naval gazing, I believe it is naval gazing with a sociological eye. It is an eye informed by a "sociological imagination." See C. Wright Mills, *The Sociological Imagination* (New York: Oxford University Press, 1959). Mills argues that sociologists, by using a sociological imagination, should seek to understand the relationship between larger structural issues and the daily problems that confront humans. For Mills a sociological imagination "consists of the capacity to shift from one perspective to another, and in

the process to build an adequate view of a total society and its components" (211). A necessary part of this approach is the researcher's ability to link his or her personal life and scholarly work. In this sense, I have coupled my personal experiences with various sociological theories as a way to lay bare the significance that the sport of basketball can have for young men.

7. The one exception to this rule is within the context of my personal stories about my playing experience. In most cases those individuals who appear in part of my biography were consulted prior to presenting this material.

Notes to the Introduction

1. D. Benson had been a starting point guard for his uncle William Benson's Northeast Knights varsity basketball team. They had an impressive team that year and finished in Georgia's state tournament Elite Eight, the remaining eight teams from the thirty-two teams that begin the state tournament. They have survived two rounds of the best basketball in the state of Georgia. This is impressive enough for most schools to hang banners in their home gymnasiums for having made it that far in the playoffs.

2. For an elaboration of the notion of "respectability," see Elijah Anderson, *Code of the Street* (New York: Norton, 1999).

3. See Harry Edwards, *Sociology of Sport* (Homewood, IL: Dorsey, 1973), 90. Edwards argues that sport in the United States buttresses values of equal opportunity and mobility through a "Dominant American Sports Creed." This creed has seven major tenets: (1) character development, (2) discipline, (3) competition; (4) physical fitness, (5) mental fitness, (6) religiosity, and (7) nationalism. In general, these ideas reinforce American values. For a detailed discussion of this creed, see Edwards, *Sociology of Sport*, 103–130.

4. Howard Nixon, *Sport and the American Dream* (New York: Leisure Press, 1984), 25.

5. For a discussion of the sports-enhances-mobility and sports-impedes-mobility perspectives, see Wilbert Leonard II, *Sociological Perspective of Sport*, 6th ed. (Boston: Allyn and Bacon, 2007). According to Leonard, the common view is the perception that sports enhances mobility. Indeed many of the young men with whom I worked could offer a variety of cases of individuals who experienced "rags-to-riches" success through basketball.

6. See John Hoberman, *Darwin's Athletes: How Sport Has Damaged Black America and Preserved the Myth of Race* (Boston: Houghton Mifflin, 1997); and Jon Entine, *Taboo: Why Black Athletes Dominate Sports and Why We Are Afraid to Talk about It* (New York: Public Affairs, 2000).

Notes to Chapter I

1. U.S. Census Bureau, http://www.census.gov.

2. For a discussion of the kinds of social factors that have transformed low-income neighborhoods into violent communities, see William Julius Wilson, *The Truly Disadvantaged* (Chicago: University of Chicago Press, 1987).

3. Although there are some blacks in the upper middle class, their numbers are few. They are prominent families in Northeast who have established themselves in professions that include medicine, law, dentistry, and auto sales.

4. According to 1999 figures, a family of four with a total income under $17,029 is considered below poverty. See Daniel Weinberg, "Press Briefing on 1999 Income and Poverty Estimates," Housing and Household Economic Statistics Division, United States Census Bureau, September 26, 2000. Although one-third of the families live in poverty, there are many more families whose children attend Northeast High School that make up what William Julius Wilson has discussed as the working poor. That is, they are families who make enough money to live above the poverty line but in fact struggle to live, oftentimes sacrificing bare necessities like health care. For a discussion of the working poor, see William Julius Wilson, *When Work Disappears: The World of the New Urban Poor* (New York: Knopf, 1996).

5. In 2003 Georgia's students statewide ranked fiftieth in national standardized testing averages. Consequently, poor educational achievement and testing continue to be central issues in Georgia politics.

6. In 2000 alone there were six bomb threats telephoned to the school's main office. These threats raised much concern among Northeast's students, teachers, and parents in light of the Columbine, Colorado, school massacre. In the Columbine high school shootings two disgruntled students, Dylan Klebold and Eric Harris, entered their high school, detonated homemade bombs, and fired an assortment of semiautomatic weapons at classmates and teachers. After the April 20, 1999, massacre thirteen were dead, several were wounded, and Klebold and Harris had committed suicide. The entire ordeal was videotaped on school surveillance cameras. The fact that these shootings took place in small-town America raised national consciousness about school safety, troubled youth, and the efficacy of law enforcement to respond to such events.

7. Presumably both Latinos and blacks felt the need to tighten allegiance along racial and ethnic lines. The Latinos represent a threat to the traditional role of blacks in Northeast's menial-labor work force. Yet the high segregation of low-income areas in Northeast prevents a great deal of interethnic conflict. For a discussion of the bonding of ethnic groups in the face of external threats by outside minorities, see Gerald Suttles, *The Social Order of the Slum: Ethnicity and Territory in the Inner City* (Chicago: University of Chicago Press, 1968).

8. According to Georgia High School Association rules preseason condi-

tioning can start a week before basketball practice. During that week the coaches are allowed to do conditioning but are not permitted to use basketballs. Some young men only came out for the team once they discovered that we had begun to do drills using basketballs.

9. Because Coach Benson grew up in the Eastridge area and his family was originally from Northeast, he had several family members throughout the city. Although he had only four nephews play for him, Coach Benson also claimed young men as distant cousins or fictive kin—those without actual blood relationships. Thus, beyond the nephews that played for him, it was difficult to know which people throughout Northeast were actually Coach Benson's blood relatives. In reality, it mattered little whether these family members were blood relatives, because Coach Benson took responsibility for their well-being. For a discussion of fictive kinships and their function within many black communities, see Carol Stack, *All Our Kin: Strategies for Survival in a Black Community* (New York: Harper and Row, 1974).

10. This was not an uncommon occurrence within Northeast, in particular, in the low-income areas. In this regard, areas like Eastridge in Northeast were like other low-income areas in cities across the United States with high rates of teen pregnancy and families composed of children who do not share the same parents.

11. In my first year as an assistant coach I volunteered. In my second year the school district approved compensation for "community" or "lay" coach—my official job title. I received $800. By my last two years of coaching I was compensated $3,000 per season. Although I was appreciative of the pay, my main motivation for participation with the team was my love of basketball. Ultimately, my annual compensation was little more than a bonus that I gave to my family to atone for spending so many hours away from them during basketball season.

Notes to Chapter 2

1. For a discussion of this topic, see Joseph J. Gruber, "Comparison of Relationships among Team Cohesion Scores and Measures of Team Success in Male Varsity Basketball Teams," *International Review of Sport Sociology* 16 (1981): 43–56.

2. For instance, William W. Clohesy, in a discussion of altruism points out, "When we act for another's welfare, then we are actually seeking our own satisfaction. . . . all aid to another is explainable as a desire for self-gratification through ensuring the other's good." See William W. Clohesy, "Altruism and the Endurance of the Good," *Voluntas: International Journal of Voluntary and Nonprofit Organizations* 11 (2000): 240. Thus, Coach Benson's motivations may be grounded in his need to see the young men survive.

3. An underlying assumption about those who compete in sport is that the majority of competitors do so because they enjoy playing. Some people choose to play informal games if organized competition is not an option. It seems that several of the nonessential players on the Northeast Knights, had Coach Benson made cuts, would have had to compete in informal pickup basketball games if they wanted to compete in basketball at all. Still, such competitors would seek to have optimal enjoyment from this activity. For an interesting discussion of wealth-maximizing norms and pickup basketball, see Jason Jimerson, "Good Times and Good Games: How Pickup Basketball Players Use Wealth-Maximizing Norms," *Journal of Contemporary Ethnography* 25(3) (1996): 353–371.

4. Brooke Harrington and Gary A. Fine have suggested that understanding small-group interaction is useful for understanding ways in which culture is created, networks formed, and social order made concrete. It is within the context of interacting small groups that important theoretical and conceptual tools are elaborated. See Brooke Harrington and Gary A. Fine, "Opening the 'Black Box': Small Groups and Twenty-First-Century Sociology," *Social Psychology Quarterly* 63 (2000): 312–323.

5. Gary A. Fine, *With the Boys* (Chicago: University of Chicago Press, 1987), 125. The notion of idioculture is particularly useful for understanding small groups like a boys' high school basketball team because it allows specification of group cultures, facilitates group comparison, identifies the relationship between environment and action, and exposes the diffusion of culture into societies and subsocieties (ibid., 126). In this chapter I employ the notion of idioculture to identify elements present that allow altruism to exist.

6. See ibid., 131.

7. According to the Centers for Disease Control, ADHD is a "neurobehavioral disorder characterized by pervasive inattention and/or hyperactivity-impulsivity and resulting in significant functional impairment." These levels of inattention and hyperactivity-impulsivity compromise an individual's ability to function. It is estimated that nearly 4.5 million youths from ages four to seventeen have been diagnosed with ADHD and currently receive medication treatment. For more information, see the Centers for Disease Control and Prevention, "Attention-Deficit/Hyperactivity Disorder," http://www.cdc.gov/ncbddd/adhd/.

8. See Fine, *With the Boys*, 134.

9. See Reuben A. Buford May, "Of Mice, Rats, and Men: Exploring the Role of Rodents in Constructing Masculinity within a Group of Young African American Males," *Qualitative Sociology* 27 (2004): 159–178.

10. My metaphorical analysis of the structure of basketball teams is generally informed by my reading of literature in the area of population ecology (PE), the study of how environmental conditions and interactions shape or-

ganizations. For a general discussion of the ideas that influence my analysis from population ecology, see Hannan and Freeman 1977. Some applications of PE are concerned with, for example, the founding of new organizations within competitive markets (Hannan and Freeman 1984, 1986), the termination of organizations that could not effectively compete within a designated population (Freeman, Carroll, and Hannan 1983; Freeman and Hannan 1983), and the study of processes that create and erode boundaries between organizations (Hannan and Freeman 1986).

Despite its popularity, scholars have also criticized PE. For instance, see Astley 1985; Young 1988; and Carroll and Hannan 2000. Others have concluded that PE is an altogether inadequate means of examining organizational structure and change. For instance, see Pfeffer 1997.

Although PE has received much criticism, it continues to be a functional means of articulating internal and external organizational structure and change. It has been used recently to illustrate ways in which internal processes inhibit organizational change (Molinsky 1999); to evaluate the spatial density and dependence of organizations (Greve 2002); to distinguish characteristics of organizations that escape isomorphic pressure (Lune and Martinez 1999); and to explain spatial dynamics of states, groups, and world-systems (Turchin and Hall 2003). PE has proven applicable to a number of diverse organizational structures and populations. I adopt elements of population ecology in an effort to explicate an idioculture on which the organizational practice of altruism in team selection is based.

11. One of the difficulties in organizational ecology is determining which organizations should be included within a specific population (Carroll and Harrison 1994). For the sake of discussion it seems appropriate to limit this particular organizational environment to the twelve teams that play one another in the Knights' region. However, I make reference throughout the discussion to various teams that play outside the Knights' region. Given the fact that these schools fall under the Georgia High School Association rules that are adopted from the National Federation of High School Associations, a collection of teams that includes most high school teams across the country could arguably be an accurate grouping as well.

12. The Northeast Knights' no-cut policy inhibits efficiency and productivity in a practical sense and threatens the viability of the team. This approach is unlike that used by business organizations that are concerned with matters like efficiency and productivity. For instance, most organizations have individuals who are focused on achieving the stated goals of the organization. In some instances, an organization may have a nonessential individual who contributes little to the organization's efforts to achieve its goals. Organizational leadership attempts to devise ways to eliminate nonessential individuals who render the organization inefficient to compete within its competitive

environment or else risk deterioration of their organization. For a discussion of this topic, see John Freeman and Michael T. Hannan, "Niche Width and the Dynamics of Organizational Populations," *American Journal of Sociology* 88 (1983): 1116–1145; and John Freeman, Glenn R. Carroll, and Michael T. Hannan, "The Liability of Newness: Age Dependence in Organizational Death Rates," *American Sociological Review* 48 (1983): 692–710.

13. Here, the Northeast Knights are much like a business organization that has an impact on what other organizations view as a particularly effective organizational model. See Michael T. Hannan and Glenn R. Carroll, *Dynamics of Organizational Populations: Density, Legitimation, and Competition* (New York: Oxford University Press, 1992).

14. In the organizational literature this is often referred to as "isomorphism." For a discussion of isomorphism, see W. Richard Scott, *Organizations: Rational, Natural, and Open Systems*, 3d ed. (Englewood Cliffs, NJ: Prentice-Hall, 1992).

Notes to Chapter 3

1. Hot Boys, "I Need a Hot Girl," *Guerilla Warfare*, Cash Money Records, Copyright 1999.

2. There have been many studies about the drug and alcohol use of both high school and college athletes. Generally, it has been found that athletes are less likely to engage in drug and alcohol use than nonathletes, but these findings may vary by region, country, or choice of drug. For a discussion of the various patterns of high school and college athlete drug and alcohol use, see Adam Naylor, Doug Gardner, and Len Zaichkowsky, "Drug Use Patterns among High School Athletes and Nonathletes," *Adolescence* 36(144) (2001): 627–639; K. M. Hildebrand, D. J. Johnson, and K. Bogle, "Comparison of Patterns of Alcohol Use between High School and College Athletes and Non-Athletes," *College Student Journal* 35(3) (2001): 358–365; F. Donato et al., "Alcohol Consumption among High School Students and Young Athletes in North Italy," *Revue d'epidemiologie et de sante publique* 42(3) (1994): 198–206; E. W. Shields Jr., "Relative Likelihood of In-Season and Off-Season Use of Alcohol by High School Athletes in North Carolina: Trends and Current Status," *Journal of Alcohol and Drug Education* 43(2) (1998): 48–63; and C. N. Carr, S. R. Kennedy, and K. M. Dimick, "Alcohol Use among High School Athletes: A Comparison of Alcohol Use and Intoxication in Male and Female High School Athletes and Non-Athletes," *Journal of Alcohol and Drug Education* 36(1) (1990): 39–43.

3. Elijah Anderson, *Code of the Street* (New York: Norton, 1999), 29–30.

4. According to several studies, blacks have higher rates of criminal violence than whites and Latinos because blacks are more likely to live in areas

with higher rates of concentrated disadvantage (e.g., heightened levels of poverty, male joblessness, female-headed families, and few professional/managerial role models). For a discussion of this topic, see Robert Sampson, Jeffrey Morenoff, and Stephen Raudenbush, "Social Anatomy of Racial and Ethnic Disparities in Violence," *American Journal of Public Health* 95 (2005): 224–232; Maria B. Velez, "Toward an Understanding of the Lower Rates of Homicide in Latino versus Black Neighborhoods," pp. 91–107 in *The Many Colors of Crime*, edited by Ruth Peterson, Lauren Krivo, and John Hagan (New York: NYU Press, 2006); Robert Sampson and William Julius Wilson, "Toward a Theory of Race, Crime, and Urban Inequality," pp. 37–54 in *Crime and Inequality*, edited by John Hagan and Ruth Peterson (Stanford, CA: Stanford University Press, 1995); and Robert Crutchfield, Ross L. Matsueda, and Devin Drakulich, "Race, Labor Markets, and Neighborhood Violence," pp. 199–220 in *The Many Colors of Crime*, edited by Ruth Peterson, Lauren Krivo, and John Hagan (New York: NYU Press, 2006).

5. *Hustle & Flow*, starring Terrence Howard, Anthony Anderson, and Taryn Manning, was directed and written by Craig Brewer and produced by John Singleton for Paramount Pictures, 2005.

6. David's academic motivation made it less likely that he would engage in drug or alcohol use in high school than if he had not focused on academics. For a discussion of the link between educational motivation and drug use among black adolescents, see Marc A. Zimmerman and Karen H. Schmeelk-Cone, "A Longitudinal Analysis of Adolescent Substance Use and School Motivation among African American Youth," *Journal of Research on Adolescence* 13(2) (2003): 185–211.

7. The disproportionate arrest and imprisonment rates of black males for drug sales have been the subject of many studies. There is frequent debate about the sources of these divergent rates. See, for instance, Debra Small, "The War on Drugs Is a War on Racial Justice," *Social Research* 68(3) (2001): 896–903; Michael Tonry, "Racial Disparities, and the War on Crime," *Crime and Delinquency* 40 (1994): 475–494; J. Knowles, "Racial Bias in Motor Vehicle Searches: Theory and Evidence," *Journal of Political Economy* 109(1) (2001): 203–229; and Erich Goode, "Drug Arrests at the Millennium," *Society* 39(5) (2002): 41–45.

8. The racial profiling of African American males has been recognized as problematic within many law enforcement agencies throughout the United States. Given the exposure of such practices against African Americans there has been a wide variety of policies implemented in an attempt to curb such profiling. For discussions of the various ways that racial profiling affects African American males, see Amg Harris, "Courting Customers: Assessing Consumer Racial Profiling and Other Marketplace Discrimination," *Journal of Public Policy and Marketing* 24(1) (2005): 163–171; Richard Lundman, "Driver Race, Ethnicity, and Gender and Citizen Reports of Vehicle Searches by Police and

Vehicle Search Hits: Toward a Triangulated Scholarly Understanding," *Journal of Criminal Law and Criminology* 94(2) (2004): 309–349; David Fasenfest, "Enforcement Mechanisms Discouraging Black-American Presence in Suburban Detroit," *International Journal of Urban and Regional Research* 29(4) (2005): 960–971; Robin Engel and Jennifer Calnon, "Examining the Influence of Driver's Characteristics during Traffic Stops with Police: Results from a National Survey," *Justice Quarterly* 21(1) (2004): 49–91.

9. For a discussion of the ways in which class might buffer blacks from discrimination, see Joe Feagin and Melvin Sikes, *Living with Racism: The Black Middle-Class Experience* (Boston: Beacon, 1994).

10. For a discussion of parents' influence on children's substance use, see Li Chaoyang, Mary Ann Pentz, and Chou Chih-Ping, "Parental Substance Use as a Modifier of Adolescent Substance Use Risk," *Addiction* 97(12) (2002): 1537–1551.

11. This is consistent with the assessment of Li et al. See ibid.

12. High school athletes often turn to over-the-counter weight-gain aids. For a discussion of the use of such aids, see Naylor, Gardner, and Zaichkowsky, "Drug Use Patterns."

13. Anderson, *Code of the Street,* 114.

14. For a discussion of the ways that affirmation of young men's delinquent behavior continues to have consequences for how masculinity is defined, see Cooper Thompston, "A New Vision of Masculinity," pp. 205–211 in *New Men, New Minds,* edited by Franklin Abbot (Freedom, CA: Crossing, 1987).

15. Students are required to attend a high school based on their home address and the school's geographic location. If they move before they begin school their freshman year, then they are permitted to enroll in the cross-town school. Because Shamar lived on the border between Northeast and Ford Heights, he was permitted to select either one. He simply registered at Northeast as a new student since he had not generated grades at Ford Heights.

Notes to Chapter 4

1. There are volumes of research on the relationship between race and athletic superiority. Oftentimes the findings of these studies of athletic differences across groups is dependent on the author's ideological bent. For a detailed discussion of various research, see Jon Entine, *Taboo: Why Black Athletes Dominate Sports and Why We Are Afraid to Talk about It* (New York: Public Affairs, 2000).

2. Despite changes in the ways in which black male athletes are represented by mass media, there continues to be an implicitly communicated "climate of differentiation" that exists. The differences most frequently identified

include the purported differences between blacks' and whites' athletic ability. For a discussion of media representation of black athletes, see Bryan E. Denham, Andrew C. Billings, and Kelby K. Halone, "Differential Accounts of Race in Broadcast Commentary of the 2000 NCAA Men's and Women's Final Four Basketball Tournaments," *Sociology of Sport Journal* 19 (2002): 315–332; and Daniel Buffington, "Contesting Race on Sundays: Making Meaning Out of the Rise in Black Quarterbacks," *Sociology of Sport Journal* 22(1) (2005): 12–19.

3. These stereotypes persist. For a discussion of such stereotypical representations of blacks, see Linda Tucker, "Blackballed: Basketball and Representations of the Black Male Athlete," *American Behavioral Scientist* 47(3) (2003): 306–328.

4. John Hoberman is especially cognizant of the ways in which blacks and their racial identity within sport are socially constructed. Indeed, throughout this book, and particularly in this chapter, I designate race as an unproblematic identifier for visible physical characteristics. This approach is based on my understanding that, for those individuals from Northeast involved in day-to-day interactions, the designations of white and black are simple and bear real consequences. See John Hoberman, *Darwin's Athletes: How Sport Has Damaged Black America and Preserved the Myth of Race* (Boston: Houghton Mifflin, 1997), chapter 12.

5. Some scholars have suggested that media representation of black athletes builds on the notion of the superior black athlete. Thus, black youths become preoccupied with the celebrity of superiority. But media presentations of the black athlete are interpreted differently by various communities. These "interpretive communities" are based on the cultural differences, social locations, and racial identities of the viewers. For a discussion of the ways in which interpretive communities shape individuals' views of representations of the black athlete, see Brian Wilson and Robert Sparks, " 'It's Gotta Be the Shoes': Youth, Race, and Sneaker Commercials," *Sociology of Sport Journal* 13 (1996): 398–427.

6. The designation of "athletic" is meant to refer to an individual who is born with physical ability that, in and of itself, distinguishes them with potential above the masses. Three elements seem to be frequently referenced as constituting natural athletes: speed, agility, and leaping ability. Thus, I interpret beliefs that black athletes are more athletic than white athletes to suggest that blacks as a group, when compared to whites as a group, are more likely to possess greater natural talent with regard to speed, agility, and leaping ability.

"Skill," on the other hand, is meant to indicate those sport-specific abilities that can be honed through repetitive practice. Skill is typically not associated with one's born athletic ability. For instance, an individual's ability to shoot the basketball has very little to do with natural attributes like the potential for speed, but more to do with constant practice using the proper technique. Although natural ability—for instance, leaping ability—can be built on through repetitive weight training, there still remains a threshold beyond which weaker leapers cannot transgress, even with constant training. Essentially, each individual is born with so much potential, and once the potential is reached, the athlete cannot move beyond it (except, of course, with performance-enhancing drugs, which continue to be a source of controversy in sports). The most effective athletes in basketball are those who are able to combine natural ability (i.e., athleticism) that has been refined through training with fundamental skills (e.g., shooting) that have been honed through practice. Michael Jordan could not only leap in the air and do acrobatic moves to the basket (athleticism), but he was also a proficient shooter (skill). Beyond athleticism and skill there are also important personality traits for those athletes that are considered elite. These notions of athleticism and skill are concepts that individuals employ as they consider the relationship between race and athletic ability.

7. "Bird: NBA 'a Black Man's Game,' " ESPN.com, http://sports.espn.go .com/nba/news/story?id=1818396.

8. Race and social class are greatly intertwined when it comes to residential patterns in the United States. For a discussion of the ways in which race figures keenly in residential patterns, see Douglas S. Massey and Nancy A. Denton, *American Apartheid: Segregation and the Making of the Underclass* (Cambridge, MA: Harvard University Press, 1993).

9. For an examination of the historical patterns of racial violence in the South, see Stewart E. Tolnay and E. M. Beck, *A Festival of Violence: An Analysis of Southern Lynchings, 1882–1930* (Urbana: University of Illinois Press, 1995). Additionally, the pictorial collection of lynchings in the South compiled by James Allen brings a visual reality to these horrendous acts. See James Allen, *Without Sanctuary: Lynching Photography in America* (Santa Fe, NM: Twin Palms, 2000).

10. For a discussion of the ways in which negative racial encounters are reified through race talk, see Reuben A. Buford May, *Talking at Trena's: Everyday Conversations at an African American Tavern* (New York: NYU Press, 2001), chapter 4.

11. For a discussion of this notion, see Entine, *Taboo*.

12. The young men's understanding of racial identity in their lives is concerned with only the socially constructed nature of race. That is, they understand that because they are identified by others as black, they may be treated differently. However, this understanding also comes with the belief that, in reality, they are no less human or American than any other individual.

Notes to Chapter 5

1. For a description of the characteristics of a man in the United States, see E. Anthony Rotundo, *American Manhood: Transformations in Masculinity from the Revolution to the Modern Era* (New York: Basic Books, 1993).

2. For a discussion of the idea of "doing gender," see Candace West and Don Zimmerman, "Doing Gender," *Gender and Society* 1 (1987): 125–151. "Doing gender involves a complex of socially guided perceptual, interactional, and micropolitical activities that cast particular pursuits as expressions of masculine and feminine natures" (126).

3. For a discussion of social perceptions of men and women, see John Berger, *Ways of Seeing* (New York: Penguin Books, 1977).

4. For a discussion of the economic changes over time that have helped define masculinity in the United States, see Rotundo, *American Manhood*.

5. For a discussion of the emphasis on material wealth as a means of enacting masculinity, see Geoff Mann, "What's a Penny Worth? Wages, Prices, and the American Working Man," *Ethnography* 6(3) (2005): 315–355; Dana Nelson, *National Manhood: Capitalist Citizenship and Imagined Fraternity of White Men* (Durham, NC: Duke University Press, 1998); and Robert W. Connell, *Masculinities* (Berkeley: University of California Press, 1995).

6. According to Ann Lombard, this notion of male independence and economic dominance was supported by the work of women. Lombard states, "This ideal of male independence was in some sense built on a fiction, because a substantial part of men's fortunes (and the authority that flowed from them) rested on the hard work, frugality, and trustworthiness of their wives." Ann Lombard, *Making Manhood: Growing Up Male in Colonial New England* (Cambridge, MA: Harvard University Press, 2003), 5.

7. For a discussion of the ways in which African American males negotiate racial and gender identity, see Lennell Dade and Lloyd Sloan, "An Investigation of Sex-Role Stereotypes in African Americans," *Journal of Black Studies* 30 (2000): 676–690; and Ian Harris, Jose Torres, and Dale Allender, "The Responses of African American Men to Dominant Norms of Masculinity within the United States," *Sex Roles* 31 (1994): 703–719.

8. See, for example, Beverly I. Fagot and Mary D. Leinbach, "The Young Child's Gender Schema: Environmental Input, Internal Organization," *Child Development* 60 (1989): 663–672; Beverly I. Fagot, "Peer Relations and the Development of Competence in Boys and Girls," *New Directions for Child Development* 65 (1994): 53–66; and IngBeth Larsson and Carl Goran Svedin, "Teachers' and Parents' Reports on 3- to 6-Year-Old Children's Sexual Behavior—A Comparison," *Child Abuse and Neglect: The International Journal* 26(3) (2002): 247–266.

9. For thorough discussions about the constructed nature of gender and

other categories, see for example Judith Lorber, *Paradoxes of Gender* (New Haven, CT: Yale University Press, 1994); Connell, *Masculinities*; and Robert W. Connell, *The Men and the Boys* (Berkeley: University of California Press, 2000).

10. For a discussion of how hegemonic masculinity flows from the culture of societies, see Connell, *Masculinities*.

11. Gary A. Fine, in his analysis of preadolescent boys' baseball found that when a player is injured, "extreme pain is recognized as so debilitating that loud complaints and even request to be removed from the game can be legitimate." Gary A. Fine, *With the Boys: Little League Baseball and Preadolescent Culture* (Chicago: University of Chicago Press, 1987), 89. In some instances, it is therefore possible for a male to acknowledge pain and maintain the impression of manliness.

12. For a discussion of games of one-upmanship, see Reuben A. Buford May, *Talking at Trena's: Everyday Conversations at an African American Tavern* (New York: NYU Press), chapter 6.

13. For a discussion of this topic, see Patricia Hill Collins, *Black Sexual Politics: African Americans, Gender, and the New Racism* (New York: Routledge, 2004).

14. The research on heterosexuals' attitudes toward gays varies across context and several dimensions. For instance, Charles Negy found that African Americans had slightly higher homophobia and homonegativity scores than whites, but there was little difference between the two groups when controlling for church attendance. Charles Negy, "A Comparison of African American and White College Students' Affective and Attitudinal Reactions to Lesbian, Gay, and Bisexual Individuals: An Exploratory Study," *Journal of Sex Research* 42(4) (2005): 291–298. In some instances, researchers have found that those respondents who attribute homosexuality to choice have stronger negative attitudes about gays than those who believe homosexuality is beyond the individual's control. For a discussion, see Gregory Herek, "Black Heterosexuals' Attitudes toward Lesbians and Gay Men in the United States," *Journal of Sex Research* 32(2) (1995): 95–105. Furthermore, blacks' attitudes toward homosexuals vary by demographic characteristics like age, income, and education. For a discussion, see Anthony Lemelle Jr. and Juan Battle, "Black Masculinity Matters in Attitudes toward Gay Males," *Journal of Homosexuality* 47(1) (2004): 39–51. Consistent across studies is the finding that religiosity is the best predictor of negative attitudes toward gays, irrespective of race. For a discussion, see Lisa Schulte and Juan Battle, "The Relative Importance of Ethnicity and Religion in Predicting Attitudes towards Gays and Lesbians," *Journal of Homosexuality* 47(2) (2004): 127–142.

15. See Negy, "Comparison of African American and White College Students' Affective and Attitudinal Reactions."

16. For the young men, the acceptability of Christianity as a common

foundation was demonstrated by the fact that no players objected to Coach Benson's pregame requests for the recitation of The Lord's Prayer. Rather, most of the players and coaches recited the prayer in unison. Those who did not recite the prayer were permitted to stand in silence. One player, white and Jewish, was the only one I noted over the seven years that did not recite the prayer.

Additionally, one year, before we departed for a tournament in Florida, the players met at the school, and then as a group we traveled to an 8:00 a.m. church service at a community Baptist church. During the church service the minister acknowledged the team's presence and then prayed for safe travel to the tournament.

For a discussion of the relationship between race, religion, and region, see Robert Taylor, Jacqueline Mattis, and Linda Chatters, "Subjective Religiosity among African Americans: A Synthesis of Findings from Five National Samples," *Journal of Black Psychology* 25(4) (1999): 524–543. For a discussion of racial differences in religiosity and health, see Luisa Franzini, "Religion, Sociodemographic and Personal Characteristics, and Self-Reported Health in Whites, Blacks, and Hispanics Living in Low-Socioeconomic Status Neighborhoods," *Ethnicity and Disease* 15(3) (2005): 469–484.

17. Despite the fact that these young men speak negatively about others who are homosexual, it is quite possible that they themselves have had homosexual thoughts or fantasies. For a discussion of this topic, see Nathaniel McConaghy, Neil Buhrich, and Derrick Silove, "Opposite Sex-Linked Behaviors and Homosexual Feelings in the Predominantly Heterosexual Male Majority," *Archives of Sexual Behavior* 23 (1994): 565–577. D. L. King has suggested that even those black men who have engaged in same-sex acts do not view themselves as homosexuals. For a discussion of this issue, see J. L. King with Karen Hunter, *On the Down Low: A Journey into the Lives of "Straight" Black Men Who Sleep with Men* (New York: Broadway Books, 2004).

18. "Facework" is the overall impression management that individuals engage in as they move through their everyday lives. For a discussion of facework, see Ervin Goffman, *Interaction Ritual: Essays in Face-to-Face Behavior* (Chicago: Aldine, 1967).

19. In the context of everyday living, men have had to fight just so that they would not be preyed upon. Thus, Meshaq's response is one of defense. It is consistent with making the overall transition into manhood. For an account of fighting as a socialization process, see G. Canada, "Learning to Fight," pp. 100–103 in *Men's Lives*, edited by M. Kimmel and M. Messner (Boston: Allyn and Bacon, 2001). For a discussion of other ways in which men negotiate masculinity in various contexts, see Michael Messner, *Politics of Masculinities: Men in Movements* (Thousand Oaks, CA: Sage, 1997); Michael A. Messner and Donald F. Sabo, *Sex, Violence and Power in Sports: Rethinking Masculinity* (Freedom,

CA: Crossing, 1994); and Michael A. Messner, *Power at Play: Sports and the Problem of Masculinity* (Boston: Beacon, 1992).

20. For an exploration of the nature of the status that high school athletes have, see H. G. Bissinger, *Friday Night Lights: A Town, a Team, and a Dream* (New York: Addison-Wesley, 1990).

21. Unlike the preadolescent boys that Gary Fine discusses, the young men of the Northeast Knights find that girls are a key component of their social lives. See Fine, *With the Boys.*

22. The Georgia High School Association has five classifications for athletic competition. Each school is generally assigned to a classification based on the number of students attending the school. Northeast High School competes in the 4A classification, and Forest County competes in the 2A classification.

23. Forest County has one of the highest rates of teen pregnancy and of female, single-headed households in the state of Georgia. See Gordon R. Freymann, James L. Tobias, and Michael A. Coletta, *A Decade of Change: The Demographic Atlas of Georgia 1990 and 2000* (Atlanta: Georgia Division of Public Health, 2002).

24. See "Where's Daddy?" *Sports Illustrated*, April 29, 1998.

25. *Two Can Play That Game*, starring Vivica Fox and Morris Chestnut, directed by Dennis Brown, and released by Sony Pictures, 2004; and *Breakin' All the Rules*, starring Jamie Foxx and Gabrielle Union, directed by Daniel Taplitz, and released by Sony Pictures, 2004.

26. Released by Shady Records/Aftermath Records and produced by Dr. Dre, Eminem, and D. Porter in 2003.

27. For a discussion of hip-hop music and misogyny, see Terri Adams, "The Words Have Changed but the Ideology Remains the Same—Misogynistic Lyrics in Rap Music," *Journal of Black Studies* 36(6) (2006): 938–957; and Edward Armstrong, "Gangsta Misogyny: A Content Analysis of the Portrayals of Violence against Women in Rap Music, 1987–1993," *Journal of Criminal Justice and Popular Culture* 8(2) (2001): 96–126.

28. The Northeast Knights' view of sex is consistent with the views of boys from various backgrounds. For a discussion of how adolescents' views of sexuality have changed over the past three decades, see Marita P. McCabe and Robert A. Cummins, "Sexuality and the Quality of Life among Young People," *Adolescence* 33 (1998): 761–773.

29. The Knights' idiocultural emphasis on sexual encounters with girls is consistent with black male sexual-intercourse patterns found by Kara Joyner and Edward Laumann. In an analysis of national data they found that being a black male about tripled the odds that one would have heterosexual intercourse before the age of eighteen. For a discussion of these findings, see Kara Joyner and Edward Laumann, "Teenage Sex and the Sexual Revolution," pp. 41–71 in *Sex, Love and Health in America: Private Choices and Public Policies,*

edited by Edward Laumann and Robert T. Michael (Chicago: University of Chicago Press, 2001). The differences between girls' and boys' attitudes suggest that sex is an important part of how boys establish masculine identities, whereas girls feel that they should avoid sexual activity. For a discussion of the differences in adolescent sexual attitudes, see Ronald Werner-Wilson, "Gender Differences in Adolescent Sexual Attitudes: The Influence of Individual and Family Factors," *Adolescence* 33 (1998): 519–531; and Laura Carpenter, *Virginity Lost: An Intimate Portrait of First Sexual Experiences* (New York: NYU Press, 2005).

30. For a discussion of this topic, see Lisa Jepson, Linda Juszczak, and Martin Fisher, "Mental Health Care in a High School Based Health Service," *Adolescence* 33 (1998): 1–15.

31. "The Place" was the name of a nightclub a mile from the high school. It was rented out to various individuals each week and patronized mostly by blacks aged eighteen and up. Occasionally, special high school parties were thrown there. The party that Turo mentions was thrown by one of the football coaches at Northeast, Coach Skye. Over the span of several months The Place had developed a notorious reputation for fights. College students from Big South University were always quick to point out that they hated to go to The Place because the "locals" were always fighting. Ultimately, it was shut down after about a year because of the constant fights—a few of which ended in stabbings or gun shots being fired.

32. There are a variety of social settings where young women feel that they are not, or in fact are not, in control of their surroundings. In such situations, sexual acts, either consensual or nonconsensual, can occur. For a discussion of sexual decision-making factors for young women, see Susan L. Rosenthal, Lisa Lewis, and Sheila S. Cohen, "Issues Related to the Sexual Decision-Making of Inner-City Adolescent Girls," *Adolescence* 31 (1996): 731–739.

33. One study suggests that this pattern holds true for adolescents in interracial romantic relationships. That is, interracial couples are less likely than intraracial couples to exhibit public and private displays of affection but do not differ from intraracial couples in intimate displays of affection. For a discussion of this topic, see Elizabeth Vaquera and Grace Kao, "Private and Public Displays of Affection among Interracial and Intra-Racial Adolescent Couples," *Social Science Quarterly* 86(2) (2005): 484–508.

34. For a discussion of the relationship between the quality of interracial relationships and the support of those relationships by significant others, see Hongyu Wang, Grace Kao, and Kara Joyner, "Stability of Interracial and Intraracial Romantic Relationships among Adolescents," *Social Science Research* 35(2) (2006): 435–453; and Justin Lehmiller and Christopher Agnew, "Marginalized Relationships: The Impact of Social Disapproval on Romantic Relation-

ship Commitment," *Personality and Social Psychology Bulletin* 32(1) (2006): 40–51.

35. For a discussion of characteristics of individuals who participate in interracial relationship as a measure of broader race relations, see George Yancey, "Who Interracially Dates? An Examination of the Characteristics of Those Who Have Interracially Dated," *Journal of Comparative Family Studies* 33(2) (2002): 179–190.

36. A 1985 study based on a convenience sample of college students from one Midwestern university found that 59 percent of the white females surveyed had performed fellatio before college, whereas only 22 percent of the black females surveyed had done so. These findings, although based on a limited sample, would seem to support the stereotype held by the young men of the Northeast Knights. See Philip Belcastro, "Sexual Behavior Differences between Black and White Students," *Journal of Sex Research* 21(1) (1985): 56–67. Additionally, a 1994 study based on a national sample of individuals aged eighteen to fifty-nine found that 18.2 percent of the white females surveyed found giving oral sex "very appealing," whereas only 7.6 percent of the black females surveyed did. See Edward Laumann, John Gagnon, Robert Michael, and Stuart Michaels, *The Social Organization of Sexuality: Sexual Practices in the United States* (Chicago: University of Chicago Press, 1994). This study also seems to support the young men's idea that white women are more willing to engage in fellatio than their black counterparts.

37. "Down low" connotes keeping one's illicit homosexual affairs "down low," or out of sight. Interestingly, there are many men who engage in the "down low" behavior that do not consider themselves closet homosexuals; rather, they consider themselves heterosexual men who enjoy sex with other men. This conceptualization of sexual behavior, typically described as bisexual by outsiders, demonstrates the intensity with which black males are expected to defend heterosexuality as a key requirement for masculinity. For a discussion of "down low" behavior, see King with Hunter, *On the Down Low*.

38. For a discussion of the ways in which these young men use rodents as a means of demonstrating this courage, see Reuben A. Buford May, "Of Mice, Rats, and Men: Exploring the Role of Rodents in Constructing Masculinity within a Group of Young African American Males," *Qualitative Sociology* 27(2) (2004): 159–177.

Notes to Chapter 6

1. Technical fouls are usually given to players whose behavior is perceived as unsportsmanlike. This behavior includes excessive rough play, use of profanity, taunting, or fighting. These behaviors have been the subject of

much social commentary because within the interpretation of the rules regarding sportsmanship are embedded important racial and cultural elements that grate against institutional rules. For a discussion of these challenges, see Herbert D. Simons, "Race and Penalized Sports Behavior," *International Review for the Sociology of Sport* 38(1) (2003): 5–22.

2. For a discussion of these ideas, see F. Bockrath and E. Franke, "Is There Any Value in Sports? About the Ethical Significance of Sport Activities," *International Review for the Sociology of Sport* 30(3–4) (1995): 283–310; R. Grough, *Character Is Everything: Promoting Excellence in Sports* (New York: Harcourt Brace, 1997); G. Papp and G. Prisztoka, "Sportsmanship as an Ethical Value," *International Review for the Sociology of Sport* 30(3–4) (1995): 375–389; and G. A. Pilz, "Performance Sport: Education in Fair Play? (Some Empirical and Theoretical Remarks)," *International Review for the Sociology of Sport* 30(3–4) (1995): 391–418.

3. For a discussion of this topic, see D. Stanley Eitzen, "Ethical Problems in American Sport," *Journal of Sport and Social Issues* 12(1) (1988): 28.

4. D. Stanley Eitzen, *Fair and Foul: Beyond the Myths and Paradoxes of Sport* (Boston: Rowman and Littlefield, 1999), 52 (emphasis added).

5. For a discussion of this problem, see G. Ramsey and B. Rank, "Rethinking Youth Sports," *Parks and Recreation* 32(12) (1997): 30–36.

6. For a discussion of these issue, see A. Knoppers, B. B. Meyers, and M. Zuidema, "Playing to Win or Playing to Play?" *Sociology of Sport Journal* 6 (1989): 70–76; D. Shields, B. Bredemeier, D. Gardner, and A. Bostrom, "Leadership, Cohesion, and Team Norms Regarding Cheating and Aggression, *Sociology of Sport Journal* 12 (1995): 324–336; T. Wandzilak, T. Carroll, and C. J. Ansorge, "Values Development through Physical Activity: Promoting Sportsmanlike Behaviors, Perceptions, and Moral Reasoning," *Journal of Teaching in Physical Education* 8(1) (1988): 13–22; K. Volkwein, "Ethics and Top-Level Sport —A Paradox?" *International Review for Sociology of Sport* 30(3–4) (1995): 311–321.

7. Wandzilak, Carroll, and Ansorge, "Values Development through Physical Activity," 15.

8. Ibid.

9. Eitzen, "Ethical Problems in American Sport."

10. See Shields et al., "Leadership, Cohesion," 326.

11. Eitzen, "Ethical Problems in American Sport," 19.

12. The "Old South" refers to a time between the late 1800s and the late 1950s, just after the end of blacks' enslavement and before the dissolution of Jim Crow segregation in the South. At that time, whites' blatant racism and racially motivated attacks against blacks were both commonplace and acceptable. The most violent attacks, in the form of lynch mobs, occurred from 1880 to 1930 in the southern states. Many blacks were lynched at that time. For a

discussion of Old South violence against blacks, see Stewart E. Tolnay and E. M. Beck, *A Festival of Violence: An Analysis of Southern Lynchings, 1882–1930* (Urbana: University of Illinois Press, 1995).

13. Whether the players have overemphasized race in their interpretation is a question raised in a multitude of ambiguous interracial encounters. Past negative racial encounters will continue to press blacks to define sometimes ambiguous interracial interactions as racist or discriminatory even when there are viable alternative interpretations. See Reuben A. Buford May, "The Sid Cartwright Incident and More: An African American Male's Interpretive Narrative of Interracial Encounters at the University of Chicago," pp. 75–100 in *Studies in Symbolic Interaction,* edited by Norman K. Denzin (New York: Elsevier Science, 2001).

14. Grough, *Character Is Everything,* 21.

15. My daughter Regina was two years old at the time the Knights had this fight in the summer league. When the fight broke out I instinctively stood to my feet and jumped in the fray to push players apart with one hand during the fight while I held my daughter in the other hand. In hindsight this was a very foolish act on my part because Regina could have easily been hit by flailing fists. The surprise of the fight had completely overtaken my thought and emotions. My rush to act was heightened by the fact that Calvin, throughout the time that I had been coaching, had always proven to be a coachable, "good" kid. Thus, when the opposing player put his hands on Calvin, I reacted.

Notes to Chapter 7

1. "Walk-ons" are players who are allowed to try out for a team during "open tryouts." Most college athletic programs offer this opportunity to only a few players, if at all. For those who make the team, their role is typically as a practice player. They are skilled but smaller or less athletic than those players offered scholarships to compete. Coaches usually substitute these walk-ons in games once the outcome of the game has been decided. In reality, even these walk-on players are above-average athletes who sometimes have success. For instance, Scottie Pippen, former NBA All-Star, started his college career as equipment manager and walk-on at Central Arkansas University. Pippen's extraordinary trip to the NBA stands as an example of the possibility of success despite long odds.

2. According to the National Federation of High School Associations the number of participants in boys' high school basketball in 2004 was 544,811. Basketball represents the second most popular sport for high school boys, behind only football. See the National Federation of High School Associations website, http://www.nfhs.org.

3. See Wilbert Leonard II, *A Sociological Perspective of Sport*, 6th ed. (Boston: Allyn and Bacon, 2007).

4. For instance, the probability that one of the 544,811 high school basketball players would move on to the professional ranks remains below .001.

5. Rick Telander, a sports writer, details the aspirations of playground players from Brooklyn who attempt to make it to college and then professionally by playing basketball. Average players like the Northeast Knights share similar aspirations as those held by the young black men from inner-city Brooklyn in the 1970s. For a fascinating description of Brooklyn playground players' lives, see Rick Telander, *Heaven Is a Playground* (Lincoln: University of Nebraska Press, 1995).

6. Although I argue that mass media is one element of the "dirty trick" that influences the young men to pursue hoop dreams, in this study I have not focused specifically on the young men's patterns of mass-media consumption. Beyond anecdotal observation or information, I have little data on the young men's home viewing of television and reading of sports magazines and newspapers. This lack of data is related to the fact that my observations of the young men were limited to very specific contexts like practice, games, bus rides, and locker-room interactions. Yet I glean the influence of mass-media information from the ways in which the young men import the ideas about professional athletics into their everyday interactions with one another. For instance, the young men buy imitation clothes similar to the brand clothing worn by professional players, adorn replica jewelry like star athletes and hip-hop entertainers, and emulate the on-the-court moves of their favorite professional players.

7. For a discussion of the case, see IMDb website, "Biography for Allen Iverson," http://www.imdb.com/name/nm1132515/bio.

8. For a discussion of the charges, see "Iverson Freed on Bail," CBS News website, July 16, 2002, available at http://www.cbsnews.com/stories/2002/07/29/national/main516750.shtml.

9. For an interesting discussion of the impact of housing segregation on other social outcomes, see Douglas Massey and Nancy Denton, *American Apartheid: Segregation and the Making of the Underclass* (Cambridge, MA: Harvard University Press, 1993).

10. For instance, see William Julius Wilson, *The Truly Disadvantaged* (Chicago: University of Chicago Press, 1987); Camille Charles, Gniesha Dinwiddie, and Douglas Massey, "The Continuing Consequences of Segregation: Family Stress and College Academic Performance," *Social Science Quarterly* 85(5) (2004): 1353–1374; David Williams and Chiquita Collins, "Reparations: A Viable Strategy to Address the Enigma of African American Health," *American Behavioral Scientist* 47(7) (2004): 977–1001; Robert Adelman, "Neighborhood Opportunities, Race, and Class: The Black Middle Class and Residential Segre-

gation," *City and Community* 3(1) (2004): 43–64; Michael Emerson, Karen Chai, and George Yancey, "Does Race Matter in Residential Segregation? Exploring Preferences of White Americans," *American Sociological Review* 66(6) (2001): 922–936; and Chenoa Flippen, "Residential Segregation and Minority Home Ownership," *Social Science Research* 30(3) (2001): 337–363.

11. For a discussion of confidence as an important aspect of athletic performance, see Sheldon Hanton, Stephen Mellalieu, and Ross Hall, "Self-Confidence and Anxiety Interpretation: A Qualitative Investigation," *Psychology of Sport and Exercise* 5(4) (2004): 477–496; Tracey Covassin and Suzanne Pero, "The Relationship between Self-Confidence, Mood State, and Anxiety among Collegiate Tennis Players," *Journal of Sport Behavior* 27(3) (2004): 230–243; and Steven Bray and K. A. Martin, "The Effect of Competition Location on Individual Athlete Performance and Psychological States," *Psychology of Sport and Exercise* 4(2) (2003): 117–124.

12. For a discussion of the ways that coaches' behaviors influence athletes' intrinsic and extrinsic motivations, see Genevieve Mageau and Robert Fallerand, "The Coach-Athlete Relationship: A Motivational Model," *Journal of Sports Sciences* 21(11) (2003): 883–905.

13. Interestingly, aspirations like those of the Northeast Knights are also held by blacks from Canada. Thus, blacks from the United States are also competing with blacks from Canada for opportunities to play professionally. See Carl E. James, "Schooling, Basketball and U.S. Scholarship Aspirations of Canadian Student Athletes," *Race, Ethnicity and Education* 6(2) (2003): 123–144.

14. Although the exact origin of this statement is not known, it continues to be part of the common lore used by intellectuals to anchor arguments against black males who focus on athletics as a means of mobility.

15. Although I mention discrimination as it relates to acquiring the skills necessary for becoming a brain surgeon, it is important to consider the myriad ways in which racial discrimination affects the life chances of blacks. From matters of racial profiling, employment discrimination, and housing discrimination, there are many facets of life in which blacks confront racial discrimination. As individual incidents or considerations of discrimination their impact is minuscule, but considered as accumulations, the impact of such discrimination is far greater. For a discussion of the cost of such discrimination, see Joe Feagin and Karyn D. McKinney, *The Many Costs of Racism* (Lanham, MD: Rowman and Littlefield, 2003).

Notes to the Methodological Appendix

1. For a systematic description of the ethnographic process, see John Lofland and Lyn Lofland, *Analyzing Social Settings*, 3d ed. (Belmont, CA: Wadsworth, 1995).

2. These studies include diverse topics. See, for instance, Gary Alan Fine, *Kitchens: The Culture of Restaurant Work* (Berkeley: University of California Press, 1996); Elijah Anderson, *Streetwise: Race, Class, and Change in an Urban Community* (Chicago: University of Chicago Press, 1990); and Sudhir Venkatesh, *American Project: The Rise and Fall of a Modern Ghetto* (Cambridge, MA: Harvard University Press, 2001). For examples of ethnographic studies of aspects of sport, see Gary Alan Fine, *With the Boys: Little League Baseball and Preadolescent Culture* (Chicago: University of Chicago Press, 1987); Patricia A. Adler and Peter Adler, *Backboards and Blackboards: College Athletics and Role Engulfment* (New York: Columbia University Press, 1990), a study of college basketball players; and Nancy Theberge, *Higher Goals: Women's Ice Hockey and the Politics of Gender* (Albany: State University of New York Press, 2000).

3. Sociologists continue to debate the various ways in which subjectivity influences data collection in both qualitative and quantitative methodological approaches to understanding social phenomena. Despite the fact that subjectivity is apparent in most forms of social inquiry, ethnography is particularly noted for the ways in which researchers' backgrounds and experiences limit the "objective" collection of data about social facts.

4. For a description of qualitative interviews, see Steiner Kvale, *Interviews: An Introduction to Qualitative Research Interviewing* (Thousand Oaks, CA: Sage, 1996); Grant McCracken, *The Long Interview* (Newbury Park, CA: Sage, 1988); and Robert Weiss, *Learning from Strangers: The Art and Method of Qualitative Interview Studies* (New York: Free Press, 1994).

5. For a discussion of the original precepts of grounded theory, see Barney Glaser and Anselm Strauss, *Discovery of Grounded Theory: Strategies of Qualitative Research* (Chicago: Aldine, 1967).

6. For a more recent discussion of grounded theory procedures, see Juliet Corbin and Anselm Strauss, "Grounded Theory Research: Procedures, Canons and Evaluative Criteria," *Qualitative Sociology* 13 (1990): 4–21.

7. Glaser and Strauss's original formulation of grounded theory procedures in *Discovery of Grounded Theory* emphasized the importance of beginning analysis of the data while the fieldworker was still in the field. The early observations would then focus the subsequent questions to be answered while in the field and thereby help the researcher develop theory. They state, "Joint collection, coding and analysis of data is the underlying operation [of generating theory]. The generation of theory, coupled with the notion of theory as a process, requires that all three operations be done together as much as possible" (43).

8. I was particularly interested in the literature on transitioning to professional leagues from high school and college athletic participation. For a discussion of these issues, see Wilbert Leonard, *A Sociological Perspective of Sport*, 6th ed. (Boston: Allyn and Bacon, 2007).

9. Roger Sanjek, an anthropologist, proposes this approach as a means for establishing ethnographic validity. See Roger Sanjek, "On Ethnographic Validity," pp. 385–418 in *Fieldnotes: The Makings of Anthropology*, edited by Roger Sanjek (Ithaca, NY: Cornell University Press, 1990).

10. I place the word "irrelevant" in quotation marks here to suggest that relevancy is dependent on a number of factors including the researcher's objectives for the final write-up and the context within which the researcher is attempting to meet those objectives.

11. For recent discussions of reflexive ethnography that capture a wide variety of definitions for it, see Michael Burawoy, "Revisits: An Outline of a Theory of Reflexive Ethnography," *American Sociological Review* 68(5) (2003): 645–679; Raymond J. Michalowski, "Ethnography and Anxiety: Field Work and Reflexivity in the Vortex of U.S.-Cuban Relations," *Qualitative Sociology* 19(1) (1996): 59–82; Douglas E. Foley, "Critical Ethnography: The Reflexive Turn," *International Journal of Qualitative Studies in Education* 15(5) (2002): 469–490; Karen M. Staller, "Relationships—Responsibilities, Once Removed and Ever Connected," *Qualitative Inquiry* 9(1) (2003): 153–160; Denise Fletcher, " 'In the Company of Men': A Reflexive Tale of Cultural Organizing in a Small Organization," *Gender, Work and Organization* 9(4) (2002): 398–419.

12. Patricia A. Adler and Peter Adler, *Membership Roles in Field Research* (Newbury Park, CA: Sage, 1987), 34.

13. In addition to my own connection to the Northeast Knights, my family became further involved with the program when my wife, with no prior experience, volunteered as head cheer coach for the Northeast Knights from 2000 to 2004. The emotional connection we shared with the team and the school manifested itself in the anticipation we shared for big games, the excitement we felt from winning, or the disappointment we experienced in a loss. I often found myself sharing intimate details about coaching with my wife. I am certain that she can also attest to the range of mood swings I experienced based on my participation with the Northeast Knights.

Bibliography

Adams, Terri. 2006. "The Words Have Changed but the Ideology Remains the Same—Misogynistic Lyrics in Rap Music." *Journal of Black Studies* 36(6): 938–957.

Adelman, Robert. 2004. "Neighborhood Opportunities, Race, and Class: The Black Middle Class and Residential Segregation." *City and Community* 3(1): 43–64.

Adler, Patricia A., and Peter Adler. 1987. *Membership Roles in Field Research.* Newbury Park, CA: Sage.

———. 1990. *Backboards and Blackboards: College Athletics and Role Engulfment.* New York: Columbia University Press.

Allen, James. 2000. *Without Sanctuary: Lynching Photography in America.* Santa Fe, NM: Twin Palms.

Anderson, Elijah. 1990. *Streetwise: Race, Class, and Change in an Urban Community.* Chicago: University of Chicago Press.

———. 1999. *Code of the Street.* New York: Norton.

Armstrong, Edward. 2001. "Gangsta Misogyny: A Content Analysis of the Portrayals of Violence against Women in Rap Music, 1987–1993." *Journal of Criminal Justice and Popular Culture* 8(2): 96–126.

Astley, Graham W. 1985. "The Two Ecologies: Population and Community Perspectives on Organizational Evolution." *Administrative Science Quarterly* 30: 224–241.

Bates, Paul E. 1995. *Vicarious Thrills: A Championship Season of High School Basketball.* Carbondale: Southern Illinois University Press.

Belcastro, Philip. 1985. "Sexual Behavior Differences between Black and White Students." *Journal of Sex Research* 21(1): 56–67.

Berger, John. 1977. *Ways of Seeing.* New York: Penguin Books.

Berkow, Ira. 1978. *The DuSable Panthers: The Greatest, Blackest, Saddest Team from the Meanest Street in Chicago.* New York: Atheneum.

Bissinger, H. G. 1990. *Friday Night Lights: A Town, a Team, and a Dream.* New York: Addison-Wesley.

Bockrath, F., and E. Franke. 1995. "Is There Any Value in Sports? About the Ethical Significance of Sport Activities." *International Review for the Sociology of Sport* 30(3–4): 283–310.

Boyd, Todd, and Kenneth L. Shropshire (eds.). 2000. *Basketball Jones: America above the Rim.* New York: NYU Press.

Bray, Steven, and K. A. Martin. 2003. "The Effect of Competition Location on Individual Athlete Performance and Psychological States." *Psychology of Sport and Exercise* 4(2): 117–124.

Buffington, Daniel. 2005. "Contesting Race on Sundays: Making Meaning Out of the Rise in Black Quarterbacks." *Sociology of Sport Journal* 22(1): 12–19.

Burawoy, Michael. 2003. "Revisits: An Outline of a Theory of Reflexive Ethnography." *American Sociological Review* 68(5): 645–679.

Canada, G. 2000. "Learning to Fight." Pp. 100–103 in *Men's Lives,* edited by M. Kimmel and M. Messner. Boston: Allyn and Bacon.

Carpenter, Laura. 2005. *Virginity Lost: An Intimate Portrait of First Sexual Experiences.* New York: NYU Press.

Carr, C., S. R. Kennedy, and K. M. Dimick. 1990. "Alcohol Use among High School Athletes: A Comparison of Alcohol Use and Intoxication in Male and Female High School Athletes and Non-Athletes." *Journal of Alcohol and Drug Education* 36(1): 39–43.

Carroll, Glenn R., and Michael T. Hannan. 2000. *The Demography of Corporations and Industries.* Princeton, NJ: Princeton University Press.

Carroll, Glenn R., and Richard J. Harrison. 1994. "On the Historical Efficiency of Competition between Organizational Populations." *American Journal of Sociology* 100: 720–749.

Charles, Camille, Gniesha Dinwiddie, and Douglas Massey. 2004. "The Continuing Consequences of Segregation: Family Stress and College Academic Performance." *Social Science Quarterly* 85(5): 1353–1374.

Clohesy, William W. 2000. "Altruism and the Endurance of the Good." *Voluntas: International Journal of Voluntary and Nonprofit Organizations* 11: 237–253.

Collins, Patricia Hill. 2004. *Black Sexual Politics: African Americans, Gender, and the New Racism.* New York: Routledge.

Connell, Robert W. 1995. *Masculinities.* Berkeley: University of California Press.

———. 2000. *The Men and the Boys.* Berkeley: University of California Press.

Corbin, Juliet, and Anselm Strauss. 1990. "Grounded Theory Research: Procedures, Canons and Evaluative Criteria." *Qualitative Sociology* 13: 4–21.

Covassin, Tracey, and Suzanne Pero. 2004. "The Relationship between Self-Confidence, Mood State, and Anxiety among Collegiate Tennis Players." *Journal of Sport Behavior* 27(3): 230–243.

Crutchfield, Robert, Ross L. Matsueda, and Devin Drakulich. 2006. "Race, Labor Markets, and Neighborhood Violence." Pp. 199–220 in *The Many Colors of Crime,* edited by Ruth Peterson, Lauren Krivo, and John Hagan. New York: NYU Press.

Dade, Lennell, and Lloyd Sloan. 2000. "An Investigation of Sex-Role Stereotypes in African Americans." *Journal of Black Studies* 30: 676–690.

Denham, Bryan E., Andrew C. Billings, and Kelby K. Halone. 2002. "Differential Accounts of Race in Broadcast Commentary of the 2000 NCAA Men's
and Women's Final Four Basketball Tournaments." *Sociology of Sport Journal* 19: 315–332.

Donato, F., D. Assanelli, M. Marconi, C. Corsini, G. Rosa, and S. Monarca. 1994.
"Alcohol Consumption among High School Students and Young Athletes
in North Italy." *Revue d'epidemiologie et de sante publique* 42(3): 198–206.

Dygard, Thomas J. 1984. *Tournament Upstart*. New York: Morrow.

Edwards, Harry. 1973. *Sociology of Sport*. Homewood, IL: Dorsey.

Eitzen, D. Stanley. 1988. "Ethical Problems in American Sport." *Journal of Sport
and Social Issues* 12(1): 17–30.

———. 1999. *Fair and Foul: Beyond the Myths and Paradoxes of Sport*. Boston:
Rowman and Littlefield.

Emerson, Michael, Karen Chai, and George Yancey. 2001. "Does Race Matter
in Residential Segregation? Exploring Preferences of White Americans."
American Sociological Review 66(6): 922–936.

Engel, Robin, and Jennifer Calnon. 2004. "Examining the Influence of Driver's
Characteristics during Traffic Stops with Police: Results from a National
Survey." *Justice Quarterly* 21(1): 49–91.

Entine, Jon. 2000. *Taboo: Why Black Athletes Dominate Sports and Why We Are
Afraid to Talk about It*. New York: Public Affairs.

Fagot, Beverly I. 1994. "Peer Relations and the Development of Competence in
Boys and Girls." *New Directions for Child Development* 65: 53–66.

Fagot, Beverly I., and Mary D. Leinbach. 1989. "The Young Child's Gender
Schema: Environmental Input, Internal Organization." *Child Development*
60: 663–672.

Fasenfest, David. 2005. "Enforcement Mechanisms Discouraging Black-American Presence in Suburban Detroit." *International Journal of Urban and Regional Research* 29(4): 960–971.

Feagin, Joe, and Karyn D. McKinney. 2003. *The Many Costs of Racism*. Lanham,
MD: Rowman and Littlefield.

Feagin, Joe, and Melvin Sikes. 1994. *Living with Racism: The Black Middle-Class
Experience*. Boston: Beacon.

Fine, Gary Alan. 1987. *With the Boys: Little League Baseball and Preadolescent Culture*. Chicago: University of Chicago Press.

———. 1996. *Kitchens: The Culture of Restaurant Work*. Berkeley: University of
California Press.

Fine, Michelle, and Lori Weis. 1996. "Writing the 'Wrongs' of Fieldwork."
Qualitative Inquiry 2: 251–274.

Fletcher, Denise. 2002. "'In the Company of Men': A Reflexive Tale of Cultural Organizing in a Small Organization." *Gender, Work and Organization* 9(4): 398–419.

Flippen, Chenoa. 2001. "Residential Segregation and Minority Home Ownership." *Social Science Research* 30(3): 337–363.

Foley, Douglas E. 2002. "Critical Ethnography: The Reflexive Turn." *International Journal of Qualitative Studies in Education* 15(5): 469–490.

Franzini, Luisa. 2005. "Religion, Socio-demographic and Personal Characteristics, and Self-Reported Health in Whites, Blacks, and Hispanics Living in Low-Socioeconomic Status Neighborhoods." *Ethnicity and Disease* 15(3): 469–484.

Freeman, John, Glenn R. Carroll, and Michael T. Hannan. 1983. "The Liability of Newness: Age Dependence in Organizational Death Rates." *American Sociological Review* 48: 692–710.

Freeman, John, and Michael T. Hannan. 1983. "Niche Width and the Dynamics of Organizational Populations." *American Journal of Sociology* 88: 1116–1145.

Frey, Darcy. 1994. *The Last Shot: City Streets, Basketball Dreams.* New York: Simon and Schuster.

Freymann, Gordon R., James L. Tobias, and Michael A. Coletta. 2002. *A Decade of Change: The Demographic Atlas of Georgia 1990 and 2000.* Atlanta: Georgia Division of Public Health.

Glaser, Barney, and Anselm Strauss. 1967. *Discovery of Grounded Theory: Strategies of Qualitative Research.* Chicago: Aldine.

Goffman, Erving. 1967. *Interaction Rituals: Essays in Face-to-Face Behavior.* Chicago: Aldine.

Goode, Erich. 2002. "Drug Arrests at the Millennium." *Society* 39(5): 41–45.

Greve, Henrich R. 2002. "An Ecological Theory of Spatial Evolution: Local Density Dependence in Tokyo Banking 1894–1936." *Social Forces* 80: 847–879.

Grough, R. 1997. *Character Is Everything: Promoting Excellence in Sports.* New York: Harcourt Brace.

Gruber, Joseph J. 1981. "Comparison of Relationships among Team Cohesion Scores and Measures of Team Success in Male Varsity Basketball Teams." *International Review of Sport Sociology* 16: 43–56.

Hannan, Michael T., and Glenn R. Carroll. 1992. *Dynamics of Organizational Populations: Density, Legitimation, and Competition.* New York: Oxford University Press.

Hannan, Michael T., and John Freeman. 1977. "The Population Ecology of Organizations." *American Journal of Sociology* 82: 929–964.

———. 1984. "Structural Inertia and Organizational Change." *American Sociological Review* 49: 149–164.

———. 1986. "Where Do Organizational Forms Come From?" *Sociological Forum* 1: 50–72.

Hanton, Sheldon, Stephen Mellalieu, and Ross Hall. 2004. "Self-Confidence and Anxiety Interpretation: A Qualitative Investigation." *Psychology of Sport and Exercise* 5(4): 477–496.

Harrington, Brooke, and Gary A. Fine. 2000. "Opening the 'Black Box': Small Groups and Twenty-First-Century Sociology." *Social Psychology Quarterly* 63: 312–323.

Harris, Amg. 2005. "Courting Customers: Assessing Consumer Racial Profiling and Other Marketplace Discrimination." *Journal of Public Policy and Marketing* 24(1): 163–171.

Harris, Ian, Jose Torres, and Dale Allender. 1994. "The Responses of African American Men to Dominant Norms of Masculinity within the United States." *Sex Roles* 31: 703–719.

Herek, Gregory. 1995. "Black Heterosexuals' Attitudes toward Lesbians and Gay Men in the United States." *Journal of Sex Research* 32(2): 95–105.

Hildebrand, K., D. J. Johnson, and K. Bogle. 2001. "Comparison of Patterns of Alcohol Use between High School and College Athletes and Non-Athletes." *College Student Journal* 35(3): 358–365.

Hoberman, John. 1997. *Darwin's Athletes: How Sport Has Damaged Black America and Preserved the Myth of Race.* Boston: Houghton Mifflin.

James, Carl E. "Schooling, Basketball and U.S. Scholarship Aspirations of Canadian Student Athletes." *Race, Ethnicity and Education* 6(2) (2003): 123–144.

Jepson, Lisa, Linda Juszczak, and Martin Fisher. 1998. "Mental Health Care in a High School Based Health Service." *Adolescence* 33: 1–15.

Jimerson, Jason. 1996. "Good Times and Good Games: How Pickup Basketball Players Use Wealth-Maximizing Norms," *Journal of Contemporary Ethnography* 25(3): 353–371.

Joyner, Kara, and Edward Laumann. 2001. "Teenage Sex and the Sexual Revolution." Pp. 41–71 in *Sex, Love, and Health in America: Private Choices and Public Policies,* edited by Edward Laumann and Robert T. Michaels. Chicago: University of Chicago Press.

King, J. L., with Karen Hunter. 2004. *On the Down Low: A Journey into the Lives of "Straight" Black Men Who Sleep with Men.* New York: Broadway Books.

Knoppers, A., B. B. Meyers, and M. Zuidema. 1989. "Playing to Win or Playing to Play?" *Sociology of Sport Journal* 6: 70–76.

Knowles, J. 2001. "Racial Bias in Motor Vehicle Searches: Theory and Evidence." *Journal of Political Economy* 109(1): 203–229.

Kvale, Steiner. 1996. *Interviews: An Introduction to Qualitative Research Interviewing.* Thousand Oaks, CA: Sage.

Larsson, IngBeth, and Carl Goran Svedin. 2002. "Teachers' and Parents' Reports on 3- to 6-Year-Old Children's Sexual Behavior—A Comparison." *Child Abuse and Neglect: The International Journal* 26(3): 247–266.

Laumann, Edward, John Gagnon, Robert Michael, and Stuart Michaels. 1994. *The Social Organization of Sexuality: Sexual Practices in the United States.* Chicago: University of Chicago Press.

Lehmiller, Justin, and Christopher Agnew. 2006. "Marginalized Relationships: The Impact of Social Disapproval on Romantic Relationship Commitment." *Personality and Social Psychology Bulletin* 32(1): 40–51.

Lemelle, Anthony, Jr., and Juan Battle. 2004. "Black Masculinity Matters in Attitudes toward Gay Males." *Journal of Homosexuality* 47(1): 39–51.

Leonard, Wilbert, II. 2007. *A Sociological Perspective of Sport.* 6th ed. Boston: Allyn and Bacon.

Li Chaoyang, Mary Ann Pentz, and Chou Chih-Ping. 2002. "Parental Substance Use as a Modifier of Adolescent Substance Use Risk." *Addiction* 97(12): 1537–1551.

Lofland, John, and Lyn Lofland. 1995. *Analyzing Social Settings.* 3d ed. Belmont, CA: Wadsworth.

Lombard, Ann. 2003. *Making Manhood: Growing Up Male in Colonial New England.* Cambridge, MA: Harvard University Press.

Lorber, Judith. 1994. *Paradoxes of Gender.* New Haven, CT: Yale University Press.

Lundman, Richard. 2004. "Driver Race, Ethnicity, and Gender and Citizen Reports of Vehicle Searches by Police and Vehicle Search Hits: Toward a Triangulated Scholarly Understanding." *Journal of Criminal Law and Criminology* 94(2): 309–349.

Lune, Howard, and Miranda Martinez. 1999. "Old Structures, New Relations: How Community Development Credit Unions Define Organizational Boundaries." *Sociological Forum* 14: 609–634.

MacLeod, Jay. 1987. *Ain't No Making It: Leveled Aspirations in a Low Income Neighborhood.* Boulder, CO: Westview.

Mageau, Genevieve, and Robert Fallerand. 2003. "The Coach-Athlete Relationship: A Motivational Model." *Journal of Sports Sciences* 21(11): 883–905.

Mann, Geoff. 2005. "What's a Penny Worth? Wages, Prices, and the American Working Man." *Ethnography* 6(3): 315–355.

Massey, Douglas S., and Nancy A. Denton. 1993. *American Apartheid: Segregation and the Making of the Underclass.* Cambridge, MA: Harvard University Press.

May, Reuben A. Buford. 2001a. "The Sid Cartwright Incident and More: An African American Male's Interpretive Narrative of Interracial Encounters at the University of Chicago." Pp. 75–100 in *Studies in Symbolic Interaction,* edited by Norman K. Denzin. New York: Elsevier Science.

———. 2001b. *Talking at Trena's: Everyday Conversations at an African American Tavern.* New York: NYU Press.

———. 2004. "Of Mice, Rats, and Men: Exploring the Role of Rodents in Constructing Masculinity within a Group of Young African American Males." *Qualitative Sociology* 27(2): 159–177.

McCabe, Marita, and Robert A. Cummins. 1998. "Sexuality and the Quality of Life among Young People." *Adolescence* 33: 761–773.

McConaghy, Nathaniel, Neil Buhrich, and Derrick Silove. 1994. "Opposite Sex-Linked Behaviors and Homosexual Feelings in the Predominantly Heterosexual Male Majority." *Archives of Sexual Behavior* 23: 565–577.

McCracken, Grant. 1988. *The Long Interview.* Newbury Park, CA: Sage.

Messner, Michael. 1992. *Power at Play: Sports and the Problem of Masculinity.* Boston: Beacon.

———. 1997. *Politics of Masculinities: Men in Movements.* Thousand Oaks, CA: Sage.

Messner, Michael, and Donald F. Sabo. 1994. *Sex, Violence and Power in Sports: Rethinking Masculinity.* Freedom, CA: Crossing.

Michalowski, Raymond J. 1996. "Ethnography and Anxiety: Field Work and Reflexivity in the Vortex of U.S.-Cuban Relations." *Qualitative Sociology* 19(1): 59–82.

Mills, C. Wright. 1959. *The Sociological Imagination.* New York: Oxford University Press.

Molinsky, Andrew. 1999. "Sanding Down the Edges: Paradoxical Impediments to Organizational Change." *Journal of Applied Behavioral Science* 35: 8–24.

Naylor, Adam, Doug Gardner, and Len Zaichkowsky. 2001. "Drug Use Patterns among High School Athletes and Nonathletes." *Adolescence* 36(144): 627–639.

Negy, Charles. 2005. "A Comparison of African American and White College Students' Affective and Attitudinal Reactions to Lesbian, Gay, and Bisexual Individuals: An Exploratory Study." *Journal of Sex Research* 42(4): 291–298.

Nelson, Dana. *National Manhood: Capitalist Citizenship and Imagined Fraternity of White Men.* Durham, NC: Duke University Press, 1998.

Nixon, Howard. 1984. *Sport and the American Dream.* New York: Leisure Press.

Papp, G., and G. Prisztoka. 1995. "Sportsmanship as an Ethical Value." *International Review for the Sociology of Sport* 30(3–4): 375–389.

Pfeffer, Jeffrey. 1997. *New Directions for Organization Theory: Problems and Prospects.* New York: Oxford University Press.

Pilz, G. A. 1995. "Performance Sport: Education in Fair Play? (Some Empirical and Theoretical Remarks)." *International Review for the Sociology of Sport* 30(3–4): 391–418.

Ramsey, G., and B. Rank. 1997. "Rethinking Youth Sports." *Parks and Recreation* 32(12): 30–36.

Reynolds, Bill. 1994. *Fall River Dreams: A Team's Quest for Glory, a Town's Search for Its Soul.* New York: St. Martin's.

Rosenthal, Susan L., Lisa Lewis, and Sheila S. Cohen. 1996. "Issues Related to the Sexual Decision-Making of Inner-City Adolescent Girls." *Adolescence* 31: 731–739.

Rotundo, E. Anthony. 1993. *American Manhood: Transformations in Masculinity from the Revolution to the Modern Era.* New York: Basic Books.

Sampson, Robert, Jeffrey Morenoff, and Stephen Raudenbush. 2005. "Social Anatomy of Racial and Ethnic Disparities in Violence." *American Journal of Public Health* 95: 224–232.

Sampson, Robert, and William Julius Wilson. 1995. "Toward a Theory of Race, Crime, and Urban Inequality." Pp. 37–54 in *Crime and Inequality,* edited by John Hagan and Ruth Peterson. Stanford, CA: Stanford University Press.

Sanjek, Roger. 1990. "On Ethnographic Validity." Pp. 385–418 in *Fieldnotes: The Makings of Anthropology,* edited by Roger Sanjek. Ithaca, NY: Cornell University Press.

Schulte, Lisa, and Juan Battle. 2004. "The Relative Importance of Ethnicity and Religion in Predicting Attitudes towards Gays and Lesbians." *Journal of Homosexuality* 47(2): 127–142.

Scott, W. Richard. 1992. *Organizations: Rational, Natural, and Open Systems.* 3d ed. Englewood Cliffs, NJ: Prentice-Hall.

Shields, D., B. Bredemeier, D. Gardner, and A. Bostrom. 1995. "Leadership, Cohesion, and Team Norms Regarding Cheating and Aggression." *Sociology of Sport Journal* 12: 324–336.

Shields, E. W., Jr. 1998. "Relative Likelihood of In-Season and Off-Season Use of Alcohol by High School Athletes in North Carolina: Trends and Current Status." *Journal of Alcohol and Drug Education* 43(2): 48–63.

Simons, Herbert D. 2003. "Race and Penalized Sports Behaviors." *International Review for the Sociology of Sport* 38(1): 5–22.

Small, Debra. 2001. "The War on Drugs Is a War on Racial Justice." *Social Research* 68(3): 896–903.

Stack, Carol. 1974. *All Our Kin: Strategies for Survival in a Black Community.* New York: Harper and Row.

Staller, Karen M. 2003. "Relationships—Responsibilities, Once Removed and Ever Connected." *Qualitative Inquiry* 9(1): 153–160.

Suttles, Gerald. 1968. *The Social Order of the Slum: Ethnicity and Territory in the Inner City.* Chicago: University of Chicago Press.

Taylor, Robert, Jacqueline Mattis, and Linda Chatters. 1999. "Subjective Religiosity among African Americans: A Synthesis of Findings from Five National Samples." *Journal of Black Psychology* 25(4): 524–543.

Telander, Rick. 1995. *Heaven Is a Playground*. Lincoln: University of Nebraska Press.

Theberge, Nancy. 2000. *Higher Goals: Women's Ice Hockey and the Politics of Gender*. Albany: State University of New York Press.

Thompston, Cooper. 1987. "A New Vision of Masculinity." Pp. 205–211 in *New Men, New Minds*, edited by Franklin Abbot. Freedom, CA: Crossing.

Tolnay, Stewart E., and E. M. Beck. 1995. *A Festival of Violence: An Analysis of Southern Lynchings, 1882–1930*. Urbana: University of Illinois Press.

Tonry, Michael. 1994. "Racial Disparities, and the War on Crime." *Crime and Delinquency* 40: 475–494.

Tucker, Linda. 2003. "Blackballed: Basketball and Representations of the Black Male Athlete." *American Behavioral Scientist* 47(3): 306–328.

Turchin, Peter, and Thomas Hall. 2003. "Spatial Synchrony among and within World-Systems: Insights from Theoretical Ecology." *Journal of World-Systems Research* 9: 37–64.

Vaquera, Elizabeth, and Grace Kao. 2005. "Private and Public Displays of Affection among Interracial and Intra-Racial Adolescent Couples." *Social Science Quarterly* 86(2): 484–508.

Velez, Maria B. 2006. "Toward an Understanding of the Lower Rates of Homicide in Latino versus Black Neighborhoods." Pp. 91–107 in *The Many Colors of Crime*, edited by Ruth Peterson, Lauren Krivo, and John Hagan. New York: NYU Press.

Venkatesh, Sudhir. 2001. *American Project: The Rise and Fall of a Modern Ghetto*. Cambridge, MA: Harvard University Press.

Volkwein, K. 1995. "Ethics and Top-Level Sport—A Paradox?" *International Review for Sociology of Sport* 30(3–4): 311–321.

Wandzilak, T., T. Carroll, and C. J. Ansorge. 1988. "Values Development through Physical Activity: Promoting Sportsmanlike Behaviors, Perceptions, and Moral Reasoning." *Journal of Teaching in Physical Education* 8(1): 13–22.

Wang, Hongyu, Grace Kao, and Kara Joyner. 2006. "Stability of Interracial and Intraracial Romantic Relationships among Adolescents." *Social Science Research* 35(2): 435–453.

Weiss, Robert. 1994. *Learning from Strangers: The Art and Method of Qualitative Interview Studies*. New York: Free Press.

Werner-Wilson, Ronald. 1998. "Gender Differences in Adolescent Sexual Attitudes: The Influence of Individual and Family Factors." *Adolescence* 33: 519–531.

West, Candace, and Don Zimmerman. 1987. "Doing Gender." *Gender and Society* 1: 125–151.

Williams, David, and Chiquita Collins. 2004. "Reparations: A Viable Strategy to Address the Enigma of African American Health." *American Behavioral Scientist* 47(7): 977–1001.

Wilson, Brian, and Robert Sparks. 1996. " 'It's Gotta Be the Shoes': Youth, Race, and Sneaker Commercials." *Sociology of Sport Journal* 13: 398–427.

Wilson, William Julius. 1987. *The Truly Disadvantaged*. Chicago: University of Chicago Press.

———. 1996. *When Work Disappears: The World of the New Urban Poor*. New York: Knopf.

Yancey, George. 2002. "Who Interracially Dates? An Examination of the Characteristics of Those Who Have Interracially Dated." *Journal of Comparative Family Studies* 33(2): 179–190.

Young, Ruth C. 1988. "Is Population Ecology a Useful Paradigm for the Study of Organizations?" *American Journal of Sociology* 94(1): 1–24.

Zimmerman, Marc A., and Karen H. Schmeelk-Cone. 2003. "A Longitudinal Analysis of Adolescent Substance Use and School Motivation among African American Youth." *Journal of Research on Adolescence* 13(2): 185–211.

Index

About the Author

Reuben A. Buford May is an associate professor of sociology at Texas A&M University. He received his Ph.D. from the University of Chicago in 1996. May served as an assistant professor of sociology at the University of Georgia from 1996 to 2002. His recent publications include one book, *Talking at Trena's: Everyday Conversation at an African American Tavern*. May currently resides in College Station, Texas, with his wife, Lyndel, and ten-year-old daughter, Regina.